Microsoft®
Windows® XP

maranGraphics®

&

THOMSON

COURSE TECHNOLOGY

Professional ■ Trade ■ Reference

MARAN ILLUSTRATED™ Microsoft® Windows® XP

© 2005 by maranGraphics Inc. All rights reserved. No part of this book may be reproduced or transmitted in any form or by any means, electronic, mechanical or otherwise, including by photocopying, recording, or by any storage or retrieval system without prior written permission from maranGraphics, except for the inclusion of brief quotations in a review.

Distributed in the U.S. and Canada by Thomson Course Technology PTR. For enquiries about Maran Illustrated™ books outside the U.S. and Canada, please contact maranGraphics at international@maran.com

For U.S. orders and customer service, please contact Thomson Course Technology at 1-800-354-9706. For Canadian orders, please contact Thomson Course Technology at 1-800-268-2222 or 416-752-9448.

ISBN: 1-59200-870-4

Library of Congress Catalog Card Number: 2005921017

Printed in the United States of America

05 06 07 08 09 BU 10 9 8 7 6 5 4 3

Trademarks

maranGraphics is a registered trademark of maranGraphics Inc. Maran Illustrated, the Maran Illustrated logos and any trade dress related to or associated with the contents or cover of this book are trademarks of maranGraphics Inc. and may not be used without written permission.

The Thomson Course Technology PTR logo is a trademark of Course Technology and may not be used without written permission.

All other trademarks are the property of their respective owners.

Permissions

CBS SportsLine
Copyright © 1996 SportsLine USA, Inc.
http://www.sportsline.com All rights reserved.

Golf
Copyright © 1999 golf.com LLC

Smithsonian Institution
Copyright © 1996 Smithsonian Institution

Wal-Mart
Copyright © 1998 Wal-Mart Stores, Inc.

YAHOO!
Text and artwork copyright © 1996 by Yahoo! Inc. All rights reserved. YAHOO! and the YAHOO! logo are trademarks of YAHOO!, Inc.

Other Permissions Granted:
Discovery Channel Online
Google
Sunkist

Important

maranGraphics and Thomson Course Technology PTR cannot provide software support. Please contact the appropriate software manufacturer's technical support line or Web site for assistance.

maranGraphics and Thomson Course Technology PTR have attempted throughout this book to distinguish proprietary trademarks by following the capitalization style used by the source. However, we cannot attest to the accuracy of the style, and the use of a word or term in this book is not intended to affect the validity of any trademark.

Copies

Educational facilities, companies, and organizations located in the U.S. and Canada that are interested in multiple copies of this book should contact Thomson Course Technology PTR for quantity discount information. Training manuals, CD-ROMs, and portions of this book are also available individually or can be tailored for specific needs.

DISCLAIMER: PURCHASERS, READERS OR USERS OF THIS BOOK AGREE TO BE BOUND BY THE FOLLOWING TERMS.

INFORMATION CONTAINED IN THIS BOOK HAS BEEN OBTAINED BY MARANGRAPHICS AND FROM SOURCES BELIEVED TO BE RELIABLE. HOWEVER, NEITHER MARANGRAPHICS INC. NOR THOMSON COURSE TECHNOLOGY PTR NOR ANY OF THEIR RESPECTIVE AFFILIATES, DISTRIBUTORS, EMPLOYEES, AGENTS, CONTENT CONTRIBUTORS OR LICENSORS, IF ANY, MAKE ANY REPRESENTATION, WARRANTY, GUARANTEE OR ENDORSEMENT AS TO THE INFORMATION CONTAINED IN THIS BOOK OR AS TO THIRD-PARTY SUPPLIERS REFERENCED IN THIS BOOK, INCLUDING WITHOUT LIMITATION REGARDING THEIR ACCURACY, CORRECTNESS, TIMELINESS, RELIABILITY, USEFULNESS OR COMPLETENESS, OR THE RESULTS THAT MAY BE OBTAINED FROM THE USE OF THIS BOOK, AND DISCLAIM ALL EXPRESS, IMPLIED OR STATUTORY WARRANTIES, INCLUDING IMPLIED WARRANTIES OF MERCHANTABILITY, FITNESS OR SUITABILITY FOR A PARTICULAR PURPOSE, TITLE AND NON-INFRINGEMENT. THE SUBJECT MATTER OF THIS BOOK IS CONSTANTLY EVOLVING AND THE INFORMATION PROVIDED IN THIS BOOK IS NOT EXHAUSTIVE. IT SHOULD NOT BE USED AS A SUBSTITUTE FOR CONSULTING WITH A QUALIFIED PROFESSIONAL WHERE PROFESSIONAL ASSISTANCE IS REQUIRED OR APPROPRIATE, INCLUDING WHERE THERE MAY BE ANY RISK TO HEALTH OR PROPERTY, AND THE PURCHASER, READER OR USER UNDERSTANDS AND ACKNOWLEDGES THAT THE AFOREMENTIONED PARTIES ARE NOT HEREBY PROVIDING ANY PROFESSIONAL ADVICE, CONSULTATION OR OTHER SERVICES.

IN NO EVENT WILL ANY OF MARANGRAPHICS INC., THOMSON COURSE TECHNOLOGY PTR, OR ANY OF THEIR RESPECTIVE AFFILIATES, DISTRIBUTORS, EMPLOYEES, AGENTS, CONTENT CONTRIBUTORS OR LICENSORS BE LIABLE OR RESPONSIBLE FOR ANY DAMAGES INCLUDING ANY DIRECT, INDIRECT, SPECIAL, CONSEQUENTIAL, INCIDENTAL, PUNITIVE OR EXEMPLARY LOSSES, DAMAGE OR EXPENSES (INCLUDING BUSINESS INTERRUPTION, LOSS OF PROFITS, LOST BUSINESS, OR LOST SAVINGS) IRRESPECTIVE OF THE NATURE OF THE CAUSE OF ACTION, DEMAND OR ACTION, INCLUDING BREACH OF CONTRACT, NEGLIGENCE, TORT OR ANY OTHER LEGAL THEORY.

maranGraphics Inc.
5755 Coopers Avenue
Mississauga, Ontario
L4Z 1R9
www.maran.com

THOMSON
COURSE TECHNOLOGY™
Professional ■ Trade ■ Reference

Thomson Course Technology PTR, a division of Thomson Course Technology
25 Thomson Place ■ Boston, MA 02210 ■ http://www.courseptr.com

maranGraphics is a family-run business.

At **maranGraphics**, we believe in producing great computer books—one book at a time.

Each maranGraphics book uses the award-winning communication process that we have been developing over the last 30 years. Using this process, we organize screen shots, text and illustrations in a way that makes it easy for you to learn new concepts and tasks.

We spend hours deciding the best way to perform each task, so you don't have to! Our clear, easy-to-follow screen shots and instructions walk you through each task from beginning to end.

Our detailed illustrations go hand-in-hand with the text to help reinforce the information. Each illustration is a labor of love—some take up to a week to draw!

We want to thank you for purchasing what we feel are the best computer books money can buy. We hope you enjoy using this book as much as we enjoyed creating it!

Sincerely,

The Maran Family

We would love to hear from you! Send your comments and feedback about our books to family@maran.com

Please visit us on the Web at:
www.maran.com

CREDITS

Authors:
Ruth Maran
Kelleigh Johnson

**Technical Consultant &
Post Production:**
Robert Maran

Project Manager:
Judy Maran

Editing and Screen Captures:
Jill Maran Dutfield

Proofreader:
Jennifer March

Layout Designer & Illustrator:
Richard Hung

Illustrator:
Russ Marini

Indexer:
Kelleigh Johnson

**President,
Thomson Course Technology:**
David R. West

**Senior Vice President of
Business Development,
Thomson Course Technology:**
Andy Shafran

**Publisher and General Manager,
Thomson Course Technology PTR:**
Stacy L. Hiquet

**Associate Director of Marketing,
Thomson Course Technology PTR:**
Sarah O'Donnell

**National Sales Manager,
Thomson Course Technology PTR:**
Amy Merrill

**Manager of Editorial Services,
Thomson Course Technology PTR:**
Heather Talbot

ACKNOWLEDGMENTS

Thanks to the dedicated staff of maranGraphics, including
Richard Hung, Kelleigh Johnson, Wanda Lawrie, Jill Maran,
Judy Maran, Robert Maran, Ruth Maran, Jennifer March,
Russ Marini and Raquel Scott.

Finally, to Richard Maran who originated the easy-to-use
graphic format of this guide. Thank you for your
inspiration and guidance.

TABLE OF CONTENTS

Chapter 3

WORKING WITH FILES

Chapter 4

MORE WORKING WITH FILES

TABLE OF CONTENTS

Chapter 5

CUSTOMIZE WINDOWS

Chapter 6

WORK WITH SONGS AND VIDEOS

Rock Favorites

Chapter 7

CREATE MOVIES

Chapter 8

SHARE YOUR COMPUTER

Chapter 9

OPTIMIZE COMPUTER PERFORMANCE

TABLE OF CONTENTS

Chapter 10

WORK ON A NETWORK

Chapter 11

BROWSE THE WEB

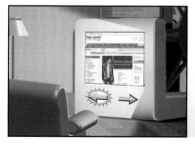

Chapter 12

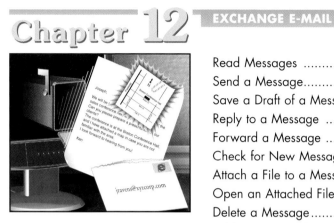

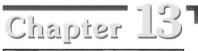

Chapter 13

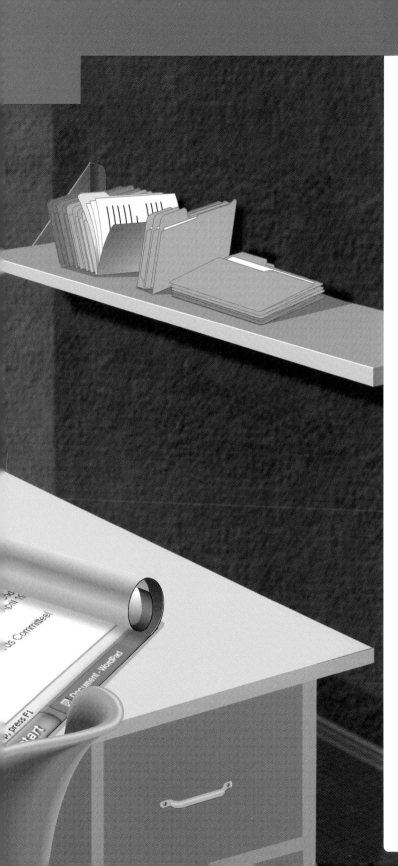

CHAPTER 1

Windows Basics

In this chapter, you will learn everything you need to know to get started using Windows XP. Find out how to navigate the Start menu, move and resize windows, use some of the programs included with Windows XP such as WordPad and Paint, and more.

INTRODUCTION TO WINDOWS

Microsoft® Windows® XP is a program that controls the overall activity of your computer.

Microsoft Windows XP ensures that all parts of your computer work together smoothly and efficiently. **XP** stands for ex**p**erience.

Windows XP Service Pack 2 (SP2) is the newest update for Windows XP and focuses on making your computer more secure. You can obtain Windows XP SP2 for free from Microsoft's Web site at www.microsoft.com.

Work with Files

Windows helps you manage the files stored on your computer. You can sort, open, rename, print, delete, move and search for files. You can also e-mail a file, publish a file to the Web and copy files to a recordable CD, memory card or other removable media.

Work with Multimedia

Windows allows you to play music CDs on your computer while you work. Windows also helps you find the latest music and videos on the Internet, organize your sound and video files and copy songs from your computer to a recordable CD or portable device. You can also transfer your home movies to your computer so you can edit the movies before sharing them with friends and family.

Share Your Computer

If you share your computer with other people, you can create user accounts to keep the personal files and settings for each person separate. You can assign a password to each user account and easily share files with other users.

Customize and Optimize Windows

You can customize Windows to suit your preferences. You can add a personalized picture to your screen and set up a screen saver to appear when you do not use your computer for a period of time.

Windows also provides tools to help you optimize your computer's performance. You can remove unnecessary programs and files to free up disk space and restore your computer to an earlier time if you experience problems.

Security

Windows offers new security features to help protect your computer. Windows uses firewall software to help prevent unauthorized people or unwanted programs, such as viruses, from accessing your computer through the Internet. Windows is also automatically set up to install the latest Windows updates for your computer from the Internet free of charge and to check regularly to see if your computer is using an up-to-date antivirus program.

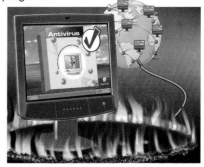

Work on a Network

Windows allows you to share information and equipment, such as a printer, with other people on a network. You can use Windows to easily set up and connect to a wired network as well as a wireless network, which allows computers to communicate without using cables.

Access the Internet

Windows allows you to browse through the information on the Web and search for Web pages of interest. When you are viewing Web pages, Windows prevents Web sites from downloading potentially harmful files and running software on your computer without your knowledge. Windows also allows you to exchange electronic mail and instant messages with people around the world. As a security feature, Windows prevents you from opening unsafe files you receive in e-mail and instant messages.

USING THE START MENU

You can use the Start menu to access programs, files, computer settings and help with Windows.

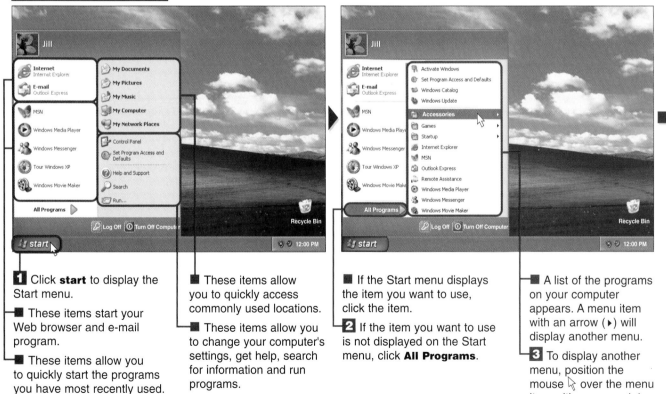

The programs available on the Start menu depend on the software installed on your computer.

USING THE START MENU

1 Click **start** to display the Start menu.

■ These items start your Web browser and e-mail program.

■ These items allow you to quickly start the programs you have most recently used.

■ These items allow you to quickly access commonly used locations.

■ These items allow you to change your computer's settings, get help, search for information and run programs.

■ If the Start menu displays the item you want to use, click the item.

2 If the item you want to use is not displayed on the Start menu, click **All Programs**.

■ A list of the programs on your computer appears. A menu item with an arrow (▸) will display another menu.

3 To display another menu, position the mouse ▨ over the menu item with an arrow (▸).

Tip

Which programs does Windows provide?

Windows comes with many useful programs. Here are some examples.

Windows Media Player is a program that allows you to find and play media files, play music CDs and listen to radio stations that broadcast on the Internet.

Windows Messenger is a program you can use to exchange instant messages and files with friends and family.

Windows Movie Maker is a program that allows you to transfer your home movies to your computer where you can then organize and edit the movies.

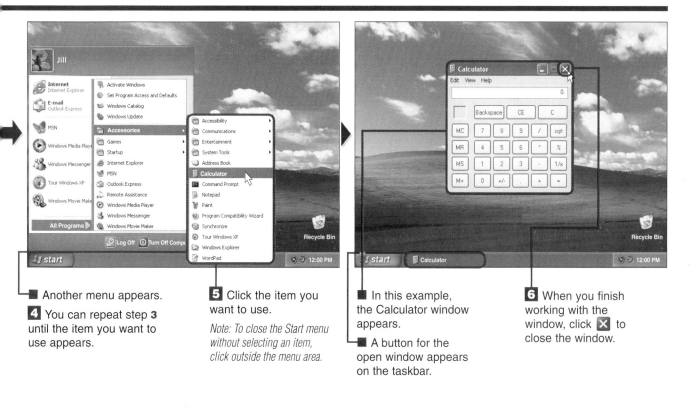

■ Another menu appears.

4 You can repeat step **3** until the item you want to use appears.

5 Click the item you want to use.

Note: To close the Start menu without selecting an item, click outside the menu area.

■ In this example, the Calculator window appears.

■ A button for the open window appears on the taskbar.

6 When you finish working with the window, click ☒ to close the window.

SCROLL THROUGH A WINDOW

You can use a scroll bar to browse through the information in a window. Scrolling is useful when a window is not large enough to display all the information it contains.

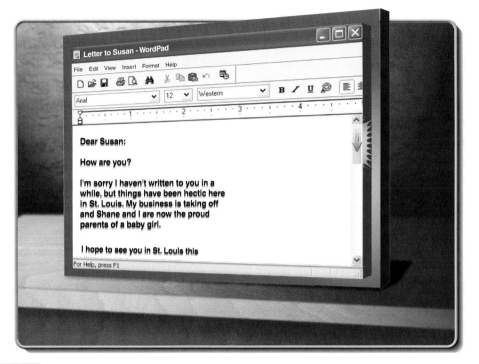

SCROLL THROUGH A WINDOW

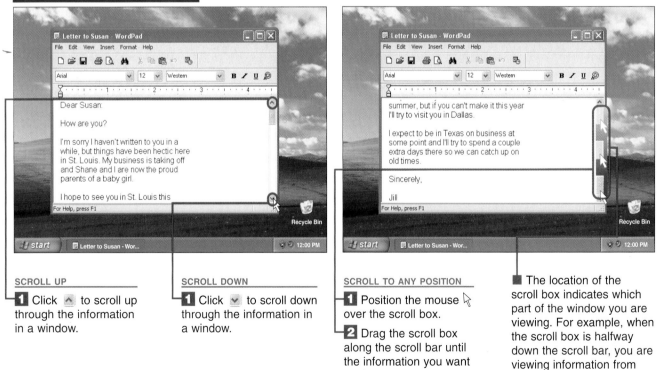

SCROLL UP

1 Click ⌃ to scroll up through the information in a window.

SCROLL DOWN

1 Click ⌄ to scroll down through the information in a window.

SCROLL TO ANY POSITION

1 Position the mouse ⍟ over the scroll box.

2 Drag the scroll box along the scroll bar until the information you want to view appears.

■ The location of the scroll box indicates which part of the window you are viewing. For example, when the scroll box is halfway down the scroll bar, you are viewing information from the middle of the window.

CLOSE A WINDOW

When you finish working with a window, you can close the window to remove it from your screen.

CLOSE A WINDOW

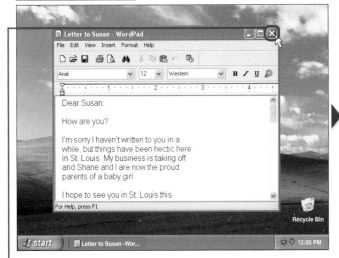

1 Click ☒ in the window you want to close.

■ The window disappears from your screen.

■ The button for the window disappears from the taskbar.

MOVE A WINDOW

If a window covers items on your screen, you can move the window to a different location.

You may want to move several windows to see the contents of multiple windows at once.

MOVE A WINDOW

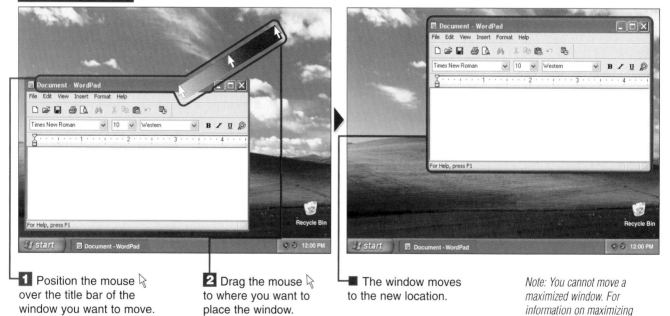

1 Position the mouse ⍺ over the title bar of the window you want to move.

2 Drag the mouse ⍺ to where you want to place the window.

■ The window moves to the new location.

Note: You cannot move a maximized window. For information on maximizing a window, see page 22.

RESIZE A WINDOW

You can easily change the size of a window displayed on your screen.

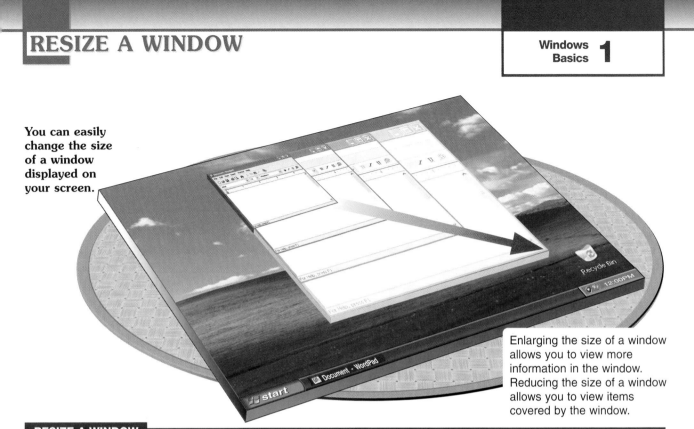

Enlarging the size of a window allows you to view more information in the window. Reducing the size of a window allows you to view items covered by the window.

RESIZE A WINDOW

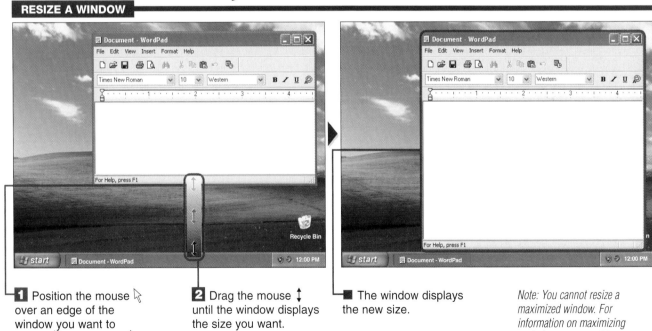

1 Position the mouse ⌖ over an edge of the window you want to resize (⌖ changes to ↕, ↔, ↖ or ↗).

2 Drag the mouse ↕ until the window displays the size you want.

■ The window displays the new size.

Note: You cannot resize a maximized window. For information on maximizing a window, see page 22.

MAXIMIZE A WINDOW

You can maximize a window to fill your entire screen. This allows you to view more of the window's contents.

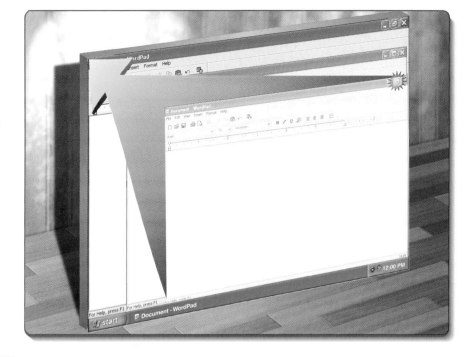

1 Click 🔲 in the window you want to maximize.

■ The window fills your entire screen.

■ To return the window to its previous size, click 🗗.

■ You can also double-click the title bar of a window to maximize the window.

22

MINIMIZE A WINDOW

If you are not using a window, you can minimize the window to temporarily remove it from your screen. You can redisplay the window at any time.

Minimizing a window allows you to temporarily put a window aside so you can work on other tasks.

MINIMIZE A WINDOW

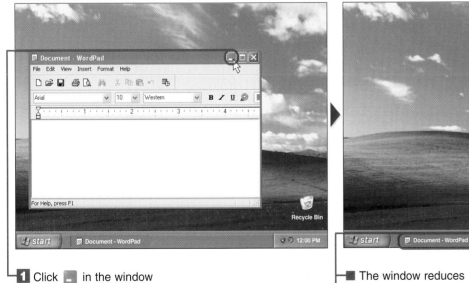

1 Click ■ in the window you want to minimize.

■ The window reduces to a button on the taskbar.

■ To redisplay the window, click its button on the taskbar.

Note: If a menu appears, displaying the names of several open windows when you click a button on the taskbar, click the name of the window you want to redisplay.

SWITCH BETWEEN WINDOWS

If you have more than one window open on your screen, you can easily switch between the windows.

Each window is like a separate piece of paper. Switching between windows is like placing a different piece of paper at the top of the pile.

You can work in only one window at a time. The active window appears in front of all other windows and displays a dark title bar.

SWITCH BETWEEN WINDOWS

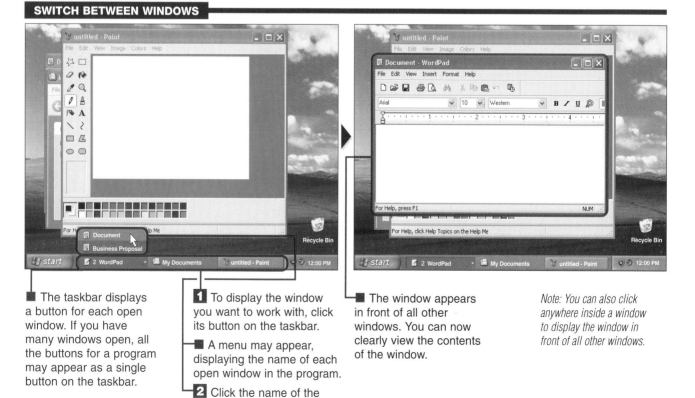

■ The taskbar displays a button for each open window. If you have many windows open, all the buttons for a program may appear as a single button on the taskbar.

1 To display the window you want to work with, click its button on the taskbar.

■ A menu may appear, displaying the name of each open window in the program.

2 Click the name of the window you want to display.

■ The window appears in front of all other windows. You can now clearly view the contents of the window.

Note: You can also click anywhere inside a window to display the window in front of all other windows.

CLOSE A MISBEHAVING PROGRAM

You can close a program that is no longer responding without having to shut down Windows.

When you close a misbehaving program, you will lose any information you did not save in the program.

Closing a misbehaving program should not affect other open programs.

CLOSE A MISBEHAVING PROGRAM

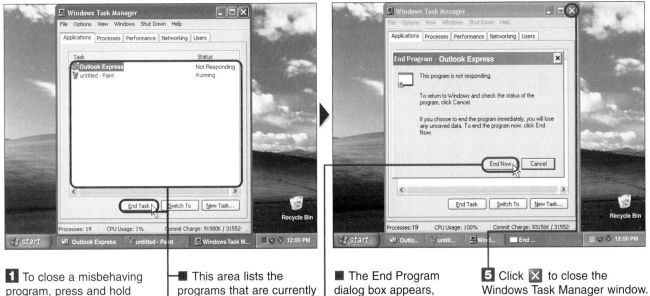

■ **1** To close a misbehaving program, press and hold down the `Ctrl` and `Alt` keys as you press the `Delete` key.

■ The Windows Task Manager window appears.

■ This area lists the programs that are currently running. The phrase **Not Responding** appears beside the name of a misbehaving program.

2 Click the program that is misbehaving.

3 Click **End Task**.

■ The End Program dialog box appears, stating that the program is not responding.

4 Click **End Now** to close the program.

5 Click ☒ to close the Windows Task Manager window.

Note: A dialog box may appear, asking if you want to send information about the misbehaving program to Microsoft to help them improve Windows. Click **Send Error Report** *or* **Don't Send**.

25

WRITE LETTERS WITH WORDPAD

You can use WordPad to create and edit documents, such as letters and memos.

If you need more advanced features than WordPad provides, you may want to obtain a more sophisticated word processor, such as Microsoft Word.

START WORDPAD

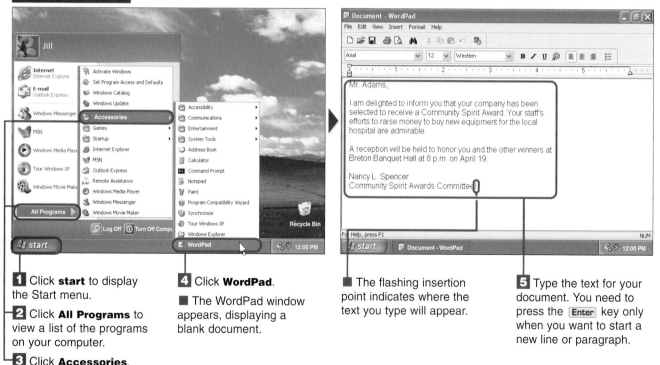

1 Click **start** to display the Start menu.

2 Click **All Programs** to view a list of the programs on your computer.

3 Click **Accessories**.

4 Click **WordPad**.

■ The WordPad window appears, displaying a blank document.

■ The flashing insertion point indicates where the text you type will appear.

5 Type the text for your document. You need to press the **Enter** key only when you want to start a new line or paragraph.

Can I cancel a change I made?

Yes. WordPad remembers the last changes you made to a document. If you regret a change, you can click the Undo button (⟲) to cancel the last change you made. You can click the Undo button repeatedly to cancel previous changes you made.

How can I emphasize text in a document?

You can **bold**, *italicize* or <u>underline</u> text to emphasize text in a document. To select the text you want to emphasize, drag the mouse over the text until the text is highlighted. Then click the Bold (**B**), Italic (*I*) or Underline (<u>U</u>) button.

EDIT TEXT

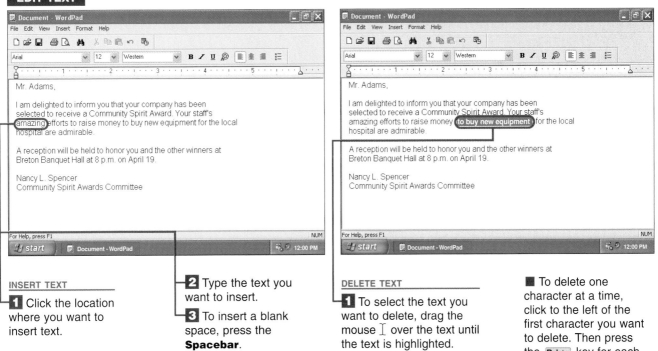

INSERT TEXT

1 Click the location where you want to insert text.

2 Type the text you want to insert.

3 To insert a blank space, press the **Spacebar**.

DELETE TEXT

1 To select the text you want to delete, drag the mouse over the text until the text is highlighted.

2 Press the Delete key to remove the text.

■ To delete one character at a time, click to the left of the first character you want to delete. Then press the Delete key for each character you want to remove.

WRITE LETTERS WITH WORDPAD

You should save your document to store it for future use. This allows you to later review and make changes to a document.

You should regularly save changes you make to a document to avoid losing your work.

SAVE A DOCUMENT

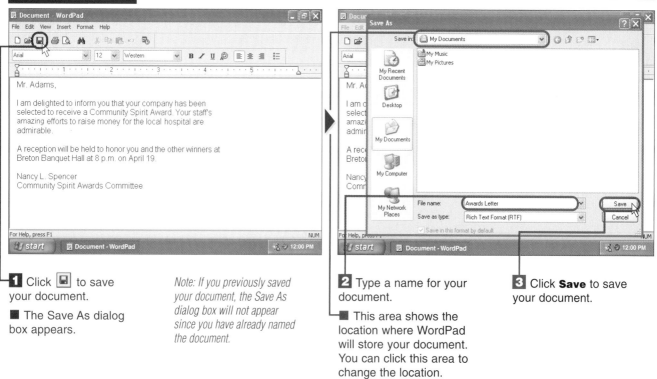

1 Click 🖫 to save your document.

■ The Save As dialog box appears.

Note: If you previously saved your document, the Save As dialog box will not appear since you have already named the document.

2 Type a name for your document.

■ This area shows the location where WordPad will store your document. You can click this area to change the location.

3 Click **Save** to save your document.

Tip

Is there a faster way to open a document?

Yes. The names of the last four documents you worked with in WordPad appear on the File menu. To open one of these documents, click **File** and then click the name of the document you want to open.

Tip

How do I print a document?

You can click the Print button (🖨) to print an entire document. Before printing a document, make sure your printer is turned on and the printer contains paper.

OPEN A SAVED DOCUMENT

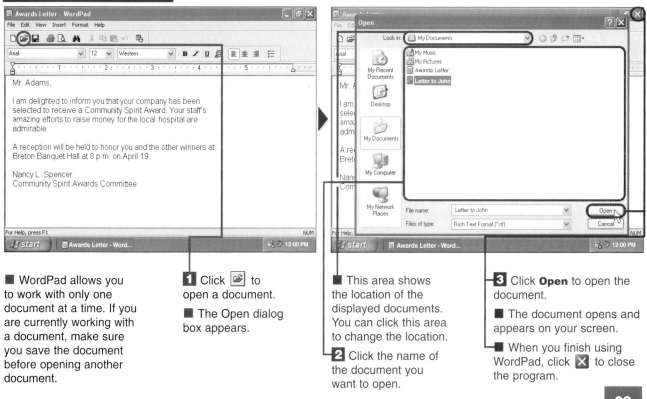

■ WordPad allows you to work with only one document at a time. If you are currently working with a document, make sure you save the document before opening another document.

1 Click 📂 to open a document.

■ The Open dialog box appears.

2 Click the name of the document you want to open.

■ This area shows the location of the displayed documents. You can click this area to change the location.

3 Click **Open** to open the document.

■ The document opens and appears on your screen.

■ When you finish using WordPad, click ✕ to close the program.

DRAW PICTURES WITH PAINT

Paint is a simple program you can use to draw pictures on your computer.

If you need more advanced features than Paint provides, you may want to obtain a more sophisticated image editing program, such as Corel Paint Shop Pro or Adobe Photoshop.

START PAINT

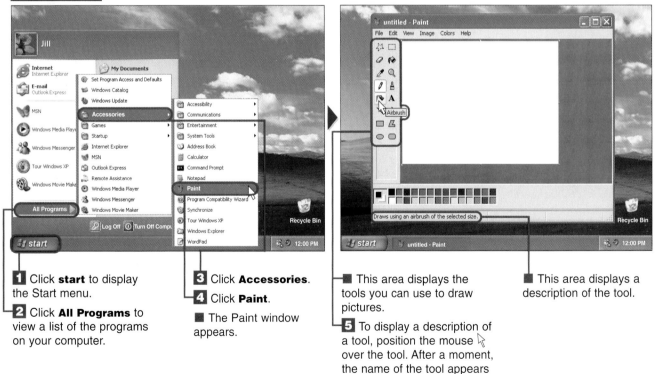

■1 Click **start** to display the Start menu.

■2 Click **All Programs** to view a list of the programs on your computer.

■3 Click **Accessories**.

■4 Click **Paint**.

■ The Paint window appears.

■ This area displays the tools you can use to draw pictures.

■5 To display a description of a tool, position the mouse over the tool. After a moment, the name of the tool appears in a yellow box.

■ This area displays a description of the tool.

Tip

How can I draw lines?

You can use the following tools to draw lines:

✏ Pencil

🖌 Brush

＼ Line

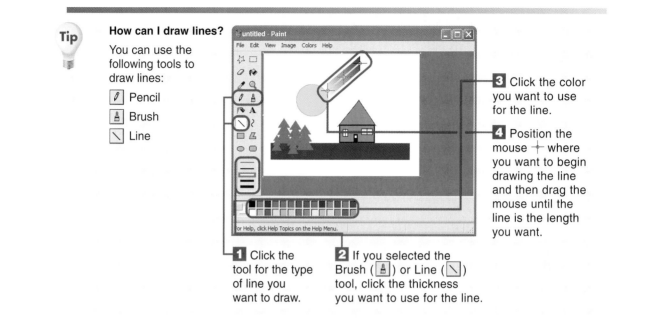

3 Click the color you want to use for the line.

4 Position the mouse ✛ where you want to begin drawing the line and then drag the mouse until the line is the length you want.

1 Click the tool for the type of line you want to draw.

2 If you selected the Brush (🖌) or Line (＼) tool, click the thickness you want to use for the line.

DRAW SHAPES

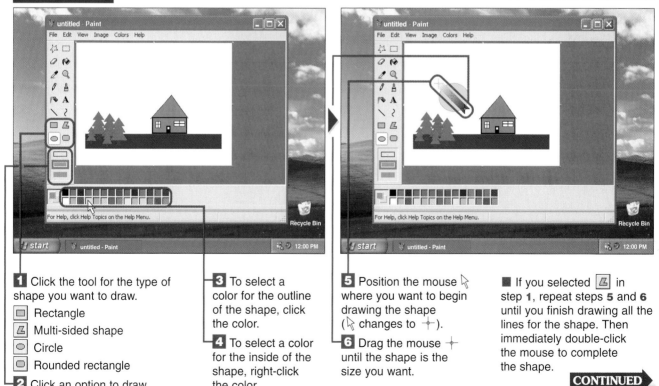

1 Click the tool for the type of shape you want to draw.

▭ Rectangle

◪ Multi-sided shape

◯ Circle

▢ Rounded rectangle

2 Click an option to draw the shape with an outline, an inside color or both.

3 To select a color for the outline of the shape, click the color.

4 To select a color for the inside of the shape, right-click the color.

5 Position the mouse ▷ where you want to begin drawing the shape (▷ changes to ✛).

6 Drag the mouse ✛ until the shape is the size you want.

■ If you selected ◪ in step **1**, repeat steps **5** and **6** until you finish drawing all the lines for the shape. Then immediately double-click the mouse to complete the shape.

CONTINUED ▶

DRAW PICTURES WITH PAINT

You should save your picture to store the picture for future use. Saving a picture allows you to later review and make changes to a picture.

You should regularly save changes you make to a picture to avoid losing your work.

SAVE A PICTURE

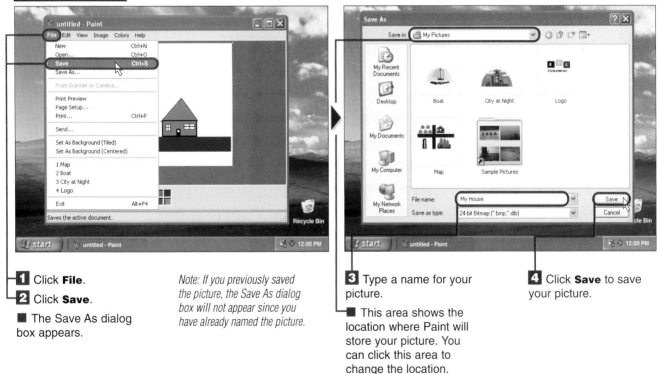

1 Click **File**.

2 Click **Save**.

■ The Save As dialog box appears.

Note: If you previously saved the picture, the Save As dialog box will not appear since you have already named the picture.

3 Type a name for your picture.

■ This area shows the location where Paint will store your picture. You can click this area to change the location.

4 Click **Save** to save your picture.

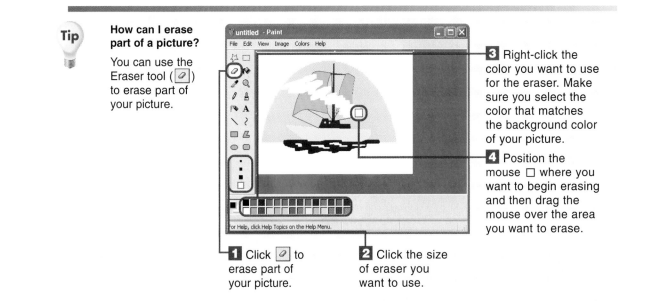

Tip

How can I erase part of a picture?

You can use the Eraser tool (🖊) to erase part of your picture.

3 Right-click the color you want to use for the eraser. Make sure you select the color that matches the background color of your picture.

4 Position the mouse □ where you want to begin erasing and then drag the mouse over the area you want to erase.

1 Click 🖊 to erase part of your picture.

2 Click the size of eraser you want to use.

OPEN A SAVED PICTURE

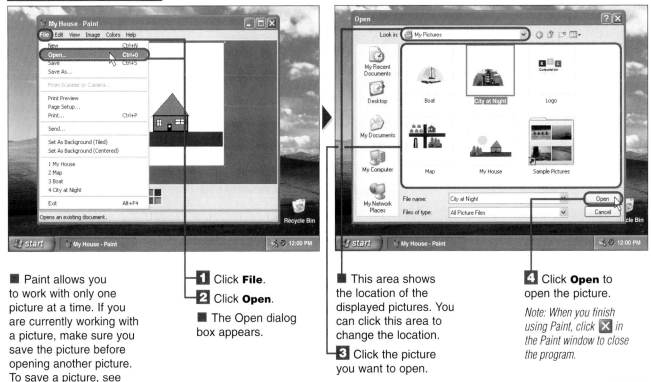

■ Paint allows you to work with only one picture at a time. If you are currently working with a picture, make sure you save the picture before opening another picture. To save a picture, see page 32.

1 Click **File**.

2 Click **Open**.

■ The Open dialog box appears.

■ This area shows the location of the displayed pictures. You can click this area to change the location.

3 Click the picture you want to open.

4 Click **Open** to open the picture.

Note: When you finish using Paint, click ✖ in the Paint window to close the program.

USING THE CALCULATOR

Windows provides a calculator that you can use to perform calculations.

You can use the Calculator to perform the same calculations you can perform on a handheld calculator.

USING THE CALCULATOR

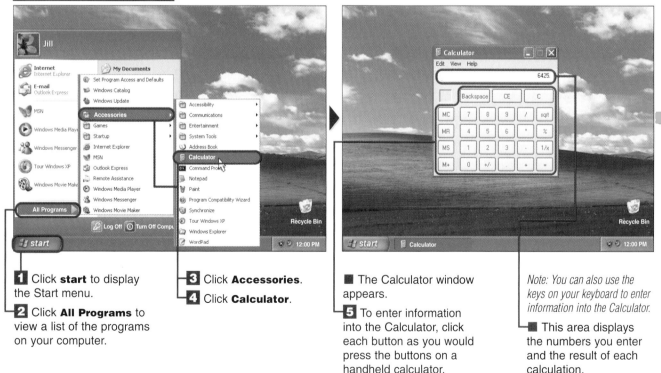

1 Click **start** to display the Start menu.

2 Click **All Programs** to view a list of the programs on your computer.

3 Click **Accessories**.

4 Click **Calculator**.

■ The Calculator window appears.

5 To enter information into the Calculator, click each button as you would press the buttons on a handheld calculator.

Note: You can also use the keys on your keyboard to enter information into the Calculator.

■ This area displays the numbers you enter and the result of each calculation.

Tip

Can I enter numbers using the keys on the right side of my keyboard?

To use the number keys on the right side of your keyboard to enter information into the Calculator, the Num Lock light must be on. To turn the light on, press the `Num Lock` key on your keyboard.

Tip

What are some useful buttons on the Calculator?

Button	Description
Backspace	Removes the last digit of the displayed number.
CE	Clears the displayed number.
C	Clears the current calculation.
MC , MR , MS	Clears, recalls and stores the number in memory.
M+	Adds the displayed number to the number in memory.
sqrt	Calculates the square root of the displayed number.
1/x	Calculates the reciprocal of the displayed number.

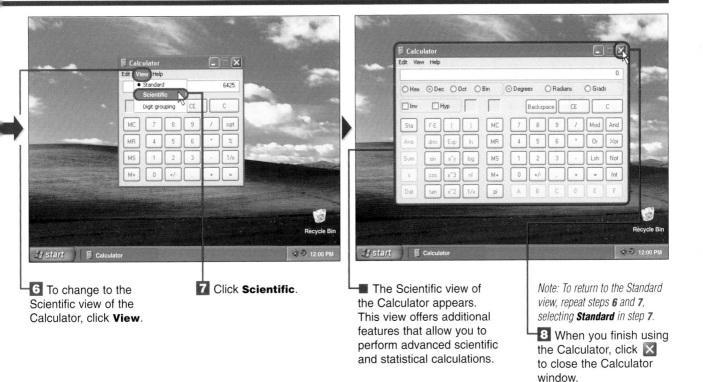

6 To change to the Scientific view of the Calculator, click **View**.

7 Click **Scientific**.

■ The Scientific view of the Calculator appears. This view offers additional features that allow you to perform advanced scientific and statistical calculations.

*Note: To return to the Standard view, repeat steps 6 and 7, selecting **Standard** in step 7.*

8 When you finish using the Calculator, click ☒ to close the Calculator window.

Windows includes several games that you can play on your computer. Games are a fun way to improve your mouse skills and hand-eye coordination.

You can play some games, such as Checkers, with other people on the Internet. Windows will match you with players from around the world. To play a game on the Internet, you will need an Internet connection.

PLAY GAMES

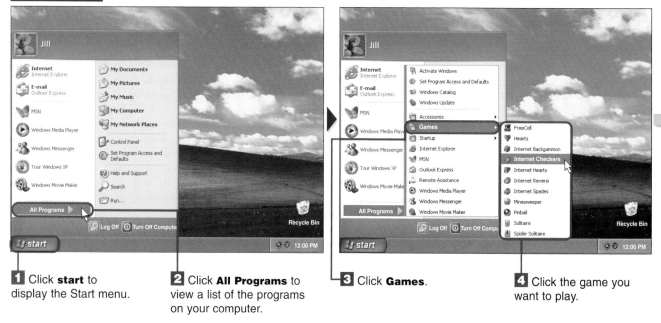

1 Click **start** to display the Start menu.

2 Click **All Programs** to view a list of the programs on your computer.

3 Click **Games**.

4 Click the game you want to play.

Tip

What games are included with Windows?

Here are some popular games included with Windows.

Minesweeper

Minesweeper is a strategy game in which you try to avoid being blown up by mines.

Pinball

Pinball is similar to a pinball game you would find at an arcade. You launch a ball and then try to score as many points as possible.

Solitaire

Solitaire is a classic card game that you play on your own. The object of the game is to place all the cards in order from ace to king in four stacks—one stack for each suit.

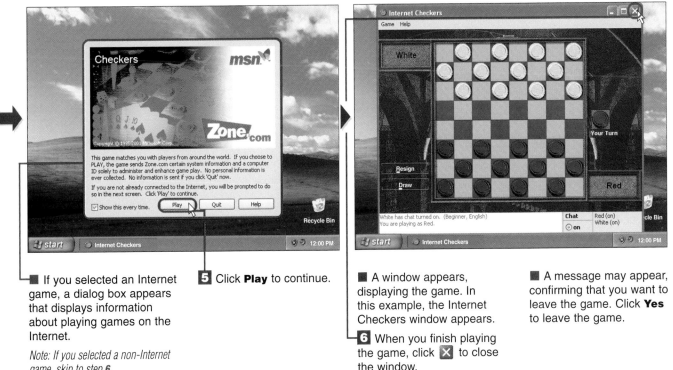

■ If you selected an Internet game, a dialog box appears that displays information about playing games on the Internet.

Note: If you selected a non-Internet game, skip to step 6.

5 Click **Play** to continue.

■ A window appears, displaying the game. In this example, the Internet Checkers window appears.

6 When you finish playing the game, click ✕ to close the window.

■ A message may appear, confirming that you want to leave the game. Click **Yes** to leave the game.

FIND HELP INFORMATION

If you do not know how to perform a task in Windows, you can use the Help feature to find information on the task.

FIND HELP INFORMATION

1 Click **start** to display the Start menu.

2 Click **Help and Support**.

■ The Help and Support Center window appears.

■ This area displays a list of common help topics, ways that you can ask for assistance and tasks for which you can receive help. You can click an item of interest to display information about the item.

3 To search for specific help information, click this area and then type a word or phrase that describes the topic of interest.

4 Press the **Enter** key to start the search.

Tip

Why do some help topics display colored text?

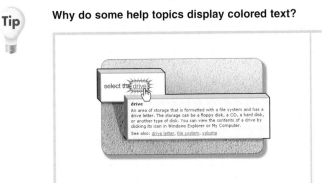

Display a Definition

You can click a word or phrase that appears in green to display a definition of the word or phrase. To hide the definition, click the definition.

Obtain Additional Help

You can click a word or phrase that appears in blue to obtain additional help. Windows may display another help topic or open a window that allows you to perform a task. If you click the phrase "Related Topics" at the bottom of a help topic, a list of related help topics appears. You can click the help topic of interest in the list.

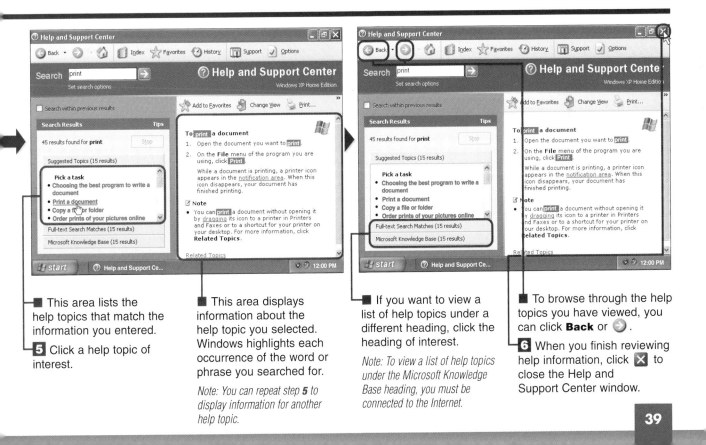

■ This area lists the help topics that match the information you entered.

5 Click a help topic of interest.

■ This area displays information about the help topic you selected. Windows highlights each occurrence of the word or phrase you searched for.

Note: You can repeat step 5 to display information for another help topic.

■ If you want to view a list of help topics under a different heading, click the heading of interest.

Note: To view a list of help topics under the Microsoft Knowledge Base heading, you must be connected to the Internet.

■ To browse through the help topics you have viewed, you can click **Back** or ⊙.

6 When you finish reviewing help information, click ✕ to close the Help and Support Center window.

RESTART YOUR COMPUTER

If your computer is not operating properly, you can restart your computer to try to fix the problem.

Before restarting your computer, make sure you close all the programs you have open.

RESTART YOUR COMPUTER

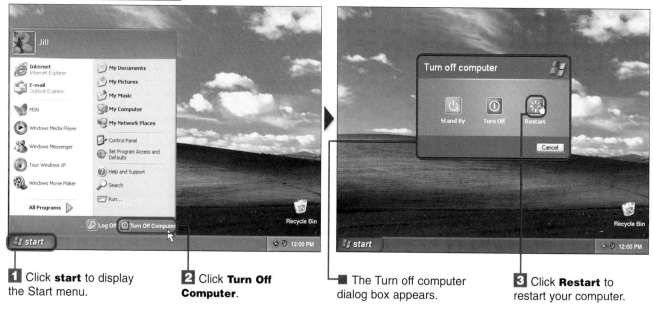

1 Click **start** to display the Start menu.

2 Click **Turn Off Computer**.

■ The Turn off computer dialog box appears.

3 Click **Restart** to restart your computer.

SHUT DOWN WINDOWS

When you finish using your computer, you should shut down Windows before turning off your computer.

Before shutting down Windows, make sure you close all the programs you have open.

SHUT DOWN WINDOWS

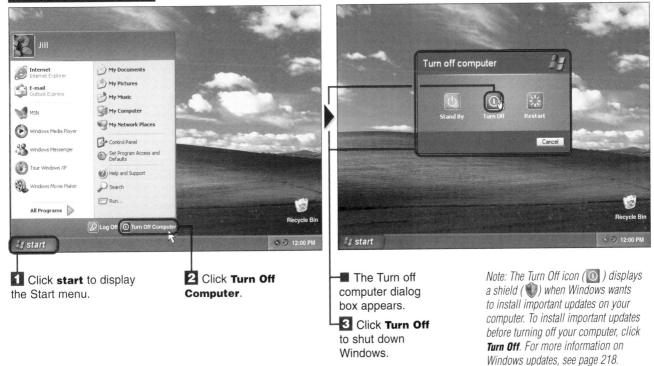

1 Click **start** to display the Start menu.

2 Click **Turn Off Computer**.

■ The Turn off computer dialog box appears.

3 Click **Turn Off** to shut down Windows.

Note: The Turn Off icon ( ) displays a shield ( ) when Windows wants to install important updates on your computer. To install important updates before turning off your computer, click Turn Off. For more information on Windows updates, see page 218.

CHAPTER 2

View Files

Read this chapter to learn how to view the files and folders stored on your computer. Discover how to view your personal files, view the contents of your entire computer as well as sort and group files and folders to suit your preferences.

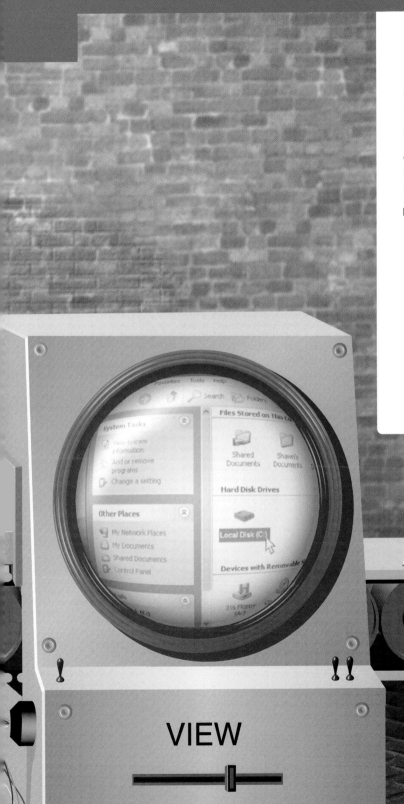

SORT

VIEW

VIEW YOUR PERSONAL FOLDERS

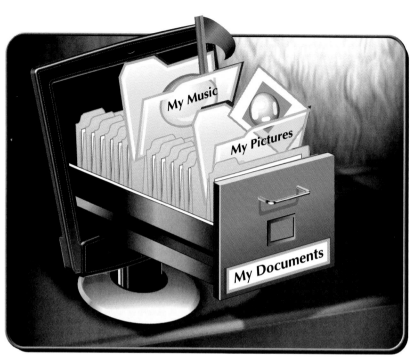

Windows provides personal folders that offer a convenient place for you to store and manage your files. You can view the contents of your personal folders at any time.

Many programs automatically store files in your personal folders.

VIEW THE MY DOCUMENTS FOLDER

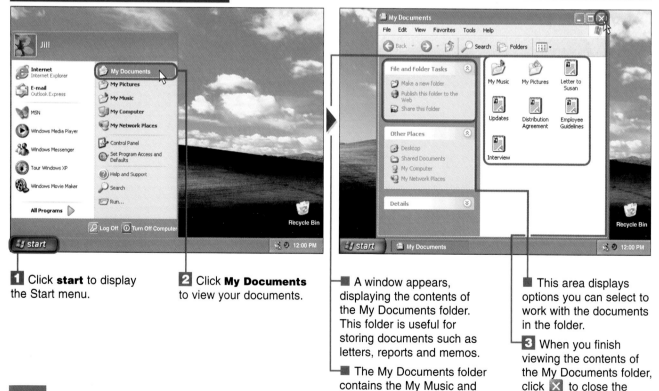

1 Click **start** to display the Start menu.

2 Click **My Documents** to view your documents.

■ A window appears, displaying the contents of the My Documents folder. This folder is useful for storing documents such as letters, reports and memos.

■ The My Documents folder contains the My Music and My Pictures folders.

■ This area displays options you can select to work with the documents in the folder.

3 When you finish viewing the contents of the My Documents folder, click ✕ to close the folder.

Tip

What tasks can I perform with the files in my personal folders?

The My Pictures and My Music folders offer several specialized options that you can select to work with your pictures and music. Here are some tasks you can perform.

MY PICTURES

View as a slide show

Displays all the pictures in the My Pictures folder as a full-screen slide show.

Order prints online

Sends the pictures you select to a Web site that allows you to order prints of the pictures.

MY MUSIC

Play all

Plays all the music in the My Music folder.

Shop for music online

Displays a Web site which allows you to listen to and purchase music.

VIEW THE MY PICTURES OR MY MUSIC FOLDER

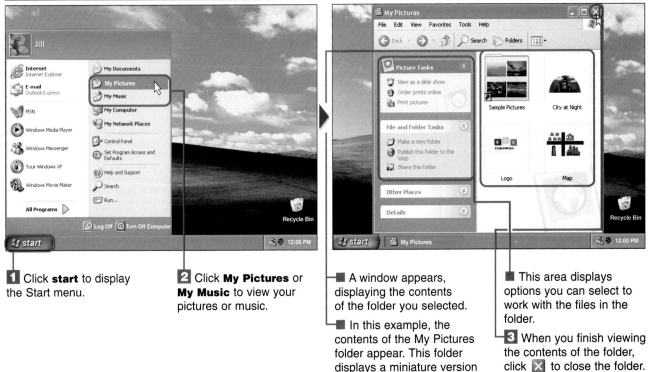

1 Click **start** to display the Start menu.

2 Click **My Pictures** or **My Music** to view your pictures or music.

■ A window appears, displaying the contents of the folder you selected.

■ In this example, the contents of the My Pictures folder appear. This folder displays a miniature version of each picture in the folder.

■ This area displays options you can select to work with the files in the folder.

3 When you finish viewing the contents of the folder, click ☒ to close the folder.

You can easily browse through the drives, folders and files on your computer.

Like a filing cabinet, Windows uses folders to organize the files, such as documents, pictures, sounds and videos, stored on your computer.

VIEW CONTENTS OF YOUR COMPUTER

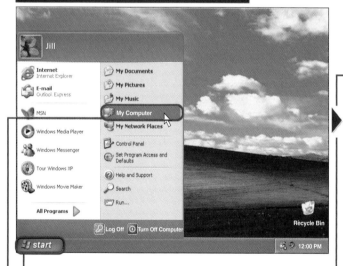

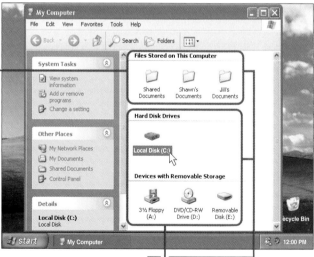

1 Click **start** to display the Start menu.

2 Click **My Computer** to view the contents of your computer.

■ The My Computer window appears.

Note: To view the contents of a CD, DVD, floppy disk or memory card, make sure you insert the disk or card into the appropriate drive or slot before continuing.

■ The folders in this area contain files that all users set up on your computer can access. For more information on these folders, see pages 194 and 195.

■ The items in this area represent the drives available on your computer, such as your hard drive, floppy drive, CD drive, DVD drive and memory card reader.

3 To display the contents of a drive or folder, double-click the item.

What do the icons in a window represent?

Each item in a window displays an icon to help you distinguish between the different types of items. Common types of items include:

	Folder
	Paint picture
	Text document
	Windows Media Player file
	Wordpad document

What is a memory card reader?

Many new computers come with a memory card reader, which is a device that reads and records information on memory cards. Memory cards are most commonly used to transfer information between a computer and an external device such as a digital camera, MP3 player or Personal Digital Assistant (PDA).

A memory card reader may have only one slot or several slots that allow the reader to accept memory cards from different manufacturers and devices. In the My Computer window, each memory card slot in a memory card reader appears as a separate drive and is often labeled as "Removable Disk."

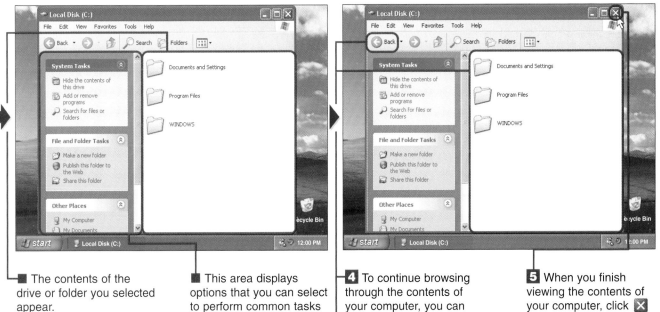

■ The contents of the drive or folder you selected appear.

Note: If the contents of the drive you selected do not appear, click **Show the contents of this folder** *in the window.*

■ This area displays options that you can select to perform common tasks and access commonly used locations on your computer. The available options depend on the selected item.

4 To continue browsing through the contents of your computer, you can double-click a folder to display its contents.

■ To return to a window you have previously viewed, click **Back**.

5 When you finish viewing the contents of your computer, click ⊠ to close the window.

CHANGE VIEW OF ITEMS

You can change the view of items in a window. The view you select determines the way files and folders will appear in the window.

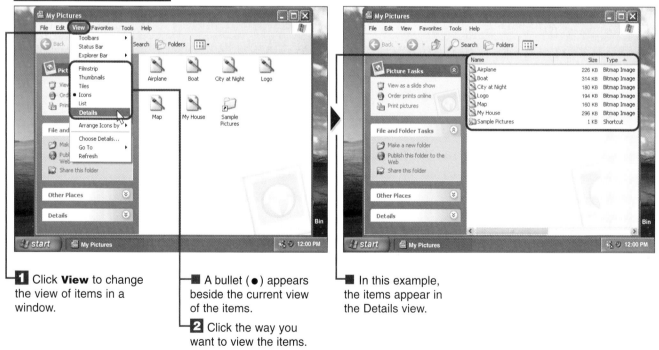

1 Click **View** to change the view of items in a window.

■ A bullet (●) appears beside the current view of the items.

2 Click the way you want to view the items.

■ In this example, the items appear in the Details view.

THE VIEWS

Filmstrip

The Filmstrip view displays pictures in a single row that you can scroll through. This view is only available in some windows, such as the My Pictures window. You can click a picture to display a larger version of the picture above the other pictures.

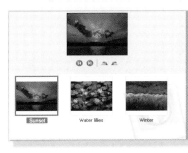

Thumbnails

The Thumbnails view displays a miniature version of each picture and some other types of files. If a miniature version of a file cannot be shown, an icon is displayed to indicate the type of file, such as a Wordpad document ( ). In this view, miniature versions of a few pictures within a folder are shown on the folder's icon.

Tiles

The Tiles view displays items as large icons and displays information about each item below the item's file name. You can sort the items to change the information that each item displays. To sort items, see page 50.

Icons

The Icons view displays items as small icons with the file name appearing below each icon.

List

The List view displays items as small icons arranged in a list. This view is useful if you want to find a particular item in a long list of items.

Details

The Details view displays information about each item, including the name, size, type and date the items were last changed.

SORT ITEMS

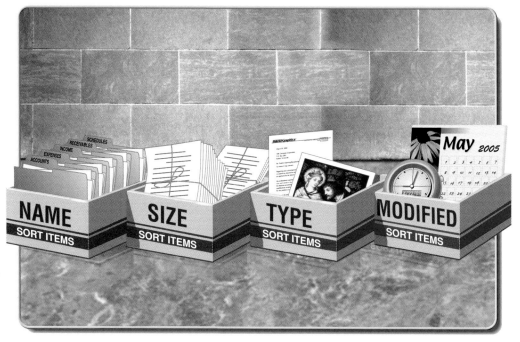

You can sort the items displayed in a window to help you find files and folders more quickly.

You can sort items by name, size, type or the date the items were last changed. Some windows allow you to sort items in other ways. For example, the My Music window allows you to sort items by artist, album title and track number.

SORT ITEMS

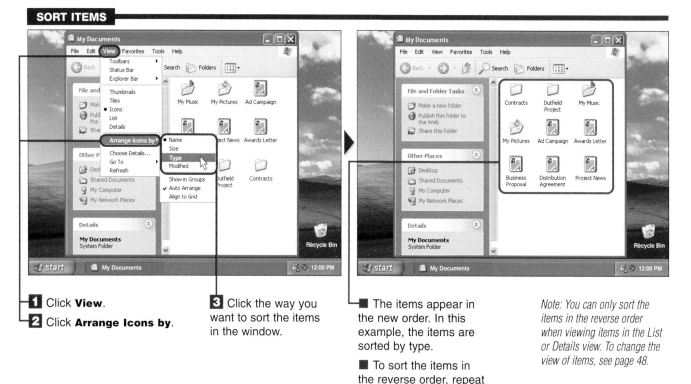

1 Click **View**.

2 Click **Arrange Icons by**.

3 Click the way you want to sort the items in the window.

■ The items appear in the new order. In this example, the items are sorted by type.

■ To sort the items in the reverse order, repeat steps **1** to **3**.

Note: You can only sort the items in the reverse order when viewing items in the List or Details view. To change the view of items, see page 48.

You can group items
to better organize
the files and folders
in a window.

GROUP ITEMS

1 Click **View**.

2 Click **Arrange Icons by**.

3 Click **Show in Groups**.

*Note: The Show in Groups
option is not available when
viewing items in the List or
Filmstrip view. To change the
view of items, see page 48.*

■ Windows groups the
items in the window.

■ You can sort the items
to change the way the items
are grouped in the window.
For example, sorting the
items by size will group the
items by size. To sort items,
see page 50.

■ If you no longer want
to group the items in a
window, repeat steps **1**
to **3**.

USING WINDOWS EXPLORER

Windows Explorer shows the organization of all the files and folders on your computer.

You can work with the files in Windows Explorer as you would work with files in any window. For example, you can move, rename and delete files in Windows Explorer. To work with files, see pages 56 to 107.

To work with files, see pages 56 to 107.

USING WINDOWS EXPLORER

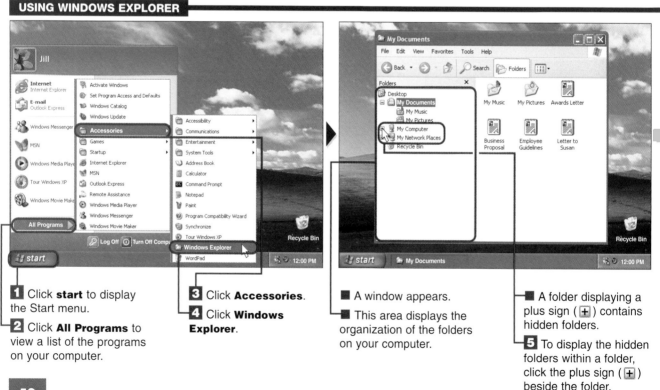

1 Click **start** to display the Start menu.

2 Click **All Programs** to view a list of the programs on your computer.

3 Click **Accessories**.

4 Click **Windows Explorer**.

■ A window appears.

■ This area displays the organization of the folders on your computer.

■ A folder displaying a plus sign (⊞) contains hidden folders.

5 To display the hidden folders within a folder, click the plus sign (⊞) beside the folder.

52

Tip

How can I quickly perform tasks with the files and folders displayed in Windows Explorer?

To quickly perform tasks in Windows Explorer, click the **Folders** button to display a list of options that you can select. The options that appear depend on the file or folder that is currently selected. To return to the organization of the folders, click the **Folders** button again.

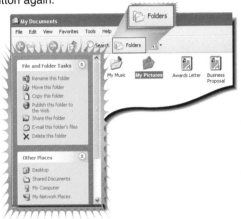

Tip

How can I view information about a file or folder displayed in Windows Explorer?

Position the mouse ⬚ over a file or folder. After a few seconds, a yellow box appears, displaying information about the file or folder.

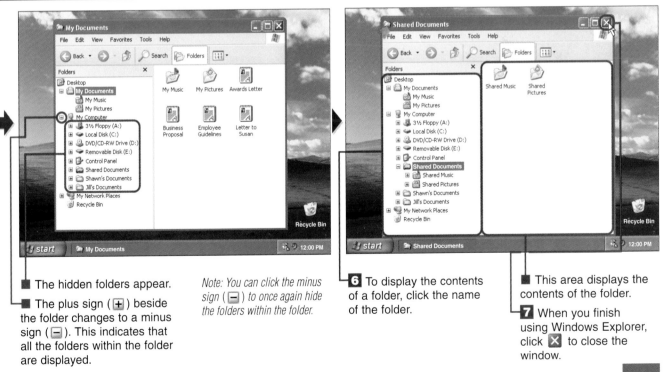

■ The hidden folders appear.

■ The plus sign (⊞) beside the folder changes to a minus sign (⊟). This indicates that all the folders within the folder are displayed.

Note: You can click the minus sign (⊟) to once again hide the folders within the folder.

6 To display the contents of a folder, click the name of the folder.

■ This area displays the contents of the folder.

7 When you finish using Windows Explorer, click ✖ to close the window.

CHAPTER 3

Working with Files

This chapter teaches you the basic tasks you will need to know to work with files on your computer. Learn how to print, move and delete files, create a shortcut to a file on your desktop and much more.

SELECT FILES

Before working with files, you often need to select the files you want to work with. Selected files appear highlighted on your screen.

You can select folders the same way you select files. Selecting a folder will select all the files in the folder.

SELECT FILES

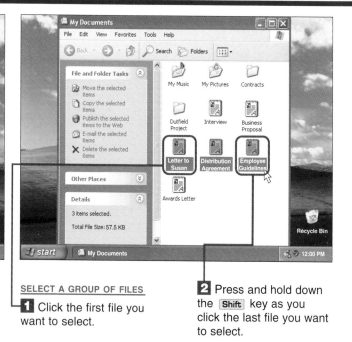

SELECT ONE FILE

1 Click the file you want to select. The file is highlighted.

2 If you want to display information about the file, click **Details**.

■ Information about the file appears, including the file type and the date and time the file was last changed.

*Note: To hide the information, click **Details** again.*

SELECT A GROUP OF FILES

1 Click the first file you want to select.

2 Press and hold down the **Shift** key as you click the last file you want to select.

Tip

How do I deselect files?

To deselect all the files in a window, click a blank area in the window.

To deselect one file from a group of selected files, press and hold down the Ctrl key as you click the file you want to deselect.

Note: You can deselect folders the same way you deselect files.

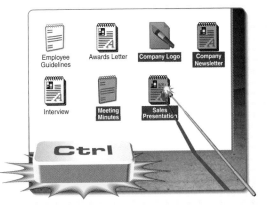

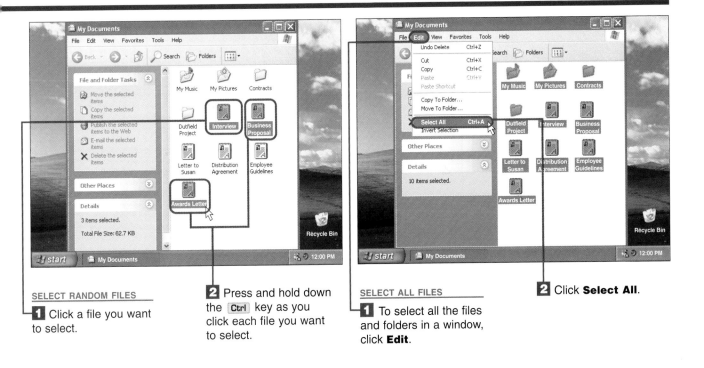

SELECT RANDOM FILES

1 Click a file you want to select.

2 Press and hold down the Ctrl key as you click each file you want to select.

SELECT ALL FILES

1 To select all the files and folders in a window, click **Edit**.

2 Click **Select All**.

OPEN A FILE

You can open a file to display its contents on your screen. Opening a file allows you to review and make changes to the file.

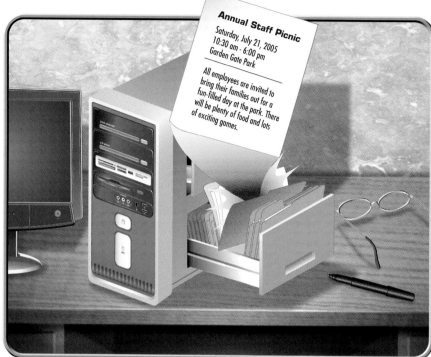

You can open folders the same way you open files.

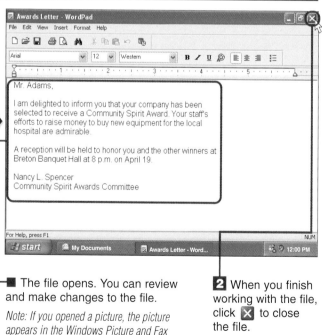

1 Double-click the file you want to open.

■ The file opens. You can review and make changes to the file.

Note: If you opened a picture, the picture appears in the Windows Picture and Fax Viewer window. To make changes to the picture, you will need to open the picture within the program you used to create the picture or in another image editing program.

2 When you finish working with the file, click ☒ to close the file.

RENAME A FILE

You can rename
a file to better
describe the
contents of the
file. Renaming
a file can help
you more
quickly locate
the file in the
future.

You can rename
folders the same
way you rename
files. You should
not rename folders
that Windows or
other programs
require to operate.

RENAME A FILE

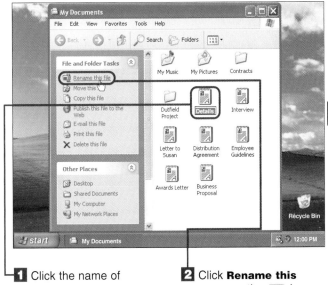

1 Click the name of
the file you want to
rename.

*Note: You should not rename
files that Windows or other
programs require to operate.*

2 Click **Rename this
file** or press the `F2` key.

■ A box appears around
the file name.

3 Type a new name for
the file and then press
the `Enter` key.

*Note: A file name cannot
contain the \ / : * ? " < > or |
characters.*

■ If you change your
mind while typing a new
file name, you can press
the `Esc` key to return to
the original file name.

PRINT A FILE

You can produce a paper copy of a file stored on your computer.

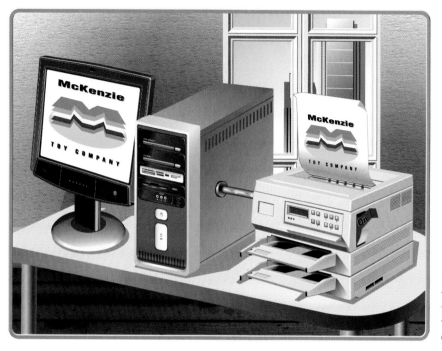

Before printing a file, make sure your printer is turned on and contains paper.

PRINT A FILE

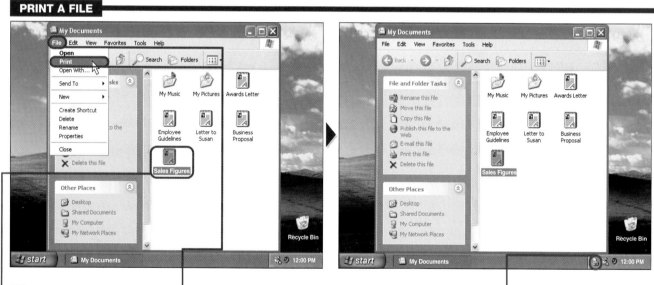

1 Click the file you want to print.

■ To print more than one file, select all the files you want to print. To select multiple files, see page 56.

2 Click **File**.

3 Click **Print**.

Note: If you selected a picture, the Photo Printing Wizard appears. For information on using the Photo Printing Wizard to print pictures, see page 80.

■ Windows quickly opens, prints and then closes the file.

■ When you print a file, a printer icon () appears in this area. The printer icon disappears when the file has finished printing.

Tip

How can I stop a file from printing?

You may want to stop a file from printing if you accidentally selected the wrong file or if you want to make last-minute changes to the file.

1 When viewing the files waiting to print, click the file you no longer want to print and then press the Delete key. To view the files waiting to print, see below.

2 A confirmation dialog box will appear. Click **Yes** to stop the file from printing.

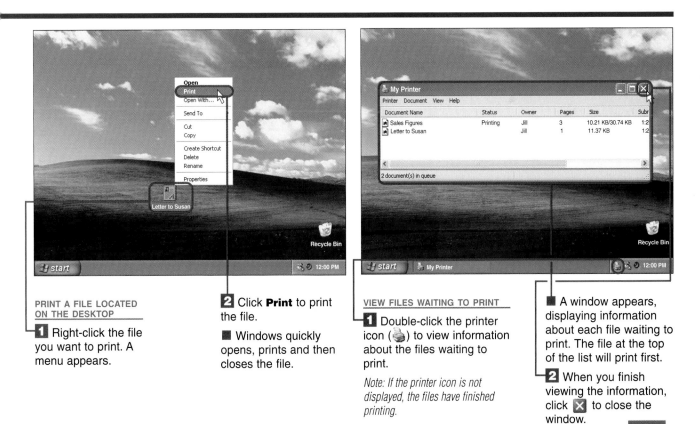

PRINT A FILE LOCATED ON THE DESKTOP

1 Right-click the file you want to print. A menu appears.

2 Click **Print** to print the file.

■ Windows quickly opens, prints and then closes the file.

VIEW FILES WAITING TO PRINT

1 Double-click the printer icon (🖨) to view information about the files waiting to print.

Note: If the printer icon is not displayed, the files have finished printing.

■ A window appears, displaying information about each file waiting to print. The file at the top of the list will print first.

2 When you finish viewing the information, click ⊠ to close the window.

DELETE A FILE

You can delete
a file you no
longer need.

Before you delete a
file, make sure you
will no longer need
the file. You should
also make sure you
do not delete a file
that Windows or
other programs
require to operate.

DELETE A FILE

1 Click the file you want
to delete.

■ To delete more than one
file, select all the files you
want to delete. To select
multiple files, see page 56.

2 Click **Delete this file**
or press the Delete key.

*Note: If you selected multiple
files, click **Delete the selected
items** in step 2.*

■ The Confirm File Delete
dialog box appears.

3 Click **Yes** to delete
the file.

Tip

**How can I permanently delete
a file from my computer?**

When you delete a file,
Windows places the file in the
Recycle Bin in case you later
want to restore the file. If you
do not want to place a deleted
file in the Recycle Bin, such as
when deleting a confidential file,
you can permanently delete the
file from your computer.

To permanently delete a
file from your computer,
perform steps **1** to **3** on
page 62, except press and
hold down the Shift key
as you perform step **2**.

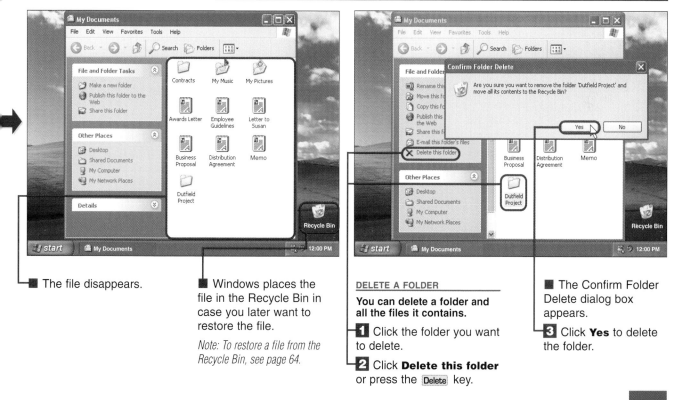

■ The file disappears.

■ Windows places the
file in the Recycle Bin in
case you later want to
restore the file.

*Note: To restore a file from the
Recycle Bin, see page 64.*

DELETE A FOLDER

**You can delete a folder and
all the files it contains.**

1 Click the folder you want
to delete.

2 Click **Delete this folder**
or press the Delete key.

■ The Confirm Folder
Delete dialog box
appears.

3 Click **Yes** to delete
the folder.

The Recycle Bin stores all the files you have deleted. You can easily restore any file in the Recycle Bin to its original location on your computer.

You can restore folders the same way you restore files. When you restore a folder, Windows restores all the files in the folder.

RESTORE A DELETED FILE

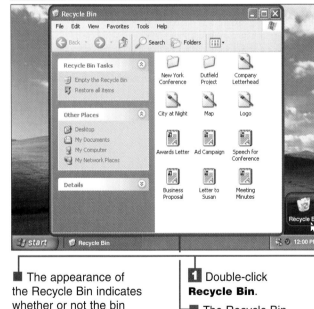

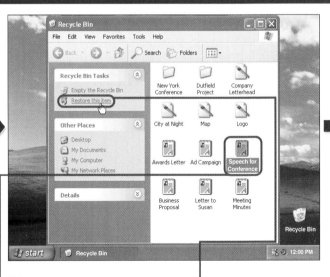

■ The appearance of the Recycle Bin indicates whether or not the bin contains deleted files.

Contains deleted files.

Does not contain deleted files.

1 Double-click **Recycle Bin**.

■ The Recycle Bin window appears, displaying all the files you have deleted.

2 Click the file you want to restore.

■ To restore more than one file, select all the files you want to restore. To select multiple files, see page 56.

3 Click **Restore this item**.

*Note: If you selected multiple files, click **Restore the selected items** in step 3.*

Tip

Why is the file I want to restore not in the Recycle Bin?

The Recycle Bin does not store files you deleted from your network or from removable storage media such as a memory card. Files deleted from these locations are permanently deleted and cannot be restored. Files that are larger than the storage capacity of the Recycle Bin are also permanently deleted.

Tip

Can I permanently remove one file from the Recycle Bin?

You may want to permanently remove one file from the Recycle Bin, such as a file that contains confidential information. You can permanently remove a file from the Recycle Bin by deleting the file in the Recycle Bin as you would delete any file on your computer. To delete a file, see page 62.

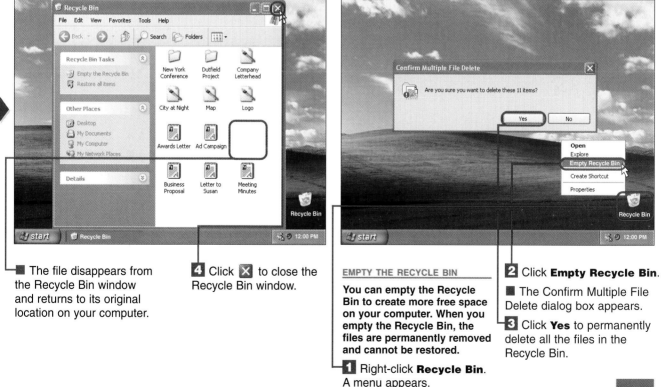

■ The file disappears from the Recycle Bin window and returns to its original location on your computer.

4 Click ☒ to close the Recycle Bin window.

EMPTY THE RECYCLE BIN

You can empty the Recycle Bin to create more free space on your computer. When you empty the Recycle Bin, the files are permanently removed and cannot be restored.

1 Right-click **Recycle Bin**. A menu appears.

2 Click **Empty Recycle Bin**.

■ The Confirm Multiple File Delete dialog box appears.

3 Click **Yes** to permanently delete all the files in the Recycle Bin.

MOVE A FILE

You can move a file to a new location on your computer to re-organize your files.

When you move a file, the file will disappear from its original location and appear in the new location.

You can move a folder the same way you move a file. When you move a folder, all the files in the folder are also moved.

MOVE A FILE

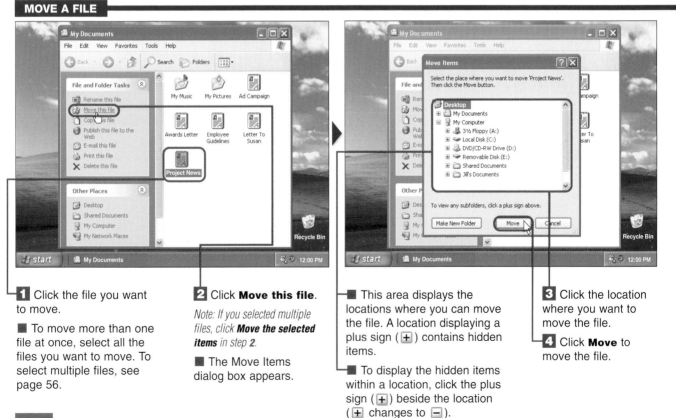

1 Click the file you want to move.

■ To move more than one file at once, select all the files you want to move. To select multiple files, see page 56.

2 Click **Move this file**.

*Note: If you selected multiple files, click **Move the selected items** in step 2.*

■ The Move Items dialog box appears.

■ This area displays the locations where you can move the file. A location displaying a plus sign (⊞) contains hidden items.

■ To display the hidden items within a location, click the plus sign (⊞) beside the location (⊞ changes to ⊟).

3 Click the location where you want to move the file.

4 Click **Move** to move the file.

Tip

Why would I want to move a file?

You may want to move a file to a different folder to keep files of the same type in one location on your computer. For example, you can move all your documents to the My Documents folder provided by Windows. Windows also includes the My Pictures and My Music folders that you can use to store your pictures and music files. To open one of these folders, see page 44.

Tip

Why does a dialog box appear when I try to move a file?

If you try to move a file to a folder that contains a file with the same name, a dialog box appears, confirming the move. You can click **Yes** or **No** in the dialog box to specify if you want to replace the existing file with the file you are moving.

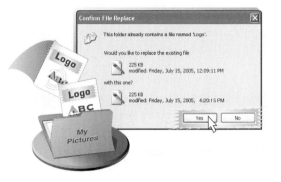

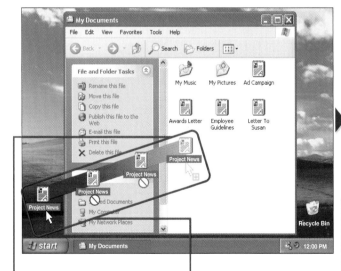

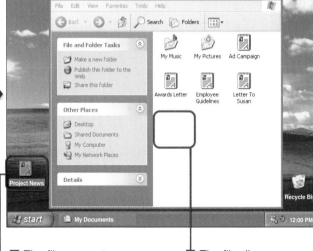

USING DRAG AND DROP

■ Before moving a file, make sure you can clearly see the location where you want to move the file.

1 Position the mouse ⌖ over the file you want to move.

■ To move more than one file at once, select all the files you want to move. Then position the mouse ⌖ over one of the files. To select multiple files, see page 56.

2 Drag the file to a new location.

■ The file moves to the new location.

■ The file disappears from its original location.

COPY A FILE

You can copy a file to a new location on your computer.

When you copy a file, the file appears in both the original and new locations.

You can copy a folder the same way you copy a file. When you copy a folder, all the files in the folder are also copied.

COPY A FILE

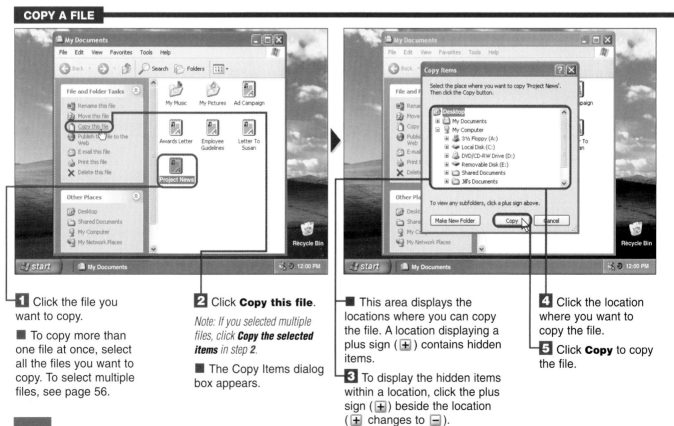

1 Click the file you want to copy.

■ To copy more than one file at once, select all the files you want to copy. To select multiple files, see page 56.

2 Click **Copy this file**.

*Note: If you selected multiple files, click **Copy the selected items** in step 2.*

■ The Copy Items dialog box appears.

■ This area displays the locations where you can copy the file. A location displaying a plus sign (+) contains hidden items.

3 To display the hidden items within a location, click the plus sign (+) beside the location (+ changes to −).

4 Click the location where you want to copy the file.

5 Click **Copy** to copy the file.

Tip

Can I copy a file to the same folder that contains the file?

Yes. If you copy a file to the same folder that contains the file, Windows will add "Copy of" to the new file name. Copying a file to the same folder is useful if you plan to make major changes to a file, but you want to keep the original copy of the file. This gives you two copies of the file—the original file and a file that you can change.

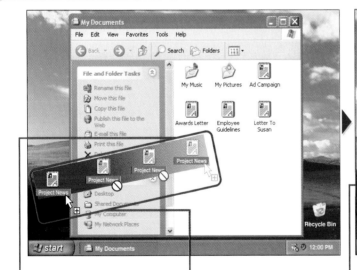

USING DRAG AND DROP

■ Before copying a file, make sure you can clearly see the location where you want to copy the file.

1 Position the mouse ⬚ over the file you want to copy.

■ To copy more than one file at once, select all the files you want to copy. Then position the mouse ⬚ over one of the files. To select multiple files, see page 56.

2 Press and hold down the **Ctrl** key as you drag the file to a new location.

■ A copy of the file appears in the new location.

■ The original file remains in the original location.

ADD A SHORTCUT TO THE DESKTOP

You can add a shortcut to the desktop that will provide a quick way of opening a file you regularly use.

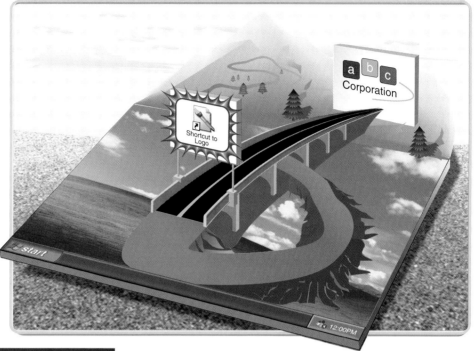

ADD A SHORTCUT TO THE DESKTOP

1 Click the file you want to create a shortcut to.

2 Click **File**.

3 Click **Send To**.

4 Click **Desktop (create shortcut)**.

Tip

How do I rename or delete a shortcut?

You can rename or delete a shortcut the same way you would rename or delete any file. Renaming or deleting a shortcut will not affect the original file. To rename a file, see page 59. To delete a file, see page 62.

Tip

Can I move a shortcut to a different location?

Yes. If you do not want a shortcut to appear on your desktop, you can move the shortcut to a different location on your computer. You can move a shortcut the same way you would move any file. To move a file, see page 66.

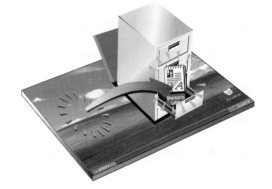

■ The shortcut appears on your desktop.

■ You can tell the difference between the shortcut and the original file because the shortcut icon displays an arrow (🔿).

■ You can double-click the shortcut to open the file at any time.

Note: You can create a shortcut to a folder the same way you create a shortcut to a file. Creating a shortcut to a folder will give you quick access to all the files in the folder.

CREATE A NEW FILE

You can instantly create, name and store a new file in the location you want without starting a program.

Creating a new file without starting a program allows you to focus on the organization of your files rather than the programs you need to accomplish your tasks.

CREATE A NEW FILE

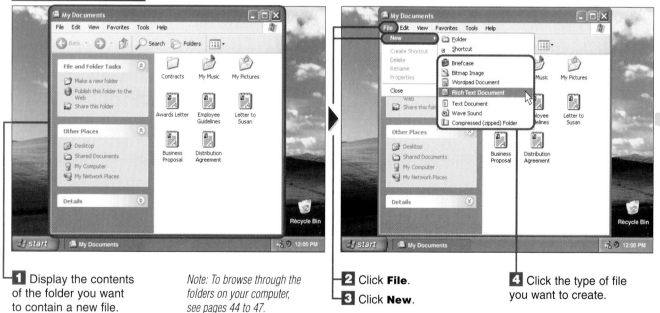

1 Display the contents of the folder you want to contain a new file.

Note: To browse through the folders on your computer, see pages 44 to 47.

2 Click **File**.

3 Click **New**.

4 Click the type of file you want to create.

Tip

What types of files can I create?

The types of files you can create depend on the programs installed on your computer. By default, Windows allows you to create the following types of files.

File Type	Description
Briefcase	Stores copies of files that you want to work with on another computer.
Bitmap Image	Creates an image file.
Wordpad Document	Creates a Wordpad document.
Rich Text Document	Creates a document that can contain formatting.
Text Document	Creates a document that cannot contain any formatting.
Wave Sound	Creates a sound file.
Compressed (zipped) Folder	Creates a folder that compresses its contents to save storage space.

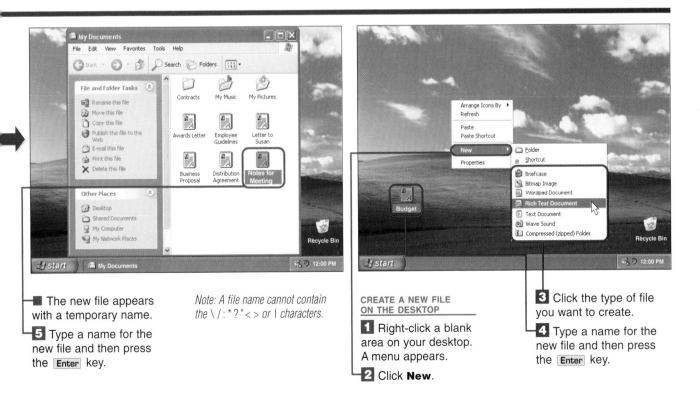

■ The new file appears with a temporary name.

5 Type a name for the new file and then press the Enter key.

*Note: A file name cannot contain the \ / : * ? " < > or | characters.*

CREATE A NEW FILE ON THE DESKTOP

1 Right-click a blank area on your desktop. A menu appears.

2 Click **New**.

3 Click the type of file you want to create.

4 Type a name for the new file and then press the Enter key.

CREATE A NEW FOLDER

You can create a
new folder to help
you organize the
files stored on
your computer.

Creating a folder is
like placing a new
folder in a filing
cabinet.

CREATE A NEW FOLDER

1 Display the contents
of the folder you want
to contain a new folder.

*Note: To browse through the
folders on your computer, see
pages 44 to 47.*

2 Click **Make a new
folder**.

*Note: If the Make a new folder
option is not available, click a
blank area in the window to
display the option.*

■ The new folder
appears, displaying
a temporary name.

3 Type a name for the
new folder and then
press the Enter key.

*Note: A folder name cannot
contain the \ / : * ? " < > or |
characters.*

Tip

How can creating a new folder help me organize the files on my computer?

You can create a new folder to store files you want to keep together, such as files for a particular project. This allows you to quickly locate the files. For example, you can create a folder named "Reports" that stores all of your reports. You can create as many folders as you need to set up a filing system that makes sense to you.

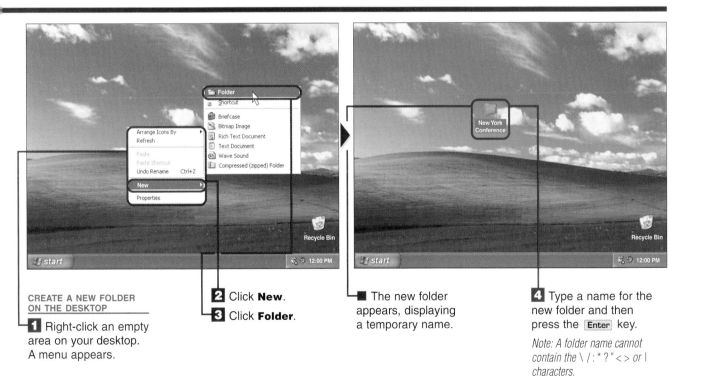

CREATE A NEW FOLDER ON THE DESKTOP

1 Right-click an empty area on your desktop. A menu appears.

2 Click **New**.

3 Click **Folder**.

■ The new folder appears, displaying a temporary name.

4 Type a name for the new folder and then press the Enter key.

*Note: A folder name cannot contain the \ / : * ? " < > or | characters.*

SEARCH FOR FILES

If you cannot remember the exact name or location of a file you want to work with, you can have Windows search for the file on your computer.

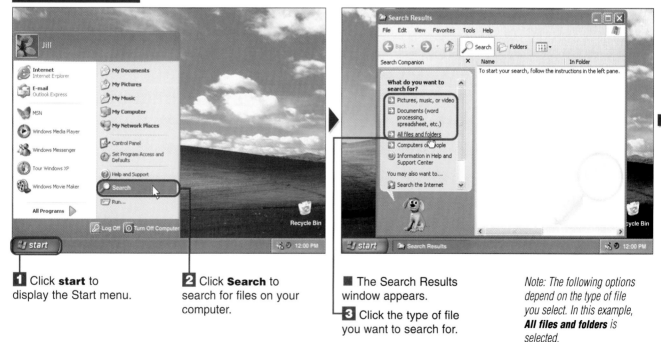

1 Click **start** to display the Start menu.

2 Click **Search** to search for files on your computer.

■ The Search Results window appears.

3 Click the type of file you want to search for.

*Note: The following options depend on the type of file you select. In this example, **All files and folders** is selected.*

Tip

**What other options does Windows offer to help
me find a file?**

Windows offers different options, depending on
the type of file you select in step **3** on page 76.

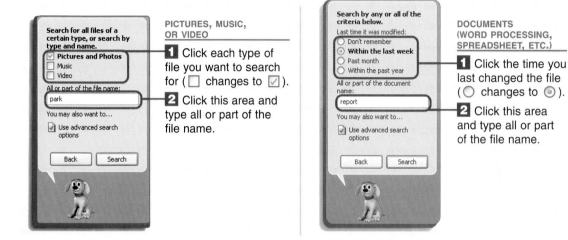

**PICTURES, MUSIC,
OR VIDEO**

1 Click each type of
file you want to search
for (☐ changes to ☑).

2 Click this area and
type all or part of the
file name.

**DOCUMENTS
(WORD PROCESSING,
SPREADSHEET, ETC.)**

1 Click the time you
last changed the file
(○ changes to ◉).

2 Click this area
and type all or part
of the file name.

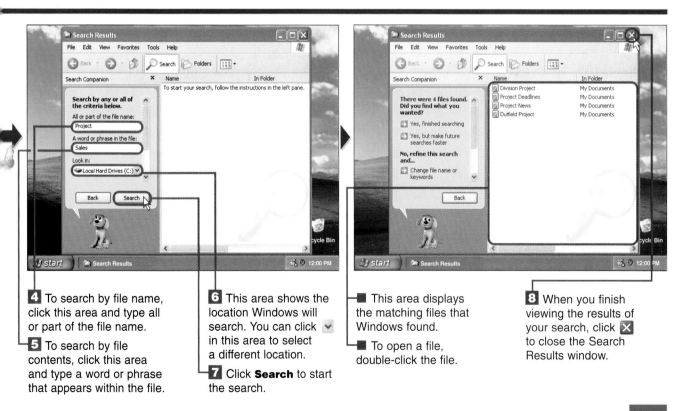

4 To search by file name,
click this area and type all
or part of the file name.

5 To search by file
contents, click this area
and type a word or phrase
that appears within the file.

6 This area shows the
location Windows will
search. You can click ✓
in this area to select
a different location.

7 Click **Search** to start
the search.

■ This area displays
the matching files that
Windows found.

■ To open a file,
double-click the file.

8 When you finish
viewing the results of
your search, click ✗
to close the Search
Results window.

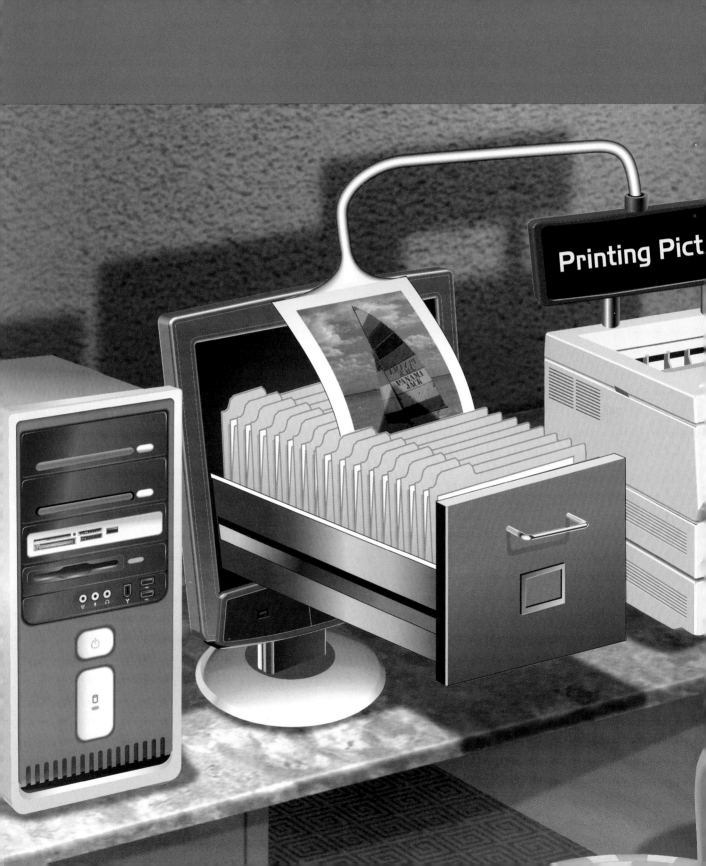

CHAPTER 4

More Working with Files

This chapter teaches you ways to work with files in Windows XP that take you beyond the basics. Learn how to copy pictures from a digital camera, scan a document into your computer, copy files from your computer to a recordable CD or memory card, e-mail a file and more.

PRINT PICTURES

You can use the Photo Printing Wizard to print your pictures.

You can obtain pictures on the Internet, use a scanner or digital camera to copy pictures into your computer, purchase pictures at computer stores or use a drawing program, such as Paint, to create your own pictures. Windows also includes a few sample pictures.

PRINT PICTURES

1 Click **start** to display the Start menu.

2 Click **My Pictures** to view the pictures stored in your My Pictures folder.

■ The contents of the My Pictures folder appear.

3 Click **Print pictures** to print the pictures in the folder.

Note: To print the pictures in a subfolder within the My Pictures folder, click the subfolder before performing step 3.

Tip

How can I get the best results when printing pictures?

Use High-Quality Paper

Your printer may allow you to use high-quality, glossy paper that is specifically designed for printing pictures. This type of paper will produce the best results when printing pictures.

Select a High Resolution

Make sure your printer is set to the highest possible resolution. A higher resolution will usually result in higher-quality pictures, but the pictures may take longer to print.

Tip

Can I use the Photo Printing Wizard to print pictures that are not stored in the My Pictures folder?

Yes. When you print a picture stored in another location on your computer, the Photo Printing Wizard will automatically appear to help you print the picture. You can print a picture stored in another location on your computer as you would print any file. For information on printing a file, see page 60.

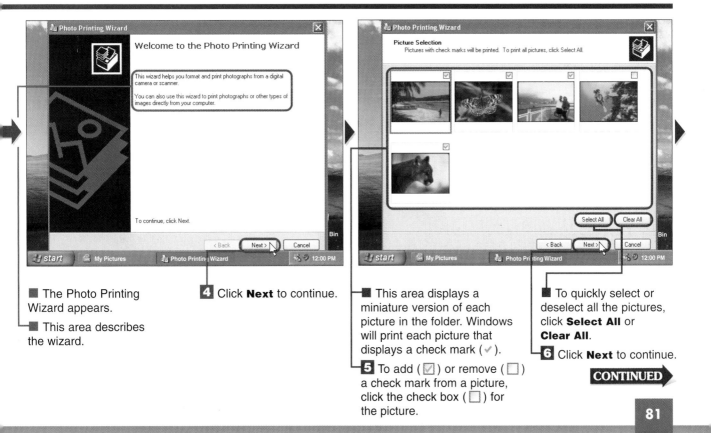

■ The Photo Printing Wizard appears.

■ This area describes the wizard.

4 Click **Next** to continue.

■ This area displays a miniature version of each picture in the folder. Windows will print each picture that displays a check mark (✓).

5 To add (☑) or remove (☐) a check mark from a picture, click the check box (☐) for the picture.

■ To quickly select or deselect all the pictures, click **Select All** or **Clear All**.

6 Click **Next** to continue.

CONTINUED

81

PRINT PICTURES

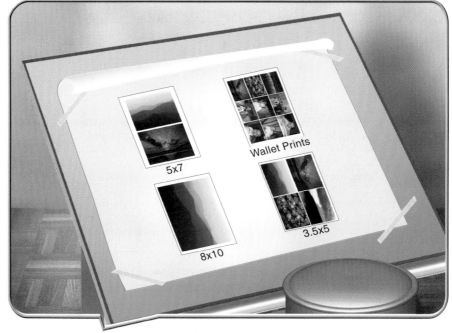

The Photo Printing Wizard allows you to select the layout you want to use for the printed pictures.

Wallet Prints

5x7

8x10

3.5x5

You can select a layout that prints more than one picture on a page. Some layouts may crop part of a large picture so the picture will fit better on a page.

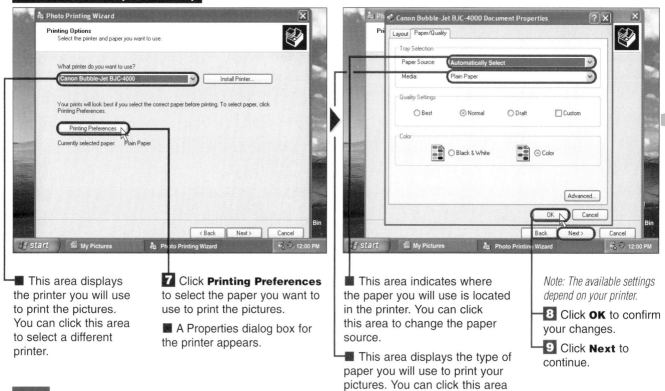

■ This area displays the printer you will use to print the pictures. You can click this area to select a different printer.

7 Click **Printing Preferences** to select the paper you want to use to print the pictures.

■ A Properties dialog box for the printer appears.

■ This area indicates where the paper you will use is located in the printer. You can click this area to change the paper source.

■ This area displays the type of paper you will use to print your pictures. You can click this area to change the type of paper.

Note: The available settings depend on your printer.

8 Click **OK** to confirm your changes.

9 Click **Next** to continue.

82

2759432q075

lllllllll

Tip

What other tasks can I perform with my pictures?

The My Pictures folder offers several options that you can select to perform tasks with your pictures.

View as a slide show

Displays all the pictures in the My Pictures folder as a full-screen slide show.

Order prints online

Sends the pictures you select to a Web site that allows you to order prints of the pictures.

Set as desktop background

Uses the picture you select as your desktop background. For information on changing the desktop background, see page 110.

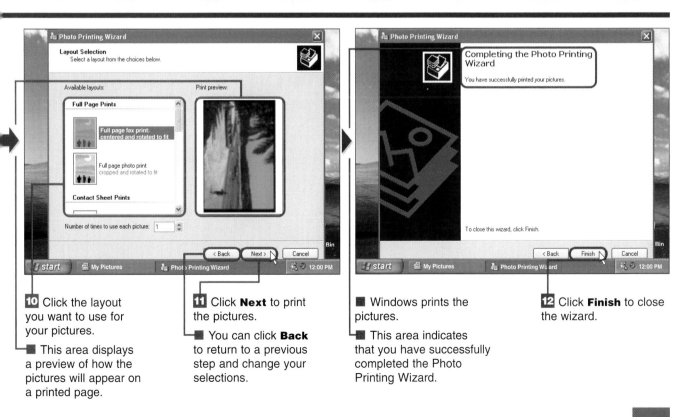

10 Click the layout you want to use for your pictures.

■ This area displays a preview of how the pictures will appear on a printed page.

11 Click **Next** to print the pictures.

■ You can click **Back** to return to a previous step and change your selections.

■ Windows prints the pictures.

■ This area indicates that you have successfully completed the Photo Printing Wizard.

12 Click **Finish** to close the wizard.

COPY PICTURES FROM A DIGITAL CAMERA

You can use the Scanner and Camera Wizard to copy pictures stored on a digital camera to your computer.

To copy pictures from a digital camera, the camera must be installed, connected to your computer and turned on. You may also need to set your camera to a specific mode, such as the Connect mode.

COPY PICTURES FROM A DIGITAL CAMERA

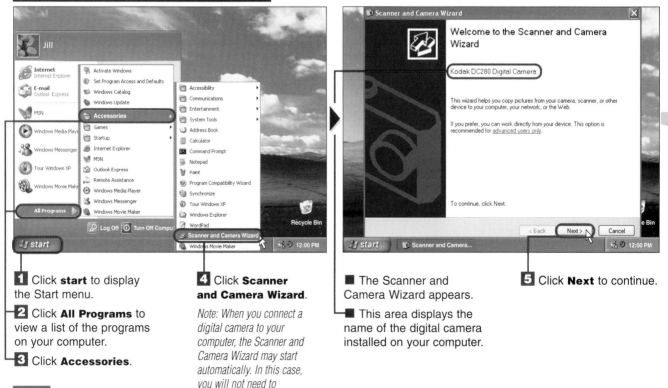

1 Click **start** to display the Start menu.

2 Click **All Programs** to view a list of the programs on your computer.

3 Click **Accessories**.

4 Click **Scanner and Camera Wizard**.

Note: When you connect a digital camera to your computer, the Scanner and Camera Wizard may start automatically. In this case, you will not need to perform steps 1 to 4.

■ The Scanner and Camera Wizard appears.

■ This area displays the name of the digital camera installed on your computer.

5 Click **Next** to continue.

Tip

Is there an easier way to copy pictures from a digital camera?

Yes. Most new digital cameras include a memory card, or flash card, which is a small card that stores pictures on a digital camera. You can remove the memory card from your digital camera and then insert the card into a memory card reader on your computer. Many new computers come with a memory card reader.

When you insert a memory card from your digital camera into your computer's memory card reader, a dialog box appears, asking what you want Windows to do. Click the **Copy pictures to a folder on my computer** option and then click **OK**. The Scanner and Camera Wizard will appear, helping you copy pictures stored on the memory card to your computer.

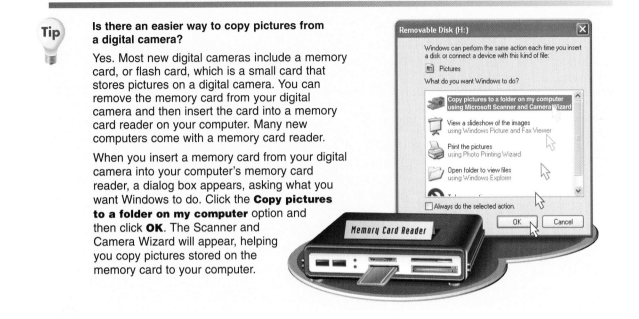

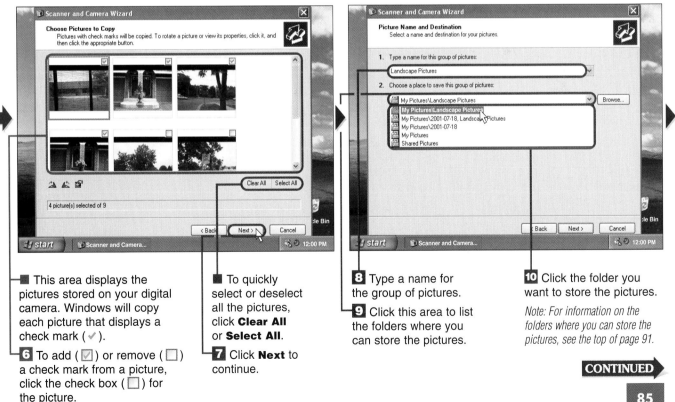

■ This area displays the pictures stored on your digital camera. Windows will copy each picture that displays a check mark (✓).

6 To add (☑) or remove (☐) a check mark from a picture, click the check box (☐) for the picture.

■ To quickly select or deselect all the pictures, click **Clear All** or **Select All**.

7 Click **Next** to continue.

8 Type a name for the group of pictures.

9 Click this area to list the folders where you can store the pictures.

10 Click the folder you want to store the pictures.

Note: For information on the folders where you can store the pictures, see the top of page 91.

CONTINUED

COPY PICTURES FROM A DIGITAL CAMERA

You can choose to delete the pictures stored on your digital camera after the pictures are copied to your computer.

If you choose to delete the pictures stored on your digital camera, you will not be able to recover the pictures.

COPY PICTURES FROM A DIGITAL CAMERA (CONTINUED)

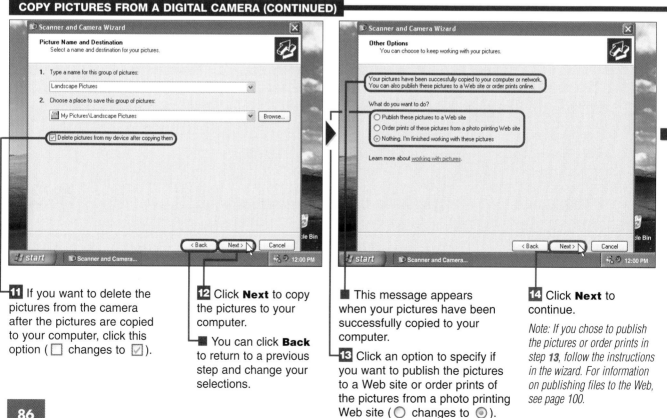

11 If you want to delete the pictures from the camera after the pictures are copied to your computer, click this option (☐ changes to ☑).

12 Click **Next** to copy the pictures to your computer.

■ You can click **Back** to return to a previous step and change your selections.

■ This message appears when your pictures have been successfully copied to your computer.

13 Click an option to specify if you want to publish the pictures to a Web site or order prints of the pictures from a photo printing Web site (○ changes to ◉).

14 Click **Next** to continue.

*Note: If you chose to publish the pictures or order prints in step **13**, follow the instructions in the wizard. For information on publishing files to the Web, see page 100.*

Tip

What tasks can I perform with my pictures after I copy them to my computer?

When viewing your pictures, Windows provides several options you can select in the window to perform tasks with the pictures. Here are some tasks you can perform.

View as a slide show

Displays your pictures as a full-screen slide show.

Print the selected pictures

Prints the pictures you select using the Photo Printing Wizard. For information on using the Photo Printing Wizard to print pictures, see page 80.

E-mail this file

E-mails a picture you select to a friend, colleague or family member. For information on e-mailing files, see page 98.

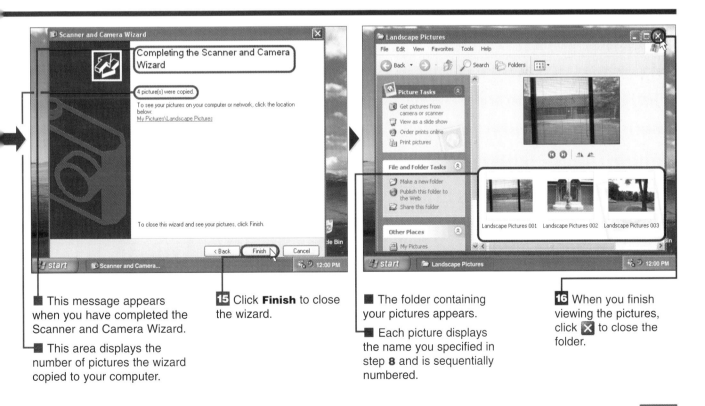

■ This message appears when you have completed the Scanner and Camera Wizard.

■ This area displays the number of pictures the wizard copied to your computer.

15 Click **Finish** to close the wizard.

■ The folder containing your pictures appears.

■ Each picture displays the name you specified in step **8** and is sequentially numbered.

16 When you finish viewing the pictures, click ⊠ to close the folder.

SCAN A DOCUMENT

You can use the Scanner and Camera Wizard to scan paper documents into your computer.

You can scan documents such as photographs, drawings, reports, newsletters, newspaper articles and forms into your computer.

SCAN A DOCUMENT

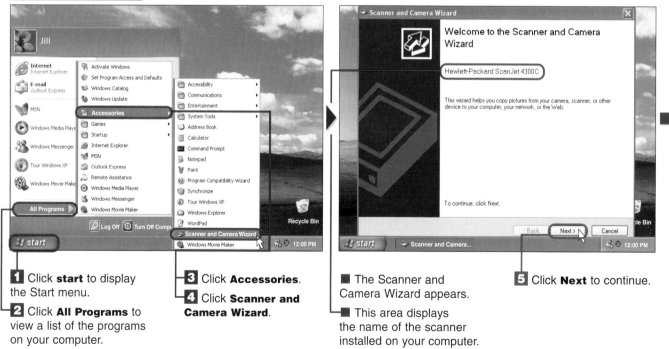

1 Click **start** to display the Start menu.

2 Click **All Programs** to view a list of the programs on your computer.

3 Click **Accessories**.

4 Click **Scanner and Camera Wizard**.

■ The Scanner and Camera Wizard appears.

■ This area displays the name of the scanner installed on your computer.

5 Click **Next** to continue.

What types of documents can I scan?

The Scanner and Camera Wizard allows you to specify the type of document you are scanning. You can scan a color, grayscale, black and white or text document. For example, if you are scanning a document that contains only shades of gray, select the **Grayscale picture** option in step **6** below.

| Color | Grayscale | Black and White | Text Document |

Which file format should I select for my scanned document?

The file format you should select depends on how you plan to use the document. The BMP and TIF file formats are useful for producing high-quality pictures. The JPG and PNG file formats are useful for pictures you plan to publish to the Web.

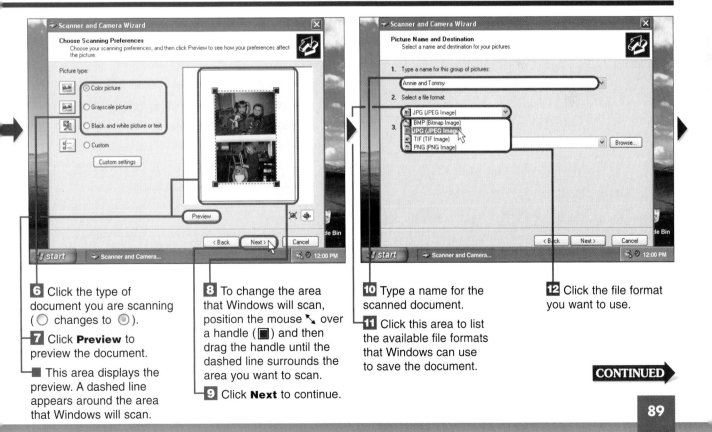

6 Click the type of document you are scanning (○ changes to ◉).

7 Click **Preview** to preview the document.

■ This area displays the preview. A dashed line appears around the area that Windows will scan.

8 To change the area that Windows will scan, position the mouse ↖ over a handle (■) and then drag the handle until the dashed line surrounds the area you want to scan.

9 Click **Next** to continue.

10 Type a name for the scanned document.

11 Click this area to list the available file formats that Windows can use to save the document.

12 Click the file format you want to use.

CONTINUED

SCAN A DOCUMENT

You can select
the folder on your
computer where you
want to store the
scanned document.

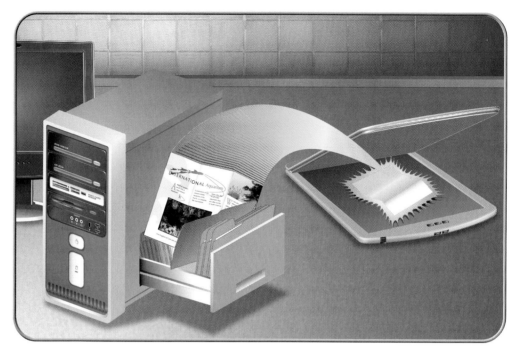

SCAN A DOCUMENT (CONTINUED)

13 Click this area to list the folders where you can store the document.

14 Click the folder you want to store the document.

15 Click **Next** to scan the document.

■ You can click **Back** to return to a previous step and change your selections.

■ This message appears when the scan is complete.

16 Click an option to specify if you want to publish the document to a Web site or order prints of the document from a photo printing Web site (○ changes to ⊙).

17 Click **Next** to continue.

Note: If you chose to publish the document or order prints in step ***16****, follow the instructions in the wizard. For information on publishing files to the Web, see page 100.*

Tip

Which folder should I use to store my scanned document?

My Pictures	**Subfolder within My Pictures**	**Shared Pictures**
If you want to be able to quickly access the scanned document in the future, store the document in the My Pictures folder. To open the My Pictures folder, see page 45.	To keep the scanned document separate from other pictures in the My Pictures folder, store the document in a subfolder within the My Pictures folder. To name the subfolder, you can select the name you gave the scanned document (Corvette), the current date (2005-01-01) or both (2005-01-01, Corvette).	If you want other users set up on your computer to be able to access the scanned document, store the document in the Shared Pictures folder. The Shared Pictures folder is stored in the Shared Documents folder on your computer. To open the Shared Documents folder, see page 194.

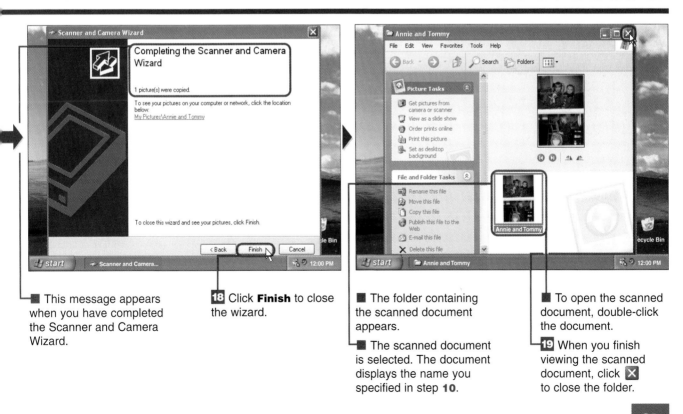

■ This message appears when you have completed the Scanner and Camera Wizard.

18 Click **Finish** to close the wizard.

■ The folder containing the scanned document appears.

■ The scanned document is selected. The document displays the name you specified in step **10**.

■ To open the scanned document, double-click the document.

19 When you finish viewing the scanned document, click ☒ to close the folder.

COPY FILES TO A CD

You can copy files, such as documents and pictures, from your computer to a CD.

You will need a recordable CD drive to copy files to a CD. For information on recordable CD drives, see the top of page 159.

If you only want to copy songs to a CD, see page 158 for information on using Windows Media Player to copy the songs.

A CD can typically store 700 MB of information.

COPY FILES TO A CD

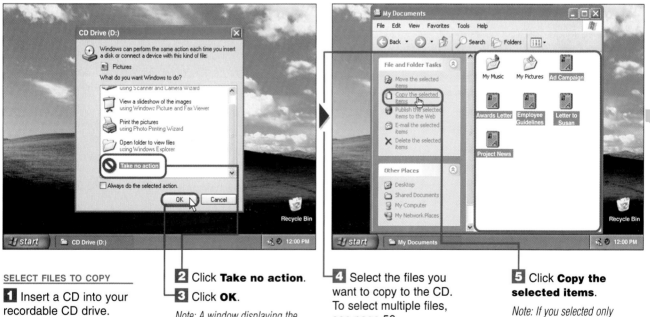

SELECT FILES TO COPY

1 Insert a CD into your recordable CD drive.

■ A dialog box may appear, asking what you want Windows to do.

2 Click **Take no action**.

3 Click **OK**.

Note: A window displaying the contents of the CD may appear instead of the dialog box. You can click ☒ *in the window to close the window.*

4 Select the files you want to copy to the CD. To select multiple files, see page 56.

5 Click **Copy the selected items**.

Note: If you selected only one file, click Copy this file in step 5.

Tip

Why would I copy files to a CD?

You can copy files to a CD to transfer large amounts of information between computers or make backup copies of the files stored on your computer. Making backup copies of your files will provide you with extra copies in case you accidentally erase the files or your computer fails.

Tip

Can I copy a folder to a CD?

Yes. You can copy a folder to a CD the same way you copy files to a CD. When you copy a folder to a CD, Windows will copy all the files in the folder. To copy a folder to a CD, perform steps **1** to **7** starting on page 92, except select **Copy this folder** in step **5**. Then perform steps **1** to **8** starting on page 93.

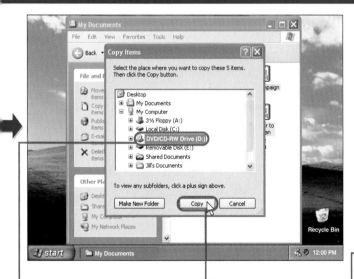

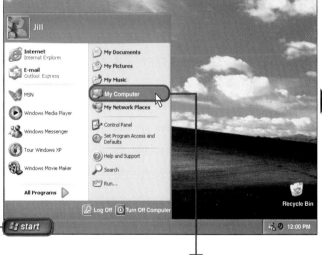

■ The Copy Items dialog box appears.

6 Click the recordable CD drive that contains the CD you want to copy the files to.

7 Click **Copy** to place a copy of the files in a temporary storage area on your computer where the files will be held until you copy them to the CD.

■ You can repeat steps **4** to **7** for each set of files you want to copy to the CD.

COPY SELECTED FILES TO A CD

1 Click **start** to display the Start menu.

2 Click **My Computer** to view the contents of your computer.

CONTINUED

COPY FILES TO A CD

Before copying the files you selected to a CD, Windows stores the files in a temporary storage area on your computer. This allows you to review the files you selected before copying the files to a CD.

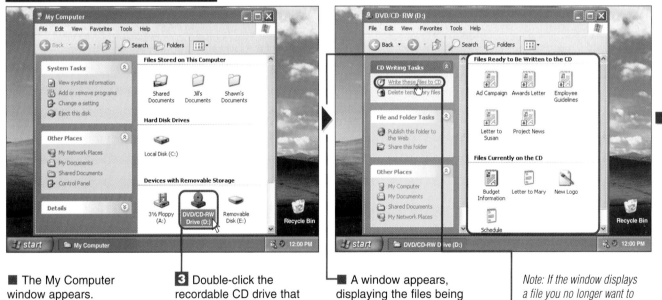

■ The My Computer window appears.

3 Double-click the recordable CD drive that contains the CD you want to copy the files to.

■ A window appears, displaying the files being held in a temporary storage area on your computer and any files currently stored on the CD.

Note: If the window displays a file you no longer want to copy to the CD, you can delete the file. To delete a file, see page 62.

4 Click **Write these files to CD** to copy the files to the CD.

Tip

Can I copy files to a CD at different times?

Yes. Each time you copy files to a CD, however, approximately 20 MB of extra information is stored on the CD. To make the best use of the storage space on the CD, you may want to copy all the files to the CD at one time.

Tip

How do I erase a CD-RW disc?

You can erase a CD-RW disc to permanently delete all the files on the disc. You cannot erase a CD-R disc.

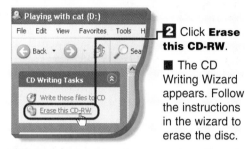

2 Click **Erase this CD-RW**.

■ The CD Writing Wizard appears. Follow the instructions in the wizard to erase the disc.

1 Display the contents of your CD-RW disc. To view the contents of a CD, see page 46.

■ The CD Writing Wizard appears.

5 Type a name for the CD.

Note: The name you specify for the CD will appear in the My Computer window when the CD is in a CD drive. To view the My Computer window, see page 46.

6 Click **Next** to copy the files to the CD.

■ This message appears when Windows has successfully copied the files to the CD.

Note: Windows will automatically eject the CD from your recordable CD drive when the copy is complete.

7 Click **Finish** to close the wizard.

8 Click ☒ to close the window for the recordable CD drive.

Note: To display the contents of a CD to confirm that the files were copied, see page 46.

COPY FILES TO A MEMORY CARD

You can copy a file stored on your computer to a memory card.

A memory card, or flash card, is a small card that stores information. Many new computers come with a memory card reader, which is a device that reads and records information on memory cards.

Copying a file to a memory card is useful when you want to transfer a file to another computer or give a friend, family member or colleague a copy of a file.

COPY FILES TO A MEMORY CARD

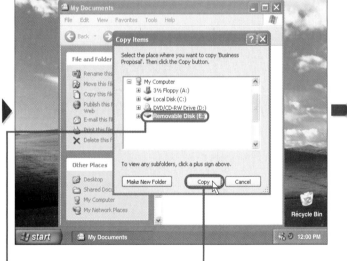

1 Insert a memory card into your computer's memory card reader.

Note: A window may appear, displaying the contents of the memory card. To close the window, click ⊠.

2 Click the file you want to copy to the memory card.

■ To copy more than one file, select all the files you want to copy. To select multiple files, see page 56.

3 Click **Copy this file**.

*Note: If you selected multiple files, click **Copy the selected items** in step 3.*

■ The Copy Items dialog box appears.

4 Click the drive that contains the memory card.

Note: Each memory card slot on your computer will appear as a separate drive and is often labeled as "Removable Disk."

5 Click **Copy** to copy the file to the memory card.

Note: Do not remove the memory card from your computer until Windows has finished copying the file to the memory card.

Tip

Can I copy a file to other types of removable media?

Yes. You can follow the steps below to copy a file stored on your computer to a flash drive or to a floppy disk.

Flash Drive

If you have a flash drive, you can copy a file stored on your computer to the flash drive. A flash drive is a small, portable, lightweight storage device that plugs into a Universal Serial Bus (USB) port on a computer. A flash drive is also known as a USB (Universal Serial Bus) key.

Floppy Disk

If your computer has a floppy drive, you can copy a file stored on your computer to a floppy disk. A floppy drive is a storage device that retrieves and stores information on floppy disks.

■ Windows places a copy of the file on the memory card.

Note: You can view the contents of a memory card as you would view the contents of any drive on your computer. To view the contents of a drive, see page 46.

COPY A FILE ON YOUR DESKTOP

1 Insert a memory card into your computer's memory card reader.

Note: A window may appear, displaying the contents of the memory card. To close the window, click **X**.

2 Right-click the file you want to copy to the memory card. A menu appears.

3 Click **Send To**.

4 Click the drive that contains the memory card.

97

E-MAIL A FILE

You can e-mail a file to a friend, colleague or family member. You must have an e-mail account set up on your computer to be able to e-mail a file.

You can e-mail many types of files, including documents, pictures, videos and sounds. The computer receiving the file must have the necessary hardware and software installed to display or play the file.

E-MAIL A FILE

1 Click the file you want to send in an e-mail message.

■ To send more than one file in an e-mail message, select all the files you want to send. To select multiple files, see page 56.

2 Click **E-mail this file**.

*Note: If you selected multiple files, click **E-mail the selected items** in step 2.*

■ A window appears that allows you to compose a message.

3 Type the e-mail address of the person you want to receive the message.

Note: To send the message to more than one person, separate each e-mail address with a semicolon (;).

4 Windows uses the name of the file as the subject. To specify a different subject, drag the mouse I over the subject and then type a new subject.

Tip

Why does a dialog box appear when I try to e-mail a picture?

Windows can change the file size and dimensions of a picture you are sending in an e-mail message so the picture will transfer faster over the Internet and fit better on a recipient's computer screen. Reducing the file size of a picture is useful when you are e-mailing a large picture, since most companies that provide e-mail accounts do not allow you to send messages larger than 10 MB.

■ Click an option to make the picture smaller or keep the original size of the picture (○ changes to ◉). Then press the **Enter** key.

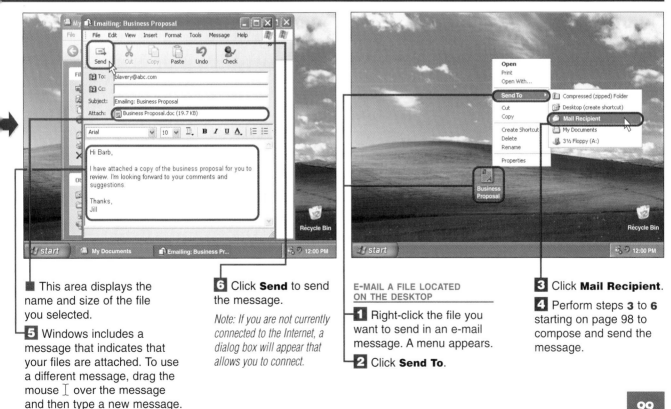

■ This area displays the name and size of the file you selected.

5 Windows includes a message that indicates that your files are attached. To use a different message, drag the mouse I over the message and then type a new message.

6 Click **Send** to send the message.

Note: If you are not currently connected to the Internet, a dialog box will appear that allows you to connect.

E-MAIL A FILE LOCATED ON THE DESKTOP

1 Right-click the file you want to send in an e-mail message. A menu appears.

2 Click **Send To**.

3 Click **Mail Recipient**.

4 Perform steps **3** to **6** starting on page 98 to compose and send the message.

PUBLISH A FILE TO THE WEB

You can publish photos, documents and other types of files to the Web to allow friends, family members and colleagues to view the files.

If you have just one or two small files that you want to share with another person, you may want to send the files in an e-mail message instead. To send files in an e-mail message, see page 278.

PUBLISH A FILE TO THE WEB

1 Click the file you want to publish to the Web.

■ To publish more than one file, select all the files you want to publish. To select multiple files, see page 56.

2 Click **Publish this file to the Web**.

*Note: If you selected multiple files, click **Publish the selected items to the Web** in step 2.*

■ The Web Publishing Wizard appears.

■ This area describes the wizard.

3 Click **Next** to continue.

Tip

Why does a wizard appear, asking me to add a Passport to my user account?

The first time you publish a file to the Web, the .Net Passport Wizard may appear, helping you add a Passport to your user account. You must add a Passport to your user account to publish a file to the Web. Follow the instructions in the wizard to add a Passport to your user account.

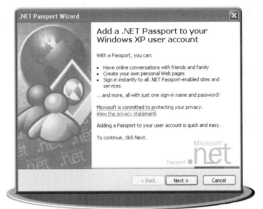

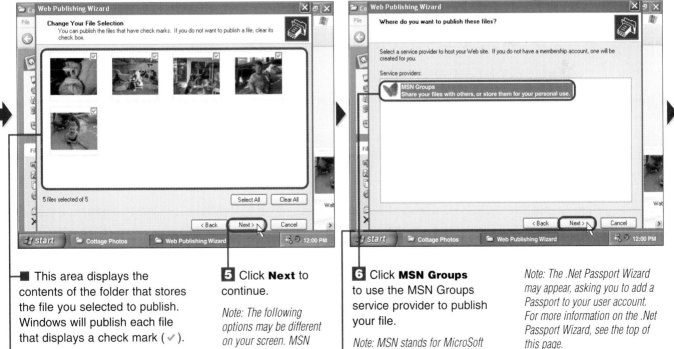

■ This area displays the contents of the folder that stores the file you selected to publish. Windows will publish each file that displays a check mark (✔).

4 To add (☑) or remove (☐) a check mark from a file, click the check box (☐) for the file.

5 Click **Next** to continue.

Note: The following options may be different on your screen. MSN may occasionally change the options to make the wizard easier to use or to provide new options.

6 Click **MSN Groups** to use the MSN Groups service provider to publish your file.

Note: MSN stands for MicroSoft Network.

7 Click **Next** to continue.

Note: The .Net Passport Wizard may appear, asking you to add a Passport to your user account. For more information on the .Net Passport Wizard, see the top of this page.

CONTINUED ▶

PUBLISH A FILE TO THE WEB

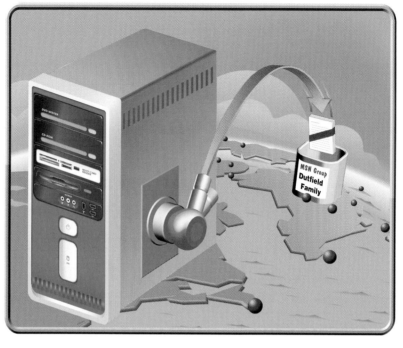

When publishing a file to the Web, you can create an MSN Group on the Web to store the file.

A group is a location on the Web that stores files you have selected to publish.

You can publish a file to share with other people or for your own private use. Storing a file for your own private use allows you to access the file from any computer that is connected to the Internet. For example, you can publish a presentation that you plan to deliver so you can access the presentation from any location.

PUBLISH A FILE TO THE WEB (CONTINUED)

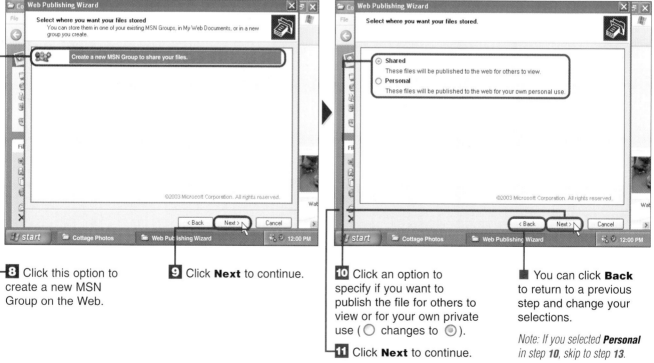

8 Click this option to create a new MSN Group on the Web.

9 Click **Next** to continue.

10 Click an option to specify if you want to publish the file for others to view or for your own private use (○ changes to ◉).

11 Click **Next** to continue.

■ You can click **Back** to return to a previous step and change your selections.

*Note: If you selected **Personal** in step 10, skip to step 13.*

Tip

Can I publish a file in a group I previously created?

Yes. If you previously published a file to the Web, you can publish a file in a group you previously created. This will keep all your published files in one location on the Web. In step **8** on page 102, click the name of the group where you want to publish the file and click **Next**. You will then need to skip to step **21** on page 104 to finish publishing the file.

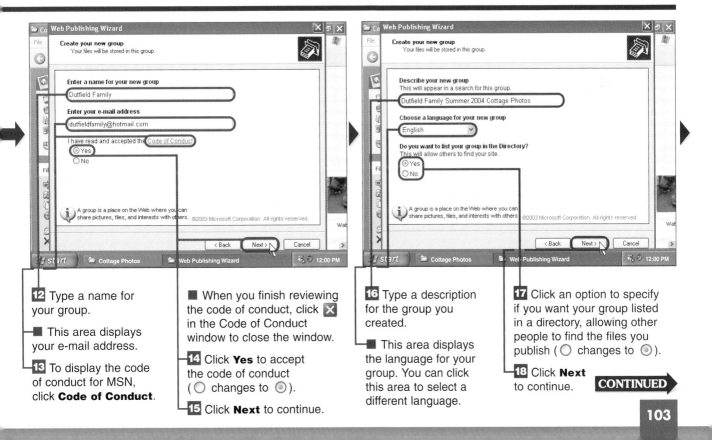

12 Type a name for your group.

■ This area displays your e-mail address.

13 To display the code of conduct for MSN, click **Code of Conduct**.

■ When you finish reviewing the code of conduct, click ☒ in the Code of Conduct window to close the window.

14 Click **Yes** to accept the code of conduct (○ changes to ◉).

15 Click **Next** to continue.

16 Type a description for the group you created.

■ This area displays the language for your group. You can click this area to select a different language.

17 Click an option to specify if you want your group listed in a directory, allowing other people to find the files you publish (○ changes to ◉).

18 Click **Next** to continue.

CONTINUED

PUBLISH A FILE TO THE WEB

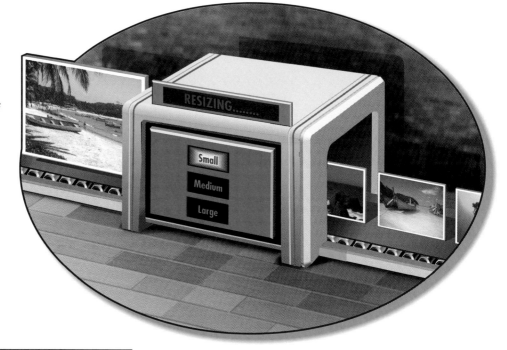

If you are publishing a picture, the Web Publishing Wizard can adjust the size of the picture so it will transfer faster and be easier to view on a computer screen.

RESIZING........

Small
Medium
Large

PUBLISH A FILE TO THE WEB (CONTINUED)

Web Publishing Wizard

How do I find my group?

Your group is located at this Web address:

http://www.msnusers.com/DutfieldFamily.

Write this address down to e-mail it to your friends and family. It will also be sent to you in e-mail.

Would you like to add the address to your browser Favorites list?
- Yes
- No

@2003 Microsoft Corporation. All rights reserved.

< Back   Next >   Cancel

start   Cottage Photos   Web Publishing Wizard   12:00 PM

Web Publishing Wizard

Your files will be published to this group

Dutfield Family
http://www.msnusers.com/DutfieldFamily.

Your non-image files will be uploaded to this folder in the group:

Documents
Change...

Your image files will be uploaded to this folder in the group:

Documents/Pictures
Change...

@2003 Microsoft Corporation. All rights reserved.

< Back   Next >   Cancel

start   Cottage Photos   Web Publishing Wizard   12:00 PM

■ This area displays the address of the Web page where you can view the published file. Make sure you write down the address for future reference.

19 Click an option to specify if you want to add the Web page address to your list of favorite Web pages in Internet Explorer (○ changes to ◉).

Note: For information on viewing the list of favorite Web pages in Internet Explorer, see page 264.

20 Click **Next** to continue.

■ This area displays the name of the group that stores the file you selected to publish.

■ This area displays the name of the folder in the group that will store your files that are not pictures.

■ This area displays the name of the folder in the group that will store your pictures.

21 Click **Next** to continue.

Tip

How do I view a file I published to the Web?

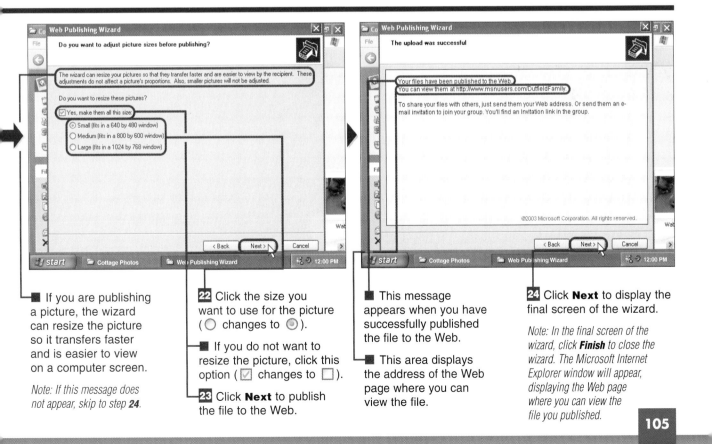

1 In a Microsoft Internet Explorer window, click this area and type the address of the Web page where you can view your published file.

2 Click **Documents** or **Pictures** to select the type of files you want to view. Documents will display files that are not pictures. Pictures will display pictures.

■ All the documents or pictures you have published appear.

3 Click the document or picture you want to view.

■ If you are publishing a picture, the wizard can resize the picture so it transfers faster and is easier to view on a computer screen.

*Note: If this message does not appear, skip to step **24**.*

22 Click the size you want to use for the picture (○ changes to ◉).

■ If you do not want to resize the picture, click this option (☑ changes to ☐).

23 Click **Next** to publish the file to the Web.

■ This message appears when you have successfully published the file to the Web.

■ This area displays the address of the Web page where you can view the file.

24 Click **Next** to display the final screen of the wizard.

*Note: In the final screen of the wizard, click **Finish** to close the wizard. The Microsoft Internet Explorer window will appear, displaying the Web page where you can view the file you published.*

105

CREATE A COMPRESSED FOLDER

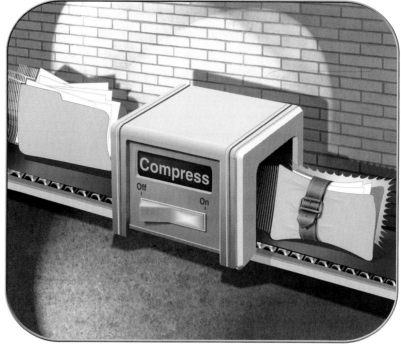

You can create a new, compressed folder that you can use to store files.

Compressed folders take up less storage space than standard folders and transfer quickly over the Internet. Creating a compressed folder is ideal when you plan to copy files to removable storage media, such as a CD or memory card, or send large files in an e-mail message.

The amount of space a compressed folder saves depends on the types of files you add to the folder. For example, text files will compress significantly more than pictures.

CREATE A COMPRESSED FOLDER

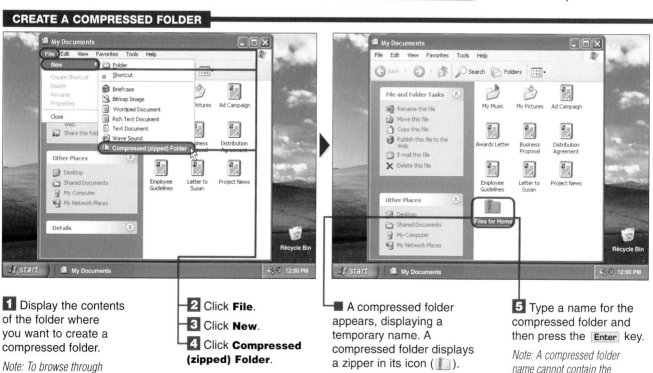

1 Display the contents of the folder where you want to create a compressed folder.

Note: To browse through the folders on your computer, see pages 44 to 47.

2 Click **File**.

3 Click **New**.

4 Click **Compressed (zipped) Folder**.

■ A compressed folder appears, displaying a temporary name. A compressed folder displays a zipper in its icon (🗎).

5 Type a name for the compressed folder and then press the **Enter** key.

*Note: A compressed folder name cannot contain the \ / : * ? " < > or | characters.*

Tip

Can other people work with my compressed folders?

Other people can work with compressed folders on their computers if they have a program that can work with compressed folders. Windows XP includes software that can work with compressed folders. People who do not have the appropriate software can obtain a program, such as WinZip, that allows them to work with compressed folders. WinZip is available at the www.winzip.com Web site.

Tip

How do I decompress a file stored in a compressed folder?

To decompress a file stored in a compressed folder, move the file to a location outside the folder. Windows will create a decompressed copy of the file in the new location. To move a file, see page 66. Decompressing a file allows you to work with the file as you would work with any file on your computer.

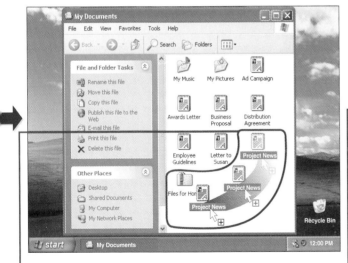

6 To add a file to the compressed folder, position the mouse ⬦ over the file and then drag the file to the folder.

■ Windows will add a compressed copy of the file to the folder. The original file will remain in its original location.

Note: You can open the files in a compressed folder as you would open any file on your computer. You cannot make changes to the files in a compressed folder.

CREATE A COMPRESSED FOLDER ON THE DESKTOP

1 Right-click an empty area on your desktop. A menu appears.

2 Click **New**.

3 Click **Compressed (zipped) Folder**.

■ A compressed folder appears, displaying a temporary name.

4 Type a name for the compressed folder and then press the Enter key.

CHAPTER 5

Customize Windows

Windows XP includes several features that help you personalize your computer. In this chapter, you will learn how to change the screen saver, add a personalized picture to your desktop, change the sounds that play when events occur on your computer and much more.

CHANGE THE DESKTOP BACKGROUND

You can select a picture, background color or both to decorate your desktop.

When selecting a picture to decorate your desktop, you can use a picture that Windows provides or your own picture.

CHANGE THE DESKTOP BACKGROUND

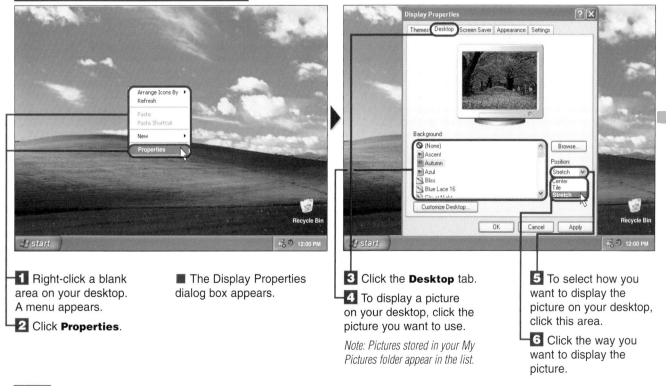

1 Right-click a blank area on your desktop. A menu appears.

2 Click **Properties**.

■ The Display Properties dialog box appears.

3 Click the **Desktop** tab.

4 To display a picture on your desktop, click the picture you want to use.

Note: Pictures stored in your My Pictures folder appear in the list.

5 To select how you want to display the picture on your desktop, click this area.

6 Click the way you want to display the picture.

Tip

How can I display a picture on my desktop?

Windows offers three ways that you can display a picture on your desktop.

Center

Displays the picture in the middle of your desktop.

Tile

Repeats the picture until it fills your entire desktop.

Stretch

Stretches the picture to cover your entire desktop.

Note: If you select a large picture that fills your entire desktop, selecting one of these options will have no effect on the way the picture will appear on your desktop.

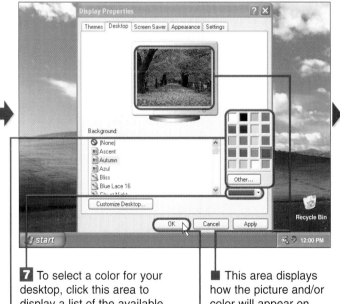

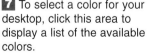

7 To select a color for your desktop, click this area to display a list of the available colors.

8 Click the color you want to use.

Note: If you selected a picture in step 4, the color you select will fill any space not covered by the picture.

■ This area displays how the picture and/or color will appear on your desktop.

9 Click **OK** to add the picture and/or color to your desktop.

■ The picture and/or color appear on your desktop.

■ To remove a picture from your desktop, perform steps **1** to **4**, selecting **(None)** in step **4**. Then perform step **9**.

CHANGE THE SCREEN SAVER

A screen saver is a moving picture or pattern that appears on the screen when you do not use your computer for a period of time.

You can use a screen saver to hide your work while you are away from your desk.

By default, Windows will display a screen saver when you do not use your computer for ten minutes.

CHANGE THE SCREEN SAVER

1 Right-click a blank area on your desktop. A menu appears.

2 Click **Properties**.

■ The Display Properties dialog box appears.

3 Click the **Screen Saver** tab.

4 Click this area to display a list of the available screen savers.

5 Click the screen saver you want to use.

■ This area will display a preview of how the screen saver will appear on your screen.

Tip

Do I need to use a screen saver?

Screen savers were originally designed to prevent screen burn, which occurs when an image appears in a fixed position on the screen for a period of time. Today's monitors are less susceptible to screen burn, but people still use screen savers for their entertainment value.

Tip

What does the My Pictures Slideshow screen saver do?

You can select the My Pictures Slideshow screen saver to have the pictures stored in your My Pictures folder appear as your screen saver. Windows will rotate through all the pictures in the folder, displaying each picture on your screen for six seconds at a time. To view the contents of your My Pictures folder, see page 45.

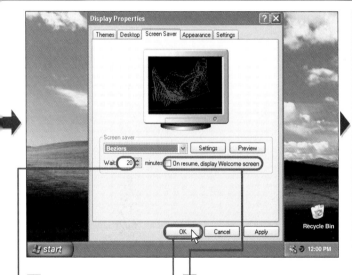

6 To specify the number of minutes your computer must be inactive before the screen saver will appear, double-click this area. Then type the number of minutes.

7 If multiple users are set up on your computer, this option requires you to log on to Windows each time you remove the screen saver. You can click this option to turn the option off (☑ changes to ☐).

Note: For information on logging on to Windows, see page 193.

8 Click **OK**.

■ The screen saver appears when you do not use your computer for the number of minutes you specified.

■ You can move the mouse or press a key on the keyboard to remove the screen saver from your screen.

■ To stop a screen saver from appearing, perform steps **1** to **5**, selecting **(None)** in step **5**. Then perform step **8**.

CHANGE THE SCREEN APPEARANCE

You can change the style and colors that Windows uses to display windows and other items on your screen.

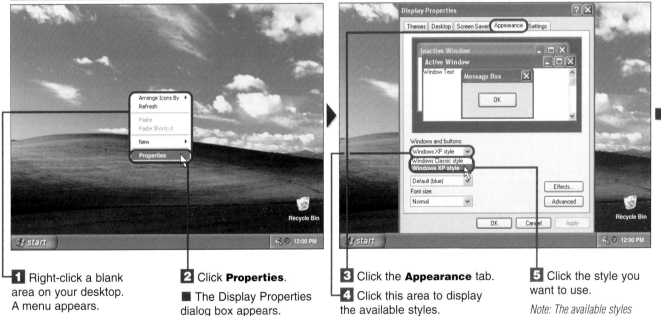

1 Right-click a blank area on your desktop. A menu appears.

2 Click **Properties**.

■ The Display Properties dialog box appears.

3 Click the **Appearance** tab.

4 Click this area to display the available styles.

5 Click the style you want to use.

Note: The available styles depend on the current theme. For information on themes, see page 116.

Tip

How can I change the appearance of my screen?

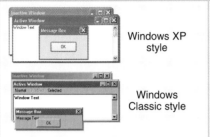

Windows XP style

Windows Classic style

Windows and buttons

By default, you can choose between the Windows XP style, which is the default style of Windows XP, and the Windows Classic style, which is the style used in previous versions of Windows.

Color scheme

You can change the colors used in items such as windows, dialog boxes and the Start menu.

Font size

You can change the size of text shown in items such as menus, icons and the title bars of windows. Changing the font size will also change the size of some buttons such as the Close button (✕). Increasing the font size is useful if you have trouble reading the text on your screen or clicking small buttons.

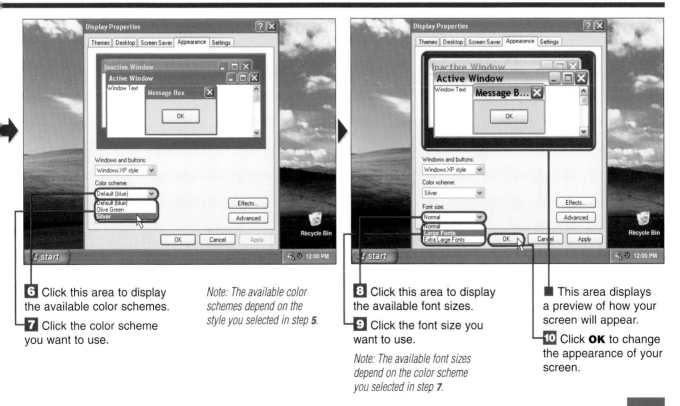

6 Click this area to display the available color schemes.

7 Click the color scheme you want to use.

Note: The available color schemes depend on the style you selected in step 5.

8 Click this area to display the available font sizes.

9 Click the font size you want to use.

Note: The available font sizes depend on the color scheme you selected in step 7.

■ This area displays a preview of how your screen will appear.

10 Click **OK** to change the appearance of your screen.

CHANGE THE DESKTOP THEME

You can use a desktop theme to personalize the overall appearance of Windows.

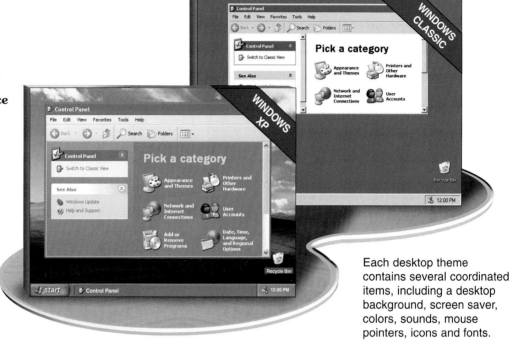

Each desktop theme contains several coordinated items, including a desktop background, screen saver, colors, sounds, mouse pointers, icons and fonts.

CHANGE THE DESKTOP THEME

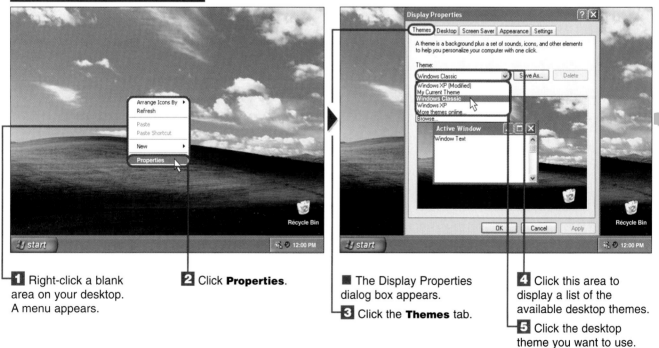

1 Right-click a blank area on your desktop. A menu appears.

2 Click **Properties**.

■ The Display Properties dialog box appears.

3 Click the **Themes** tab.

4 Click this area to display a list of the available desktop themes.

5 Click the desktop theme you want to use.

Tip

What desktop themes are available?

My Current Theme
The theme you are currently using.

Windows Classic
This theme resembles the style used in previous versions of Windows.

Windows XP
The theme initially displayed on Windows XP.

More themes online
You can select this option to obtain additional themes on the Internet. The Microsoft Internet Explorer window will appear and display a Web page that allows you to obtain additional themes.

Theme Name (Modified)
If you make changes to a theme, such as changing the desktop background, a new theme appears with the word **Modified** in its name.

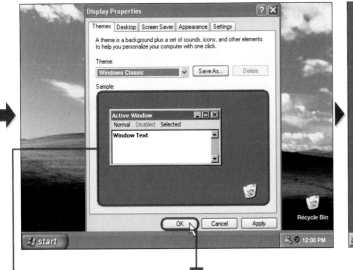

■ This area displays a preview of the desktop theme you selected.

6 Click **OK** to confirm your change.

■ Windows applies the desktop theme you selected.

■ To return to the original desktop theme, perform steps **1** to **6**, selecting **Windows XP** in step **5**.

117

CHANGE THE SCREEN RESOLUTION

You can change the screen resolution to adjust the amount of information that can fit on your screen.

Your monitor and video adapter determine which screen resolutions are available on your computer.

You will not usually change the screen resolution of a Liquid Crystal Display (LCD) monitor, since this can reduce the image quality. An LCD monitor is a thin, lightweight monitor compared to the bulkier Cathode Ray Tube (CRT) monitor.

CHANGE THE SCREEN RESOLUTION

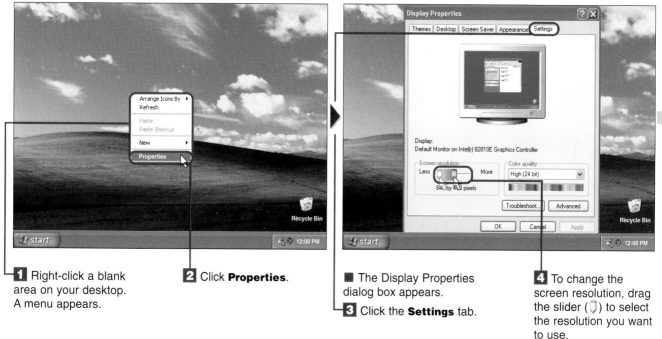

1 Right-click a blank area on your desktop. A menu appears.

2 Click **Properties**.

■ The Display Properties dialog box appears.

3 Click the **Settings** tab.

4 To change the screen resolution, drag the slider (⬚) to select the resolution you want to use.

Tip

Which screen resolution should I use?

The screen resolution is measured by the number of horizontal and vertical pixels displayed on a screen. A pixel is the smallest point on a screen. The screen resolution you should choose depends on the size of your monitor and the amount of information you want to view on your screen at once.

Lower screen resolutions display larger images so you can see the information on your screen more clearly.

Higher screen resolutions display smaller images so you can display more information on your screen at once.

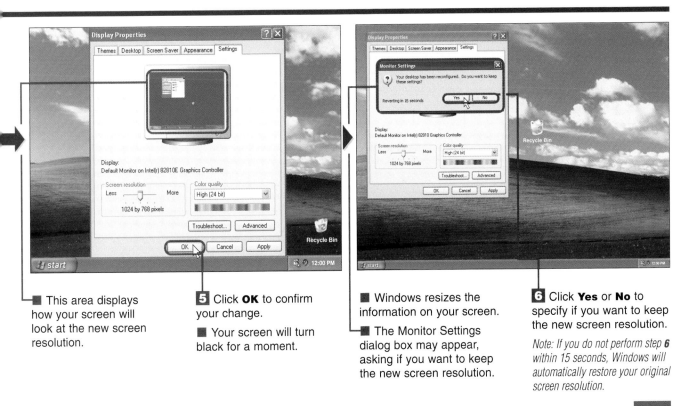

■ This area displays how your screen will look at the new screen resolution.

5 Click **OK** to confirm your change.

■ Your screen will turn black for a moment.

■ Windows resizes the information on your screen.

■ The Monitor Settings dialog box may appear, asking if you want to keep the new screen resolution.

6 Click **Yes** or **No** to specify if you want to keep the new screen resolution.

Note: If you do not perform step 6 within 15 seconds, Windows will automatically restore your original screen resolution.

119

ARRANGE DESKTOP ITEMS

You can have Windows neatly arrange the items on your desktop.

Windows can arrange desktop items by name, size, type or the date the items were last modified.

ARRANGE DESKTOP ITEMS

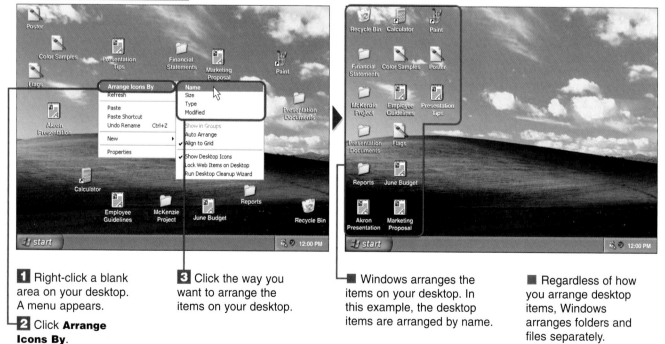

1 Right-click a blank area on your desktop. A menu appears.

2 Click **Arrange Icons By**.

3 Click the way you want to arrange the items on your desktop.

■ Windows arranges the items on your desktop. In this example, the desktop items are arranged by name.

■ Regardless of how you arrange desktop items, Windows arranges folders and files separately.

ADJUST THE VOLUME

You can adjust
the volume of
sound on your
computer.

ADJUST THE VOLUME

1 Click 🔊 to
display the Volume
control.

■ The Volume
control appears.

2 Drag this slider (▭)
up or down to increase
or decrease the sound
volume on your computer.

3 To turn off the sound,
click **Mute** (☐ changes
to ☑).

*Note: When you turn off the
sound, the icon on the taskbar
changes from 🔊 to 🔇 . To once
again turn on the sound, repeat
step 3 (☑ changes to ☐).*

4 When you finish
adjusting the volume,
click a blank area on
your desktop to hide
the Volume control.

ASSIGN SOUNDS TO PROGRAM EVENTS

Windows can play sound effects when certain program events occur on your computer. For example, you can hear a short tune when you start Windows.

You can change the sounds assigned to many events at once by selecting a sound scheme. A sound scheme consists of a set of related sounds.

ASSIGN SOUNDS TO PROGRAM EVENTS

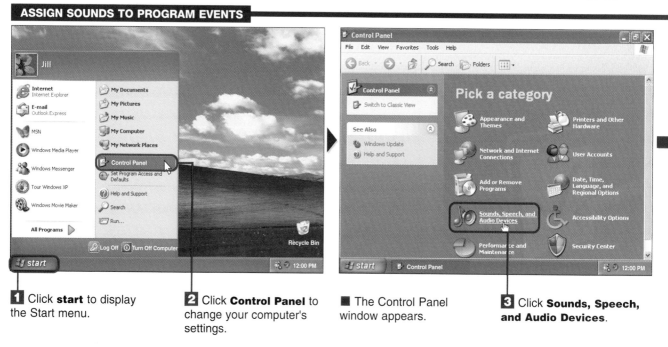

1 Click **start** to display the Start menu.

2 Click **Control Panel** to change your computer's settings.

■ The Control Panel window appears.

3 Click **Sounds, Speech, and Audio Devices**.

Tip

What program events can Windows assign sounds to?

Windows can assign sounds to over 40 events on your computer. Here are some examples.

Exit Windows

A sound will play each time you exit Windows.

New Mail Notification

A sound will play each time you receive a new e-mail message.

Empty Recycle Bin

A sound will play each time you empty the Recycle Bin.

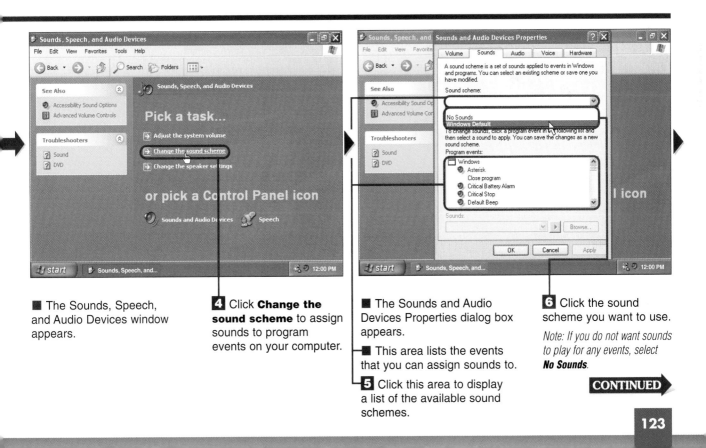

■ The Sounds, Speech, and Audio Devices window appears.

4 Click **Change the sound scheme** to assign sounds to program events on your computer.

■ The Sounds and Audio Devices Properties dialog box appears.

■ This area lists the events that you can assign sounds to.

5 Click this area to display a list of the available sound schemes.

6 Click the sound scheme you want to use.

Note: If you do not want sounds to play for any events, select **No Sounds***.*

CONTINUED

ASSIGN SOUNDS TO PROGRAM EVENTS

When assigning sounds to program events, you can test the sound that Windows will play for each event.

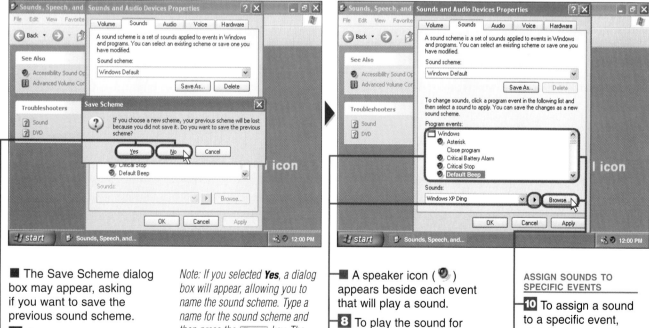

■ The Save Scheme dialog box may appear, asking if you want to save the previous sound scheme.

7 Click **Yes** or **No** to specify if you want to save the previous sound scheme.

*Note: If you selected **Yes**, a dialog box will appear, allowing you to name the sound scheme. Type a name for the sound scheme and then press the* Enter *key. The sound scheme will appear in the list of available sound schemes.*

■ A speaker icon (🔊) appears beside each event that will play a sound.

8 To play the sound for an event, click the event.

9 Click ▶ to play the sound.

ASSIGN SOUNDS TO SPECIFIC EVENTS

10 To assign a sound to a specific event, click the event.

11 Click **Browse** to search for the sound you want to use.

Where can I obtain sounds that I can assign to specific program events?

You can use the sounds included with Windows, purchase collections of sounds at computer stores or obtain sounds on the Internet. The sounds you use must be in the Wave format. Wave files have the .wav extension, such as chimes.wav. You can obtain sounds at the following Web sites.

www.favewavs.com

www.wavlist.com

www.thepocket.com

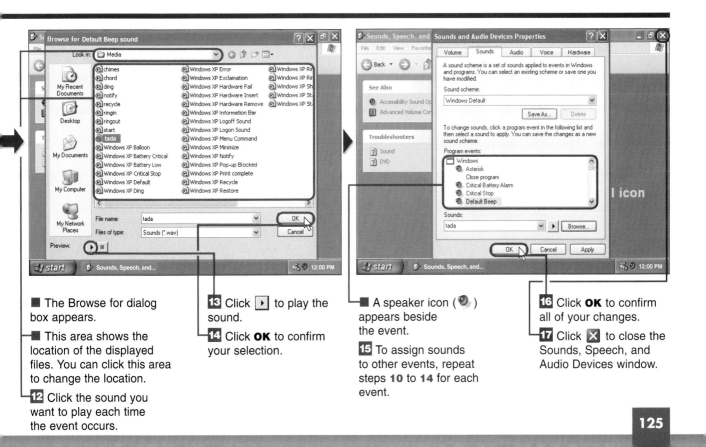

■ The Browse for dialog box appears.

■ This area shows the location of the displayed files. You can click this area to change the location.

12 Click the sound you want to play each time the event occurs.

13 Click ▶ to play the sound.

14 Click **OK** to confirm your selection.

■ A speaker icon ( ) appears beside the event.

15 To assign sounds to other events, repeat steps **10** to **14** for each event.

16 Click **OK** to confirm all of your changes.

17 Click ✕ to close the Sounds, Speech, and Audio Devices window.

CHANGE THE DATE AND TIME

You should make sure the correct date and time are set in your computer. Windows uses the date and time to determine when you create and update your files.

Your computer has a built-in clock that keeps track of the date and time even when you turn off your computer.

CHANGE THE DATE AND TIME

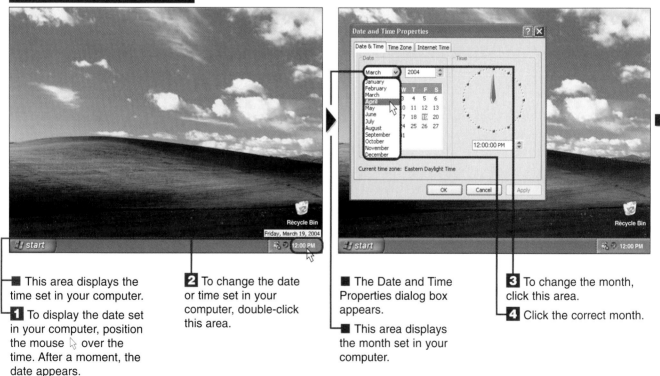

■ This area displays the time set in your computer.

1 To display the date set in your computer, position the mouse ⟍ over the time. After a moment, the date appears.

2 To change the date or time set in your computer, double-click this area.

■ The Date and Time Properties dialog box appears.

■ This area displays the month set in your computer.

3 To change the month, click this area.

4 Click the correct month.

Tip

Will Windows ever change the time automatically?

Windows will change the time automatically to compensate for daylight saving time. When you turn on your computer after daylight saving time occurs, Windows will have automatically changed the time.

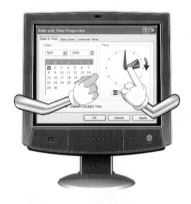

Tip

Can Windows ensure that my computer's clock is accurate?

Windows automatically synchronizes your computer's clock with a time server on the Internet approximately once a week. You must be connected to the Internet for the synchronization to occur. If you are on a network that uses a firewall to protect against unauthorized access, Windows may not be able to synchronize your computer's clock.

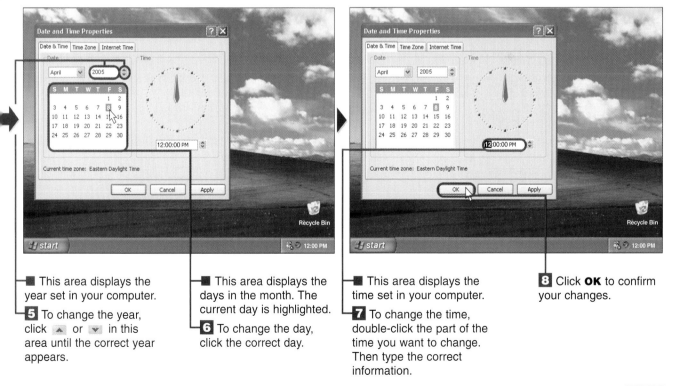

■ This area displays the year set in your computer.

5 To change the year, click ▲ or ▼ in this area until the correct year appears.

■ This area displays the days in the month. The current day is highlighted.

6 To change the day, click the correct day.

■ This area displays the time set in your computer.

7 To change the time, double-click the part of the time you want to change. Then type the correct information.

8 Click **OK** to confirm your changes.

CHANGE THE MOUSE SETTINGS

You can change
the way your
mouse works to
make the mouse
easier to use.

CHANGE THE MOUSE SETTINGS

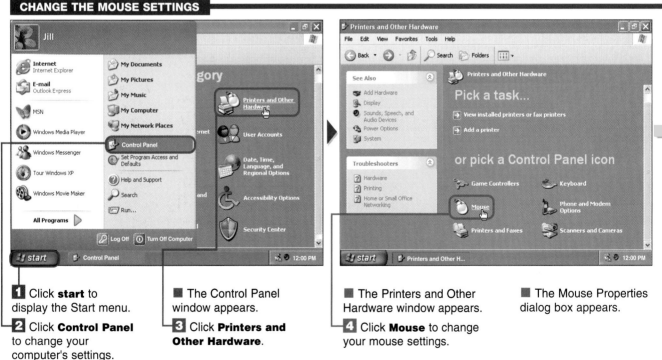

1 Click **start** to
display the Start menu.

2 Click **Control Panel**
to change your
computer's settings.

■ The Control Panel
window appears.

3 Click **Printers and
Other Hardware**.

■ The Printers and Other
Hardware window appears.

4 Click **Mouse** to change
your mouse settings.

■ The Mouse Properties
dialog box appears.

Should I use a mouse pad?

When you use a mechanical mouse, which detects movement using a ball on the bottom of the mouse, a mouse pad provides a smooth, flat surface for moving the mouse and helps reduce the amount of dirt that enters the mouse. When you use an optical mouse, which detects movement using a beam of light, you do not need to use a mouse pad. For the best results when using an optical mouse, you should use the mouse on a flat surface that is a solid color.

Mechanical Mouse

Optical Mouse

 How fast should I set the double-click speed for my mouse?

You should set the double-click speed so it is appropriate for you. If you are a new mouse user or you have difficulty double-clicking the mouse, you may find a slower double-click speed easier to use. A more experienced user may find a faster double-click speed easier to use.

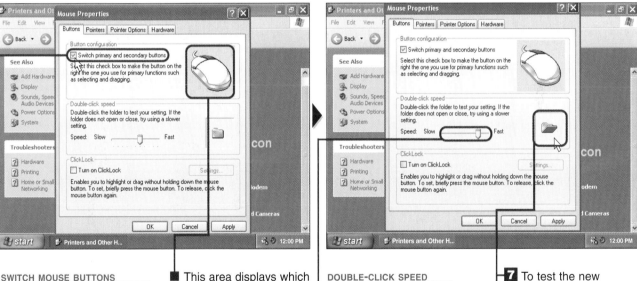

SWITCH MOUSE BUTTONS

5 If you are left-handed and want to use the right mouse button to perform most tasks, click this option to switch the functions of the left and right mouse buttons (☐ changes to ☑).

■ This area displays which mouse button you will use to perform most tasks.

Note: When you change some mouse settings, Windows immediately changes the way your mouse works.

DOUBLE-CLICK SPEED

6 To change the amount of time that can pass between two clicks of the mouse button for Windows to recognize a double-click, drag this slider (🖰) to a new position.

7 To test the new double-click speed, double-click the folder in this area.

■ The folder opens or closes when you double-click at the correct speed.

CONTINUED

129

CHANGE THE MOUSE SETTINGS

You can personalize the way your mouse works by changing how fast the mouse wheel scrolls through information. You can also change the appearance of the mouse pointers that Windows displays.

Wheel Speed   **Pointer Appearance**

CHANGE THE MOUSE SETTINGS (CONTINUED)

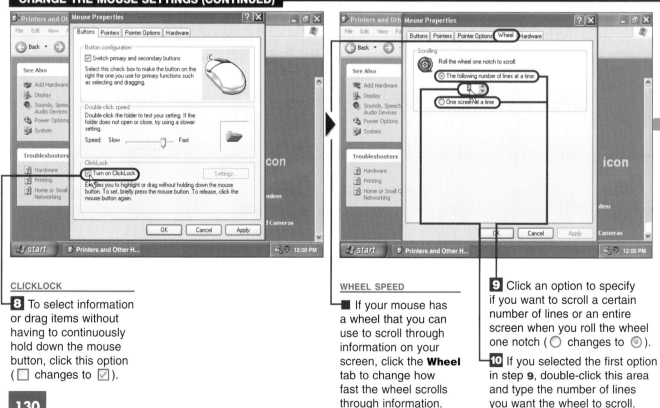

CLICKLOCK

8 To select information or drag items without having to continuously hold down the mouse button, click this option (☐ changes to ☑).

WHEEL SPEED

■ If your mouse has a wheel that you can use to scroll through information on your screen, click the **Wheel** tab to change how fast the wheel scrolls through information.

9 Click an option to specify if you want to scroll a certain number of lines or an entire screen when you roll the wheel one notch (○ changes to ◉).

10 If you selected the first option in step **9**, double-click this area and type the number of lines you want the wheel to scroll.

130

Tip

How can I use the ClickLock mouse setting to select text?

The ClickLock mouse setting allows you to select text without having to continuously hold down the mouse button.

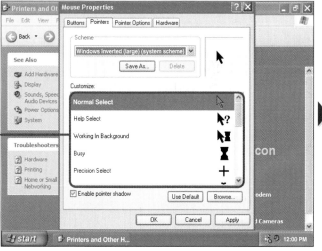

1 To select text using the ClickLock mouse setting, position the mouse I to the left of the text you want to select and then briefly press and hold down the mouse button.

2 Position the mouse I at the end of the text you want to select and then click the mouse button again.

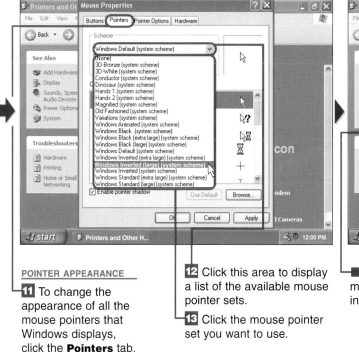

POINTER APPEARANCE

11 To change the appearance of all the mouse pointers that Windows displays, click the **Pointers** tab.

12 Click this area to display a list of the available mouse pointer sets.

13 Click the mouse pointer set you want to use.

■ This area lists the mouse pointers included in the set you selected.

Note: The mouse pointer assumes different shapes. Each shape offers a visual cue to indicate what Windows is doing or the task you can perform.

CONTINUED

CHANGE THE MOUSE SETTINGS

You can change how fast the mouse pointer moves on your screen. You can also have the mouse pointer automatically appear over the default button in most dialog boxes.

The default button in most dialog boxes is the **OK** button.

Pointer Speed

Snap to Default Button

CHANGE THE MOUSE SETTINGS (CONTINUED)

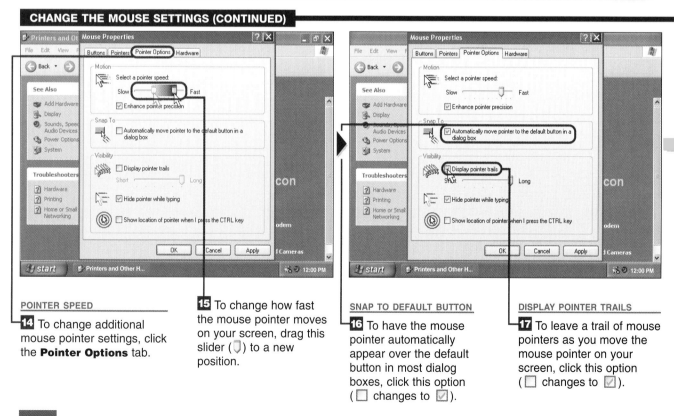

POINTER SPEED

14 To change additional mouse pointer settings, click the **Pointer Options** tab.

15 To change how fast the mouse pointer moves on your screen, drag this slider ( ) to a new position.

SNAP TO DEFAULT BUTTON

16 To have the mouse pointer automatically appear over the default button in most dialog boxes, click this option (☐ changes to ☑).

DISPLAY POINTER TRAILS

17 To leave a trail of mouse pointers as you move the mouse pointer on your screen, click this option (☐ changes to ☑).

Tip

How can I make the mouse pointer easier to see on my screen?

Windows offers two mouse settings that can help you more clearly see the mouse pointer on your screen. These settings are especially useful on notebook computer screens where the mouse pointer can be difficult to follow.

Display pointer trails

Displays mouse pointer trails to help you follow the movement of the mouse pointer on your screen.

Show location of pointer

Shows the location of the mouse pointer when you press the `Ctrl` key. Moving circles will briefly appear around the mouse pointer to help you quickly locate the mouse pointer on your screen.

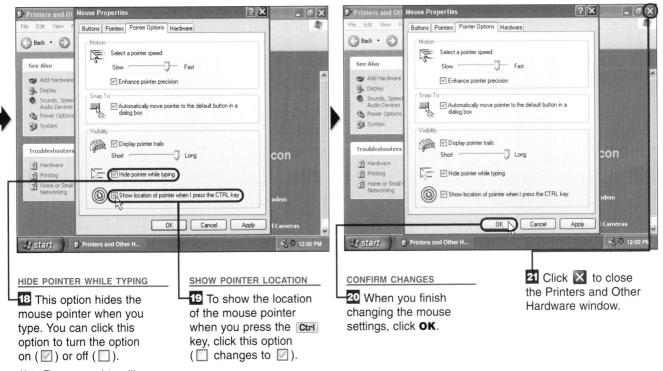

HIDE POINTER WHILE TYPING

18 This option hides the mouse pointer when you type. You can click this option to turn the option on (☑) or off (☐).

Note: The mouse pointer will re-appear when you move the mouse.

SHOW POINTER LOCATION

19 To show the location of the mouse pointer when you press the `Ctrl` key, click this option (☐ changes to ☑).

CONFIRM CHANGES

20 When you finish changing the mouse settings, click **OK**.

21 Click ☒ to close the Printers and Other Hardware window.

START A PROGRAM AUTOMATICALLY

If you use the same program every day, you can have the program start automatically each time you turn on your computer.

To have a program start automatically, you need to place a shortcut for the program in the Startup folder. A shortcut is a link to the program.

START A PROGRAM AUTOMATICALLY

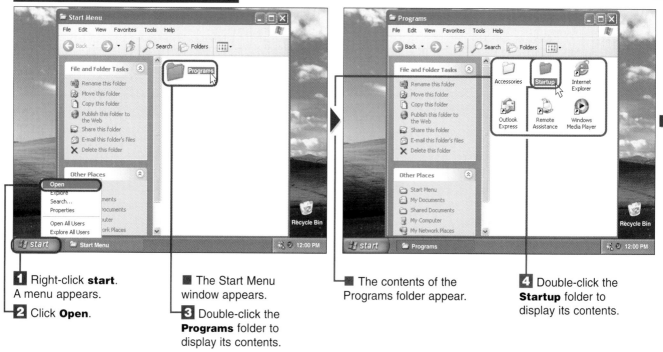

1 Right-click **start**. A menu appears.

2 Click **Open**.

■ The Start Menu window appears.

3 Double-click the **Programs** folder to display its contents.

■ The contents of the Programs folder appear.

4 Double-click the **Startup** folder to display its contents.

Tip

How do I stop a program from starting automatically?

To stop a program from starting automatically, you must remove the shortcut for the program from the Startup folder. Deleting a shortcut for a program from the Startup folder will not remove the program from your computer.

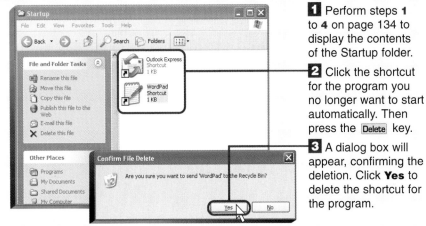

1 Perform steps **1** to **4** on page 134 to display the contents of the Startup folder.

2 Click the shortcut for the program you no longer want to start automatically. Then press the Delete key.

3 A dialog box will appear, confirming the deletion. Click **Yes** to delete the shortcut for the program.

■ The contents of the Startup folder appear.

5 Click **start** to display the Start menu.

6 Click **All Programs** to view a list of the programs on your computer.

7 Position the mouse over the program you want to start automatically.

8 Press and hold down the Ctrl key as you drag the program to a blank area in the Startup window.

■ A shortcut for the program appears in the Startup window. A shortcut displays an arrow ( ) in its icon.

9 Click ✗ to close the Startup window.

■ The program will now start automatically each time you turn on your computer.

CHAPTER 6

Work with Songs and Videos

In this chapter, you will learn how to use the Windows Media Player program to play music CDs and find music and video on the Internet. You will also learn how to copy songs to a CD or portable device, play DVD movies and much more.

PLAY A VIDEO OR SOUND

You can use Windows Media Player to play many types of video and sound files on your computer.

You can obtain video and sound files on the Internet or from friends, family members or colleagues in e-mail messages you receive.

PLAY A VIDEO OR SOUND

1 Double-click the video or sound file you want to play.

■ The Windows Media Player window appears.

Note: The first time Windows Media Player starts, a Welcome to Windows Media Player wizard appears, helping you set up the player. See the top of page 139 for more information on the wizard.

■ If you selected a video file, this area displays the video.

Note: If you selected a sound file, the sound plays. The area displays splashes of color and shapes that change as the sound plays.

■ This slider (⬭) indicates the progress of the video or sound file.

2 To use the entire screen to view the video that is currently playing, click 🖵.

Why does a Welcome wizard appear when I try to play a video or sound file?

The first time Windows Media Player starts, a Welcome to Windows Media Player wizard appears, helping you set up the player on your computer. In the wizard, click **Next** twice to accept all the settings that the wizard suggests and then click **Finish** to finish setting up Windows Media Player.

Tip

Why does my Windows Media Player window look different than the window shown below?

You may be using an older version of Windows Media Player. When Windows Media Player starts, a dialog box may appear, stating that a Windows Media update is available. To obtain the latest version of Windows Media Player, click **Yes** in the dialog box. You can also visit the www.microsoft.com Web site to obtain the latest version of Windows Media Player.

■ The video continues to play using the entire screen.

3 To once again view the video in a window, click 🔲 or press the **Esc** key.

4 To adjust the volume, drag this slider (⊖) left or right to decrease or increase the volume.

5 To pause or stop the play of the video or sound file, click the pause (⏸) or stop (⏹) button (⏸ changes to ▶).

■ You can click ▶ to resume the play of the sound or video file.

6 When you finish playing the sound or video file, click ✖ to close the Windows Media Player window.

PLAY A MUSIC CD

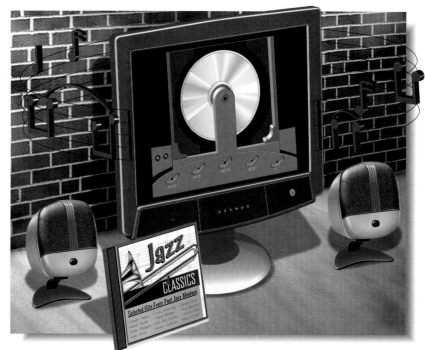

You can use your computer to play music CDs while you work.

You need an updated version of Windows Media Player to perform the steps as shown below. To obtain an updated version of Windows Media Player, see the top of page 139.

PLAY A MUSIC CD

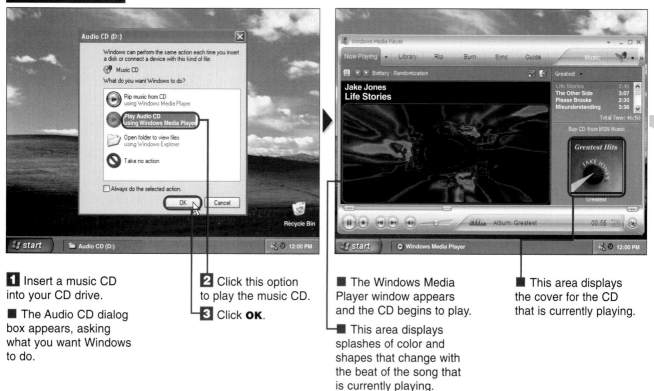

1 Insert a music CD into your CD drive.

■ The Audio CD dialog box appears, asking what you want Windows to do.

2 Click this option to play the music CD.

3 Click **OK**.

■ The Windows Media Player window appears and the CD begins to play.

■ This area displays splashes of color and shapes that change with the beat of the song that is currently playing.

■ This area displays the cover for the CD that is currently playing.

Tip

How does Windows Media Player know the CD cover and the name of each song on my music CD?

If you are connected to the Internet when you play a music CD, Windows Media Player attempts to obtain information about the CD from the Internet, including the CD cover and track names. If you are not connected to the Internet or information about the CD is unavailable, Windows Media Player displays a generic CD cover and the track number of each song instead. If Windows Media Player is able to obtain information about the CD, Windows will recognize the CD and display the appropriate information each time you insert the CD.

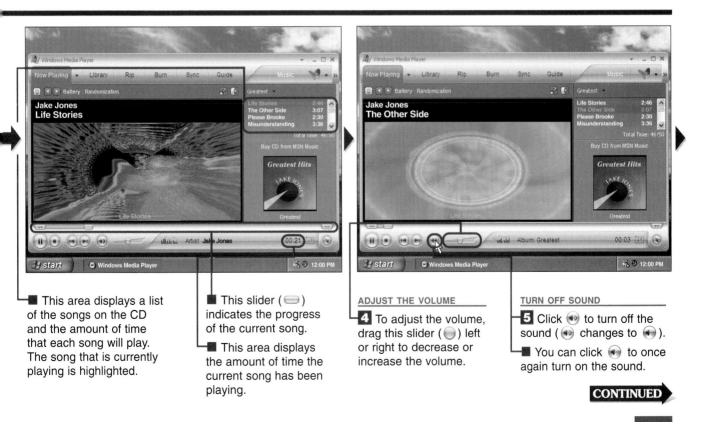

■ This area displays a list of the songs on the CD and the amount of time that each song will play. The song that is currently playing is highlighted.

■ This slider ( ) indicates the progress of the current song.

■ This area displays the amount of time the current song has been playing.

ADJUST THE VOLUME

4 To adjust the volume, drag this slider ( ) left or right to decrease or increase the volume.

TURN OFF SOUND

5 Click to turn off the sound (changes to).

■ You can click to once again turn on the sound.

CONTINUED

PLAY A MUSIC CD

When playing a music CD, you can pause or stop the play of the CD at any time. You can also play a specific song or play the songs in random order.

PLAY A MUSIC CD (CONTINUED)

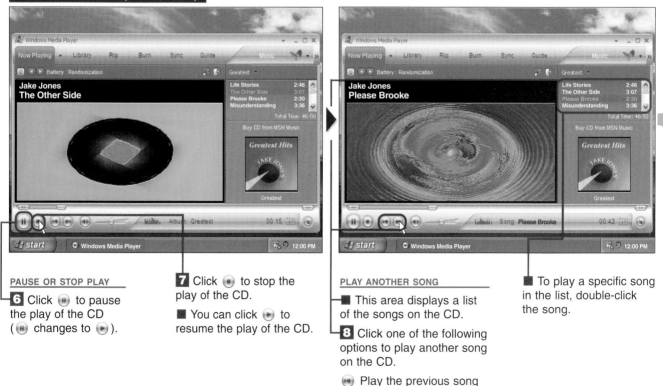

PAUSE OR STOP PLAY

6 Click ⏸ to pause the play of the CD (⏸ changes to ▶).

7 Click ⏹ to stop the play of the CD.

■ You can click ▶ to resume the play of the CD.

PLAY ANOTHER SONG

■ This area displays a list of the songs on the CD.

8 Click one of the following options to play another song on the CD.

⏮ Play the previous song

⏭ Play the next song

■ To play a specific song in the list, double-click the song.

Tip

Can I play a music CD while performing other tasks on my computer?

Yes. If you want to perform other tasks on your computer while playing a music CD, you can display the Windows Media Player window in the mini player mode. The mini player mode displays the most commonly used Windows Media Player playback controls in a toolbar on the taskbar. For information on the mini player mode, see page 152.

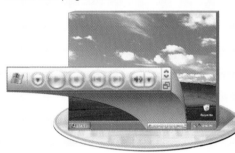

Tip

Can I listen to a music CD privately?

You can listen to a music CD privately by plugging headphones into the jack at the front or back of your computer or into your speakers.

PLAY SONGS RANDOMLY

9 To play the songs on the CD in random order, click the name of the CD.

10 Click **Play Shuffled**.

Note: A check mark (✔) appears beside Play Shuffled when this option is on.

■ To once again play the songs on the CD in order, repeat steps **9** and **10**.

CLOSE WINDOWS MEDIA PLAYER

11 When you finish listening to the CD, click ✖ to close the Windows Media Player window.

12 Remove the CD from your CD drive.

USING THE GUIDE

The Guide is like an electronic magazine that allows you to access the latest music and movies on the Internet. You can also use the Guide to obtain information on various topics such as news, sports and entertainment.

You must have a connection to the Internet to use the Guide.

You need an updated version of Windows Media Player to perform the steps as shown below. To obtain an updated version of Windows Media Player, see the top of page 139.

USING THE GUIDE

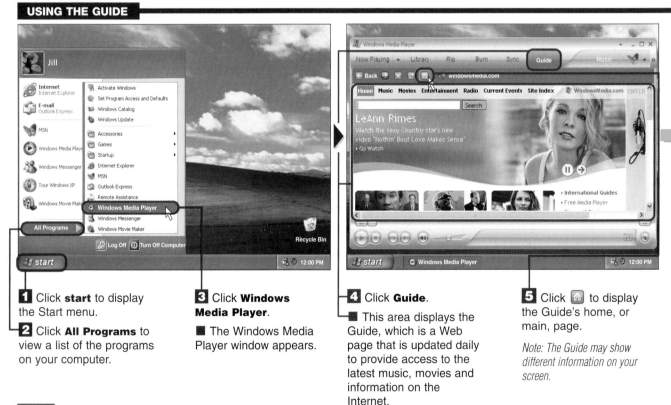

1 Click **start** to display the Start menu.

2 Click **All Programs** to view a list of the programs on your computer.

3 Click **Windows Media Player**.

■ The Windows Media Player window appears.

4 Click **Guide**.

■ This area displays the Guide, which is a Web page that is updated daily to provide access to the latest music, movies and information on the Internet.

5 Click 🏠 to display the Guide's home, or main, page.

Note: The Guide may show different information on your screen.

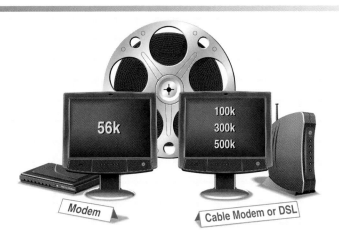

Tip

Why are different speeds listed for a media file in the Guide?

The Guide offers files for different connection speeds that you can select to transfer and play a media file such as a music video or movie clip. The connection speed you should select depends on the type of connection you have to the Internet. If problems occur while transferring or playing a media file, try selecting a slower connection speed.

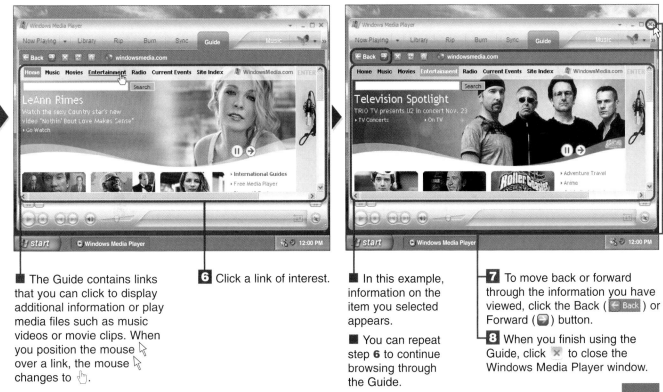

■ The Guide contains links that you can click to display additional information or play media files such as music videos or movie clips. When you position the mouse over a link, the mouse changes to ⏬.

6 Click a link of interest.

■ In this example, information on the item you selected appears.

■ You can repeat step **6** to continue browsing through the Guide.

7 To move back or forward through the information you have viewed, click the Back (← Back) or Forward (➡) button.

8 When you finish using the Guide, click ✕ to close the Windows Media Player window.

USING THE LIBRARY

You can use the Library to view, organize and play all the sound and video files on your computer.

You need an updated version of Windows Media Player to perform the steps as shown below. To obtain an updated version of Windows Media Player, see the top of page 139.

USING THE LIBRARY

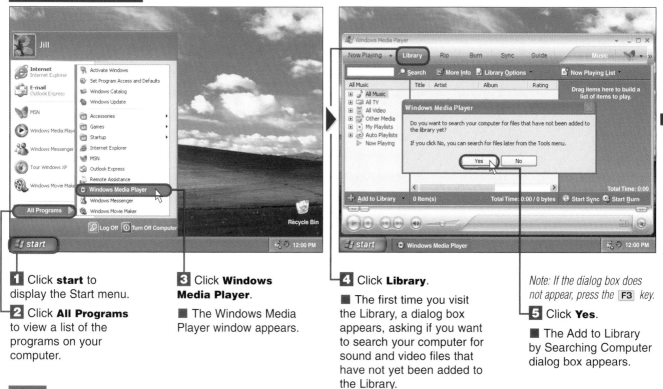

1 Click **start** to display the Start menu.

2 Click **All Programs** to view a list of the programs on your computer.

3 Click **Windows Media Player**.

■ The Windows Media Player window appears.

4 Click **Library**.

■ The first time you visit the Library, a dialog box appears, asking if you want to search your computer for sound and video files that have not yet been added to the Library.

Note: If the dialog box does not appear, press the **F3** *key.*

5 Click **Yes**.

■ The Add to Library by Searching Computer dialog box appears.

Tip

Where can I obtain media files?

The Guide

You can use the Guide that Windows Media Player provides to access the latest music, music videos and movie previews on the Internet. For more information on the Guide, see page 144.

The Internet

Many Web sites on the Internet offer sound and video files free of charge that you can play on your computer. You can also purchase the latest music and videos on the Internet. Windows Media Player offers several online stores, such as MSN Music and Napster, that you can visit. To access these online stores, click ▼ at the top of the Windows Media Player window and then click the store you want to visit from the menu that appears.

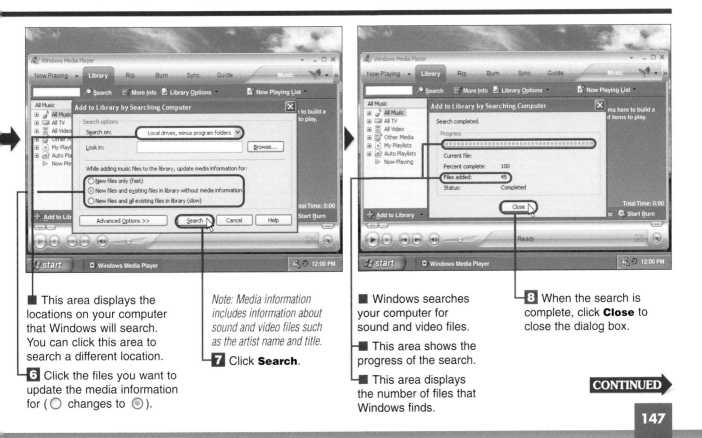

■ This area displays the locations on your computer that Windows will search. You can click this area to search a different location.

6 Click the files you want to update the media information for (○ changes to ⊙).

Note: Media information includes information about sound and video files such as the artist name and title.

7 Click **Search**.

■ Windows searches your computer for sound and video files.

■ This area shows the progress of the search.

■ This area displays the number of files that Windows finds.

8 When the search is complete, click **Close** to close the dialog box.

CONTINUED ▶

You can play
sound and
video files
that are listed
in the Library.

USING THE LIBRARY (CONTINUED)

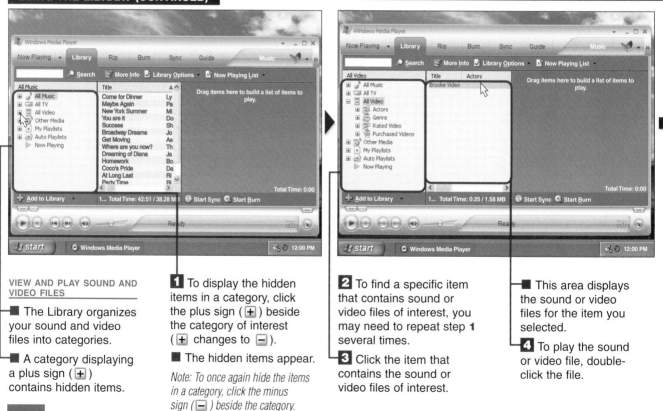

VIEW AND PLAY SOUND AND VIDEO FILES

■ The Library organizes your sound and video files into categories.

■ A category displaying a plus sign (⊞) contains hidden items.

1 To display the hidden items in a category, click the plus sign (⊞) beside the category of interest (⊞ changes to ⊟).

■ The hidden items appear.

Note: To once again hide the items in a category, click the minus sign (⊟) beside the category.

2 To find a specific item that contains sound or video files of interest, you may need to repeat step **1** several times.

3 Click the item that contains the sound or video files of interest.

■ This area displays the sound or video files for the item you selected.

4 To play the sound or video file, double-click the file.

Tip

**What categories does the Library use
to organize my sound and video files?**

All Music	Lists all your music files.
All TV	Lists television shows you have recorded.
All Video	Lists video files, including videos you have downloaded from the Internet and videos you have created using Windows Movie Maker.
Other Media	Lists sound and video files that do not belong in any other category.
My Playlists	Lists playlists that you have created. To create a playlist, see page 150.
Auto Playlists	Lists playlists that Windows Media Player has automatically created for you.
Now Playing	Lists the music and video files that are currently playing in Windows Media Player.

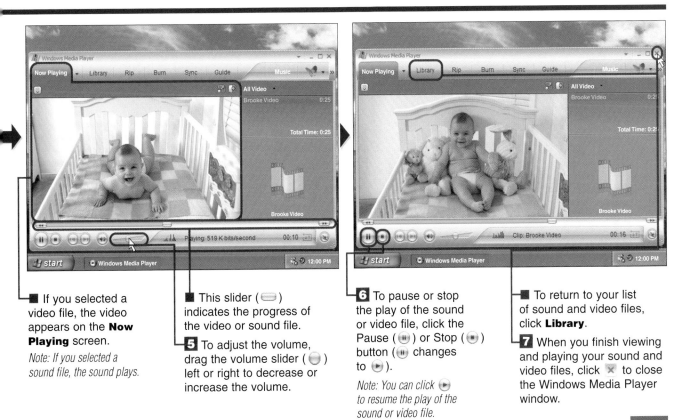

■ If you selected a video file, the video appears on the **Now Playing** screen.

Note: If you selected a sound file, the sound plays.

■ This slider (⬭) indicates the progress of the video or sound file.

5 To adjust the volume, drag the volume slider (⬭) left or right to decrease or increase the volume.

6 To pause or stop the play of the sound or video file, click the Pause (⏸) or Stop (⏹) button (⏸ changes to ▶).

Note: You can click ▶ to resume the play of the sound or video file.

■ To return to your list of sound and video files, click **Library**.

7 When you finish viewing and playing your sound and video files, click ✕ to close the Windows Media Player window.

CREATE A PLAYLIST

Windows Media Player allows you to create personalized lists of your favorite sound and video files, called playlists.

Creating a playlist is useful when you want to listen to a specific group of songs. You can select a playlist and Windows Media Player will play all the songs in the playlist. For example, you can create and play a playlist that contains all your favorite rock songs.

You need an updated version of Windows Media Player to perform the steps as shown below. To obtain an updated version of Windows Media Player, see the top of page 139.

CREATE A PLAYLIST

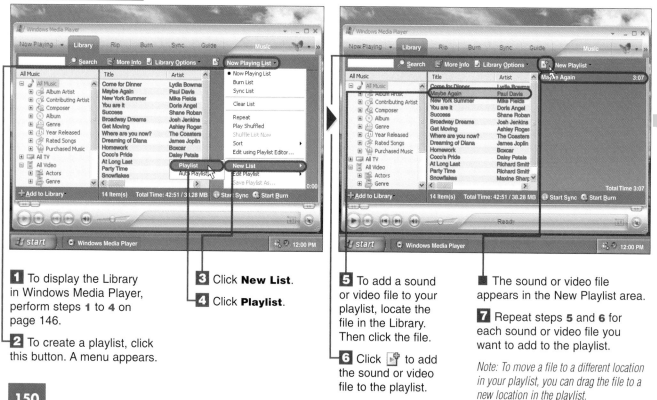

1 To display the Library in Windows Media Player, perform steps **1** to **4** on page 146.

2 To create a playlist, click this button. A menu appears.

3 Click **New List**.

4 Click **Playlist**.

5 To add a sound or video file to your playlist, locate the file in the Library. Then click the file.

6 Click 🖼 to add the sound or video file to the playlist.

■ The sound or video file appears in the New Playlist area.

7 Repeat steps **5** and **6** for each sound or video file you want to add to the playlist.

Note: To move a file to a different location in your playlist, you can drag the file to a new location in the playlist.

Tip

How do I play all the sound or video files in a playlist?

In the Library of Windows Media Player, click the plus sign (➕) beside **My Playlists** to view all the playlists you have created (➕ changes to ➖). To start playing all the sound and video files in a playlist, double-click the playlist.

Tip

Can Windows Media Player automatically create playlists for me?

Yes. In the Library of Windows Media Player, the Auto Playlists category contains playlists that Windows has automatically created for you. For example, Windows Media Player creates a playlist of the sound and video files you play most often on weekdays and another playlist of files you play most often at night.

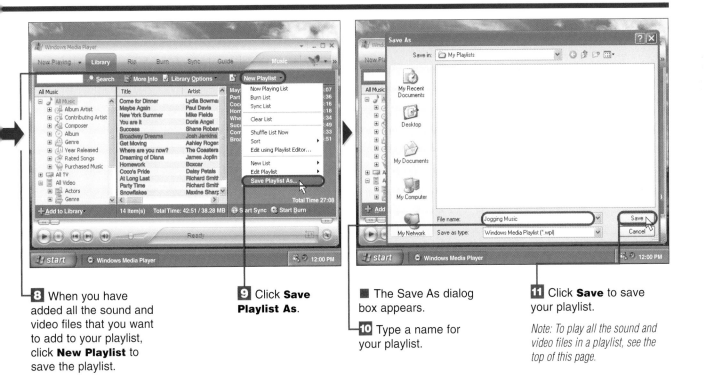

8 When you have added all the sound and video files that you want to add to your playlist, click **New Playlist** to save the playlist.

9 Click **Save Playlist As**.

■ The Save As dialog box appears.

10 Type a name for your playlist.

11 Click **Save** to save your playlist.

Note: To play all the sound and video files in a playlist, see the top of this page.

SWITCH BETWEEN DISPLAY MODES

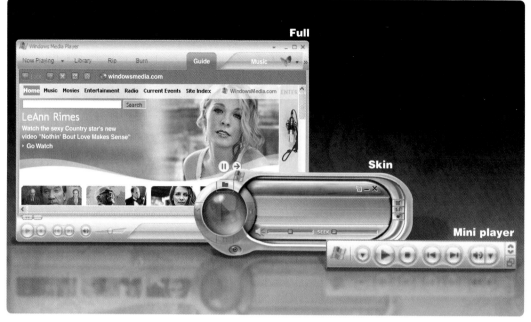

Full

Skin

Mini player

You can change the appearance of Windows Media Player by switching between three different display modes.

You need an updated version of Windows Media Player to perform the steps as shown below. To obtain an updated version of Windows Media Player, see the top of page 139.

SWITCH BETWEEN DISPLAY MODES

FULL MODE

■ Windows Media Player initially appears in the full mode. The full mode allows you to access all the features that Windows Media Player provides.

1 To display Windows Media Player in the skin mode, click 🖳.

SKIN MODE

■ The skin mode offers a distinct design and usually takes up less room on your screen but offers fewer features than the full mode.

Note: Windows Media Player offers different skins that you can choose from. To choose a different skin, see page 154.

■ To once again display Windows Media Player in the full mode, click 🖳.

Note: The location and appearance of 🖳 depends on the current skin.

Tip

**What playback controls are available
in mini player mode?**

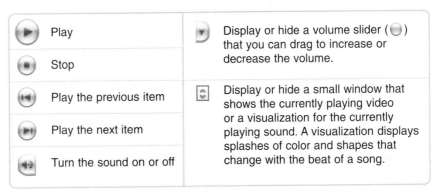

	Play		Display or hide a volume slider ( ) that you can drag to increase or decrease the volume.
	Stop		
	Play the previous item		Display or hide a small window that shows the currently playing video or a visualization for the currently playing sound. A visualization displays splashes of color and shapes that change with the beat of a song.
	Play the next item		
	Turn the sound on or off		

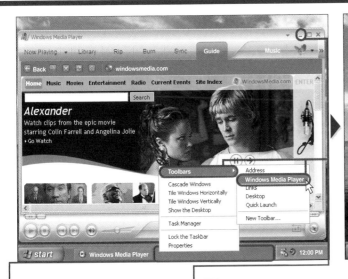

MINI PLAYER MODE

■ The mini player mode displays the most commonly used Windows Media Player playback controls in a toolbar on the taskbar.

1 To turn on the mini player mode, right-click a blank area on the taskbar. A menu appears.

2 Click **Toolbars**.

3 Click **Windows Media Player**.

4 To display Windows Media Player in the mini player mode, click  to minimize the window.

■ Windows Media Player appears as a toolbar on the taskbar.

Note: You only need to perform steps 1 to 3 once.

■ To return Windows Media Player to the full or skin mode, click . Windows Media Player will appear in the mode the player was previously in.

Note: If you want Windows Media Player to once again appear as a regular button on the taskbar when you minimize the window, repeat steps 1 to 3 to turn off the mini player mode.

CHANGE SKIN OF WINDOWS MEDIA PLAYER

You can change the skin of Windows Media Player to customize how the player looks and functions.

You need an updated version of Windows Media Player to perform the steps as shown below. To obtain an updated version of Windows Media Player, see the top of page 139.

CHANGE SKIN OF WINDOWS MEDIA PLAYER

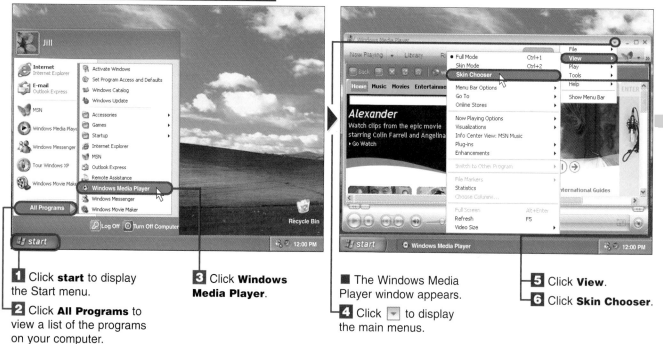

1 Click **start** to display the Start menu.

2 Click **All Programs** to view a list of the programs on your computer.

3 Click **Windows Media Player**.

■ The Windows Media Player window appears.

4 Click ▼ to display the main menus.

5 Click **View**.

6 Click **Skin Chooser**.

Tip

**Where can I obtain more skins for
Windows Media Player?**

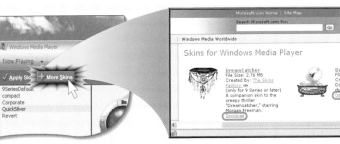

You can obtain more skins
for Windows Media Player
on the Internet.

When viewing the list of
skins in Windows Media
Player, click **More Skins**.

Windows will open Microsoft Internet
Explorer and display a Web page that offers
skins that you can choose from. Select the
Download link for the skin you want to use
and then click **Yes** and then **Close** in the
dialog boxes that appear. The skin will
transfer to your computer and appear in
your list of available skins.

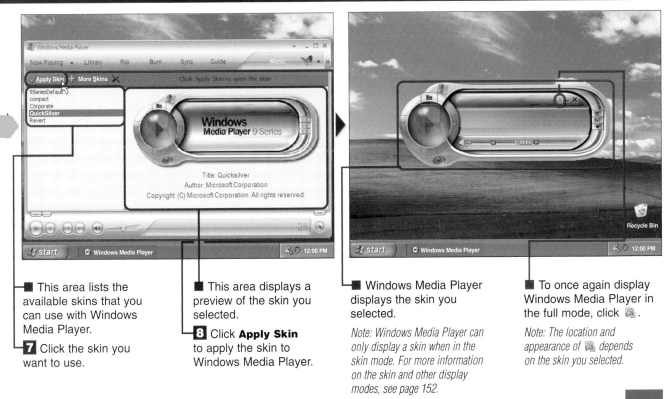

■ This area lists the
available skins that you
can use with Windows
Media Player.

7 Click the skin you
want to use.

■ This area displays a
preview of the skin you
selected.

8 Click **Apply Skin**
to apply the skin to
Windows Media Player.

■ Windows Media Player
displays the skin you
selected.

*Note: Windows Media Player can
only display a skin when in the
skin mode. For more information
on the skin and other display
modes, see page 152.*

■ To once again display
Windows Media Player in
the full mode, click ▣.

*Note: The location and
appearance of ▣ depends
on the skin you selected.*

COPY SONGS FROM A MUSIC CD

You can copy songs from a music CD onto your computer.

Copying songs from a music CD, also known as "ripping" music, allows you to play the songs at any time without having to insert the CD into your computer. Copying songs from a music CD also allows you to later copy the songs to a recordable CD or a portable device, such as an MP3 player.

You need an updated version of Windows Media Player to perform the steps as shown below. To obtain an updated version of Windows Media Player, see the top of page 139.

COPY SONGS FROM A MUSIC CD

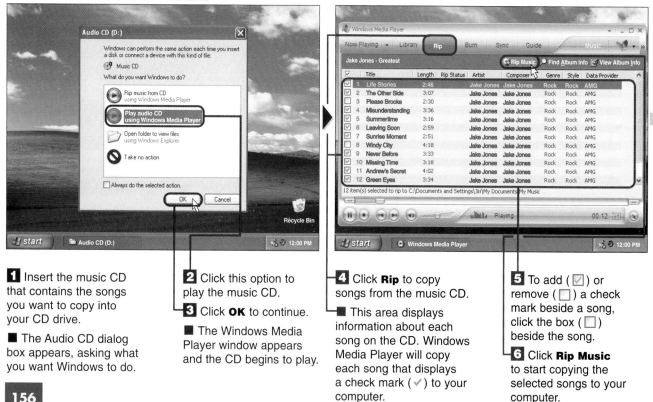

1 Insert the music CD that contains the songs you want to copy into your CD drive.

■ The Audio CD dialog box appears, asking what you want Windows to do.

2 Click this option to play the music CD.

3 Click **OK** to continue.

■ The Windows Media Player window appears and the CD begins to play.

4 Click **Rip** to copy songs from the music CD.

■ This area displays information about each song on the CD. Windows Media Player will copy each song that displays a check mark (✓) to your computer.

5 To add (☑) or remove (☐) a check mark beside a song, click the box (☐) beside the song.

6 Click **Rip Music** to start copying the selected songs to your computer.

Tip

How can I play a song I copied from a music CD?

Windows offers two ways that you can play a song you copied from a music CD.

Use the My Music Folder

Songs you copy from a music CD are stored in the My Music folder on your computer. The My Music folder contains a subfolder for each artist whose songs you have copied to your computer. To open the My Music folder, see page 45. To play a song, double-click the song.

Use Windows Media Player

Songs you copy from a music CD are listed in the Library in Windows Media Player. To play a song in the Library, see page 148.

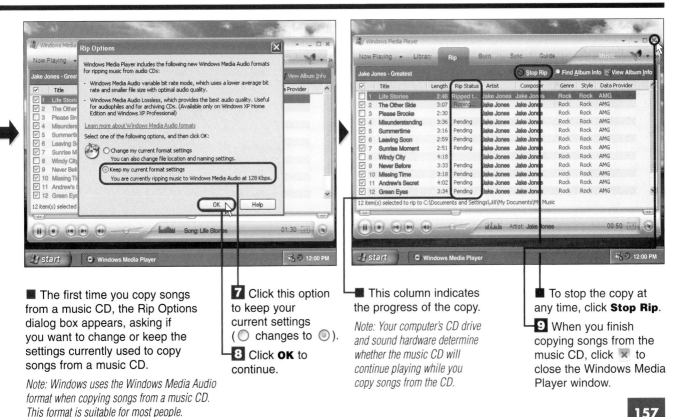

■ The first time you copy songs from a music CD, the Rip Options dialog box appears, asking if you want to change or keep the settings currently used to copy songs from a music CD.

Note: Windows uses the Windows Media Audio format when copying songs from a music CD. This format is suitable for most people.

7 Click this option to keep your current settings (○ changes to ◉).

8 Click **OK** to continue.

■ This column indicates the progress of the copy.

Note: Your computer's CD drive and sound hardware determine whether the music CD will continue playing while you copy songs from the CD.

■ To stop the copy at any time, click **Stop Rip**.

9 When you finish copying songs from the music CD, click ✕ to close the Windows Media Player window.

COPY SONGS TO A CD

You can use Windows Media Player to copy songs on your computer to a CD. Copying songs to a CD is also known as "burning" a CD.

You need an updated version of Windows Media Player to perform the steps as shown below. To obtain an updated version of Windows Media Player, see the top of page 139.

COPY SONGS TO A CD

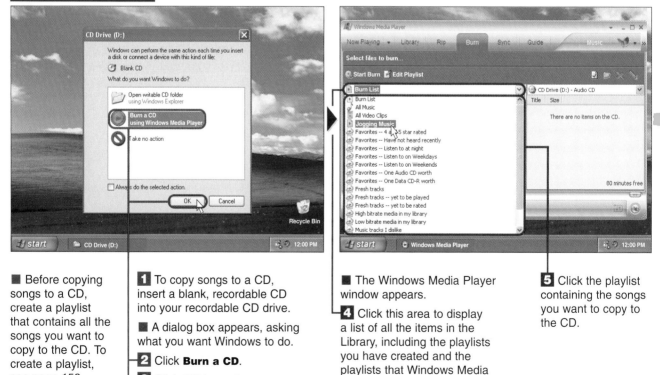

■ Before copying songs to a CD, create a playlist that contains all the songs you want to copy to the CD. To create a playlist, see page 150.

1 To copy songs to a CD, insert a blank, recordable CD into your recordable CD drive.

■ A dialog box appears, asking what you want Windows to do.

2 Click **Burn a CD**.

3 Click **OK** to continue.

■ The Windows Media Player window appears.

4 Click this area to display a list of all the items in the Library, including the playlists you have created and the playlists that Windows Media Player has automatically created for you.

5 Click the playlist containing the songs you want to copy to the CD.

Tip

What hardware do I need to copy songs to a CD?

You will need a recordable CD drive to copy songs to a CD.

CD-R Drive

A CD-R (Compact Disc-Recordable) drive allows you to permanently record data on CD-R discs. You cannot erase the contents of a CD-R disc.

CD-RW Drive

A CD-RW (Compact Disc-ReWritable) drive allows you to record data on CD-RW or CD-R discs. You can erase the contents of a CD-RW disc in order to copy new data to the disc. To erase the contents of a CD-RW disc, see the top of page 95.

Tip

Can I copy songs to a CD at different times?

You can copy songs to a CD only once using Windows Media Player. Since you must copy all the songs to a CD at the same time, make sure you carefully select all the songs you want to copy.

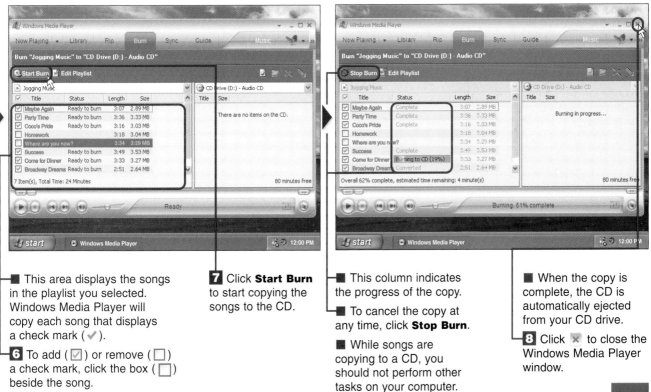

■ This area displays the songs in the playlist you selected. Windows Media Player will copy each song that displays a check mark (✓).

6 To add (☑) or remove (☐) a check mark, click the box (☐) beside the song.

7 Click **Start Burn** to start copying the songs to the CD.

■ This column indicates the progress of the copy.

■ To cancel the copy at any time, click **Stop Burn**.

■ While songs are copying to a CD, you should not perform other tasks on your computer.

■ When the copy is complete, the CD is automatically ejected from your CD drive.

8 Click ✕ to close the Windows Media Player window.

COPY SONGS TO A PORTABLE DEVICE

You can use Windows Media Player to copy songs on your computer to a portable device, such as an MP3 player.

You can copy songs that you have saved from a music CD or downloaded from the Internet to a portable device. Copying songs to a portable device is also known as "synchronizing" or "syncing" songs.

You need an updated version of Windows Media Player to perform the steps as shown below. To obtain an updated version of Windows Media Player, see the top of page 139.

COPY SONGS TO A PORTABLE DEVICE

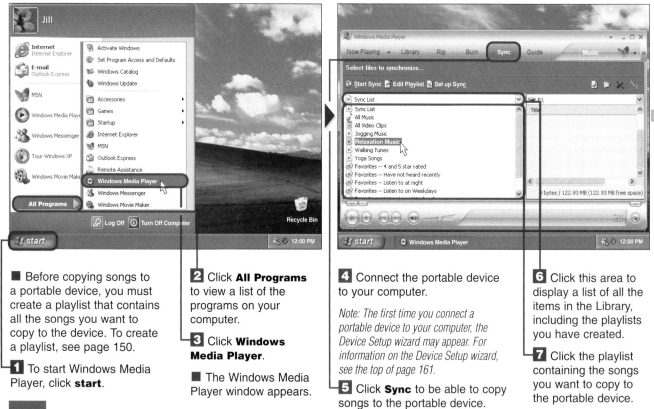

■ Before copying songs to a portable device, you must create a playlist that contains all the songs you want to copy to the device. To create a playlist, see page 150.

1 To start Windows Media Player, click **start**.

2 Click **All Programs** to view a list of the programs on your computer.

3 Click **Windows Media Player**.

■ The Windows Media Player window appears.

4 Connect the portable device to your computer.

Note: The first time you connect a portable device to your computer, the Device Setup wizard may appear. For information on the Device Setup wizard, see the top of page 161.

5 Click **Sync** to be able to copy songs to the portable device.

6 Click this area to display a list of all the items in the Library, including the playlists you have created.

7 Click the playlist containing the songs you want to copy to the portable device.

Tip

**Why does a Device Setup wizard
appear when I connect a portable
device to my computer?**

The first time you connect a
portable device to your computer,
the Device Setup wizard may
appear, allowing you to specify
how you want to copy, or
synchronize, songs to the device.

1 To select the songs
you want to copy to
the portable device
each time you connect
the device to your
computer, click **Manual**
(○ changes to ⊚).

2 Click **Finish** to
continue.

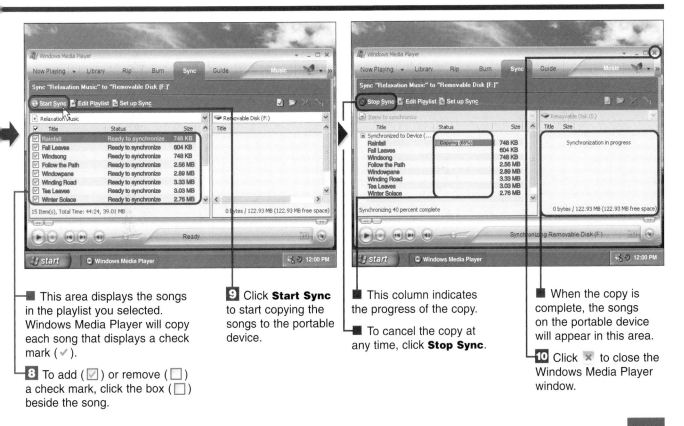

■ This area displays the songs
in the playlist you selected.
Windows Media Player will copy
each song that displays a check
mark (✓).

8 To add (☑) or remove (☐)
a check mark, click the box (☐)
beside the song.

9 Click **Start Sync**
to start copying the
songs to the portable
device.

■ This column indicates
the progress of the copy.

■ To cancel the copy at
any time, click **Stop Sync**.

■ When the copy is
complete, the songs
on the portable device
will appear in this area.

10 Click ✕ to close the
Windows Media Player
window.

PLAY A DVD MOVIE

You can use
Windows Media
Player to play
DVD movies on
your computer.

If you have a
notebook computer,
using your computer
to play DVD movies
can be especially
useful when traveling.

You need an updated
version of Windows
Media Player to
perform the steps
as shown below. To
obtain an updated
version of Windows
Media Player, see
the top of page 139.

PLAY A DVD MOVIE

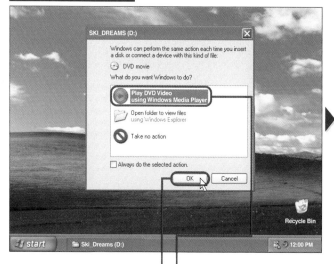

1 Insert a DVD movie
into your computer's
DVD drive.

■ A dialog box appears,
asking what you want
Windows to do.

2 Click **Play DVD Video**
to play the DVD movie
using Windows Media
Player.

3 Click **OK** to continue.

■ The Windows Media
Player window appears
and the movie begins to
play.

■ The DVD movie plays
in this area. After a few
moments, the DVD's main
menu usually appears,
displaying a list of options
you can select, such as
playing the movie or
playing a specific scene.
To select an option, click
the option.

■ To display the DVD's
main menu at any time,
click **Menu**.

Tip

Why can't I play a DVD movie?

Before you can play DVD movies, your computer must have a DVD drive and a DVD decoder installed. A DVD decoder is software that allows your computer to play DVD movies. Most new computers with a DVD drive come with a DVD decoder installed. If your computer has a DVD drive but does not have a DVD decoder installed, you can purchase a DVD decoder for Windows XP from companies such as InterVideo (www.intervideo.com) and CyberLink (www.gocyberlink.com).

Tip

How can I play a DVD movie using the entire screen?

To play a DVD movie using the entire screen, click 🖳 in the Windows Media Player window, directly above the area where the movie is playing. The 🖳 button is available only when the movie is playing. To once again display the movie in the Windows Media Player window, press the Esc key.

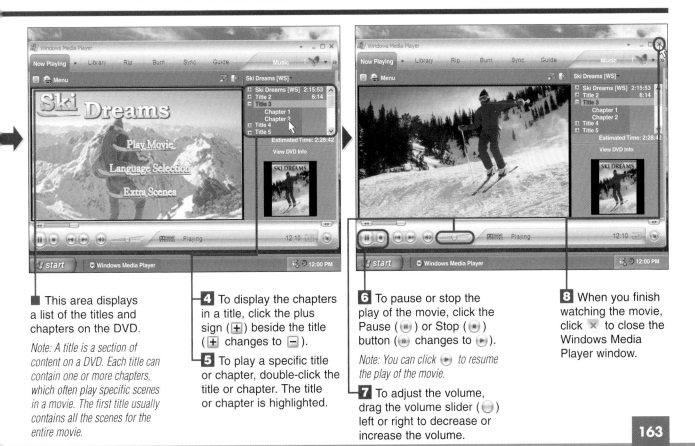

■ This area displays a list of the titles and chapters on the DVD.

Note: A title is a section of content on a DVD. Each title can contain one or more chapters, which often play specific scenes in a movie. The first title usually contains all the scenes for the entire movie.

4 To display the chapters in a title, click the plus sign (⊞) beside the title (⊞ changes to ⊟).

5 To play a specific title or chapter, double-click the title or chapter. The title or chapter is highlighted.

6 To pause or stop the play of the movie, click the Pause (⏸) or Stop (⏹) button (⏸ changes to ▶).

Note: You can click ▶ to resume the play of the movie.

7 To adjust the volume, drag the volume slider (⬤) left or right to decrease or increase the volume.

8 When you finish watching the movie, click ✖ to close the Windows Media Player window.

CHAPTER 7

Create Movies

Read this chapter to find out how to use the Windows Movie Maker program to transfer your home movies to your computer and then edit and play the movies on your computer.

TRANSFER VIDEO TO YOUR COMPUTER

You can use Windows Movie Maker to transfer home movies from your camcorder to your computer.

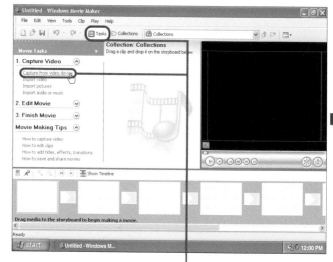

After you transfer video to your computer, you can edit the video on your computer to create your own movies.

For the best results when working with Windows Movie Maker, your screen resolution should be set at 1024x768 or higher. To change your screen resolution, see page 118.

TRANSFER VIDEO TO YOUR COMPUTER

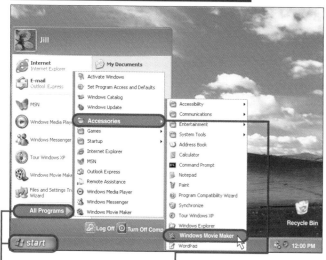

START WINDOWS MOVIE MAKER

1 Click **start** to display the Start menu.

2 Click **All Programs** to view a list of the programs on your computer.

3 Click **Accessories**.

4 Click **Windows Movie Maker**.

Note: Windows Movie Maker may appear in a different location on the Start menu.

■ The Windows Movie Maker window appears.

TRANSFER VIDEO

■ Make sure your camcorder is connected to your computer, turned on and set to the mode that plays back recorded video. Also make sure the video tape is at the point where you want to begin transferring the video.

1 Click **Capture from video device** to transfer video to your computer.

■ If the Capture from video device option is not displayed, click **Tasks** to display the Task pane.

Tip

Which setting should I choose when transferring video to my computer?

When transferring video to your computer, you can select two different ways to record video onto your computer.

Digital Device Format

Best quality for playback on my computer

This option is ideal if you want to play the final video on your computer, copy the video to a CD, send the video in an e-mail message or publish the video on the Web. This option is recommended by Windows Movie Maker.

Digital device format

This option is useful if you plan to record your final video back to the tape cartridge in your camcorder. This option produces high quality video, but very large file sizes.

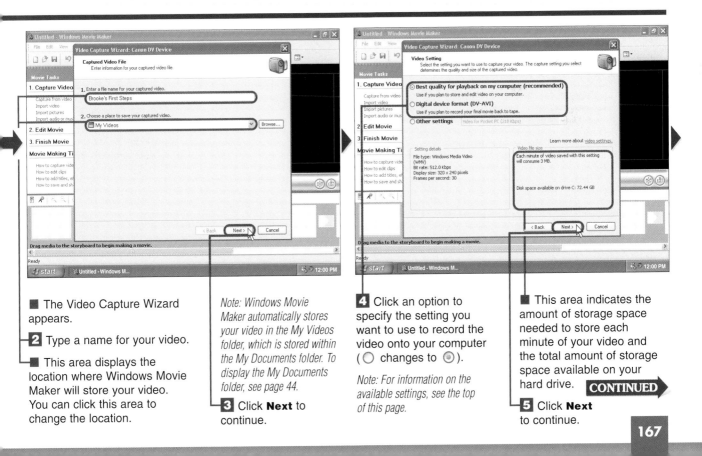

■ The Video Capture Wizard appears.

2 Type a name for your video.

■ This area displays the location where Windows Movie Maker will store your video. You can click this area to change the location.

Note: Windows Movie Maker automatically stores your video in the My Videos folder, which is stored within the My Documents folder. To display the My Documents folder, see page 44.

3 Click **Next** to continue.

4 Click an option to specify the setting you want to use to record the video onto your computer (○ changes to ◉).

Note: For information on the available settings, see the top of this page.

■ This area indicates the amount of storage space needed to store each minute of your video and the total amount of storage space available on your hard drive. **CONTINUED**

5 Click **Next** to continue.

TRANSFER VIDEO TO YOUR COMPUTER

When you transfer video to your computer, Windows Movie Maker automatically breaks up the video into smaller, more manageable segments, called clips.

A clip is created each time Windows Movie Maker detects a different sequence in a video, such as when you turn on your camcorder or when you switch from pause to once again begin recording.

TRANSFER VIDEO TO YOUR COMPUTER (CONTINUED)

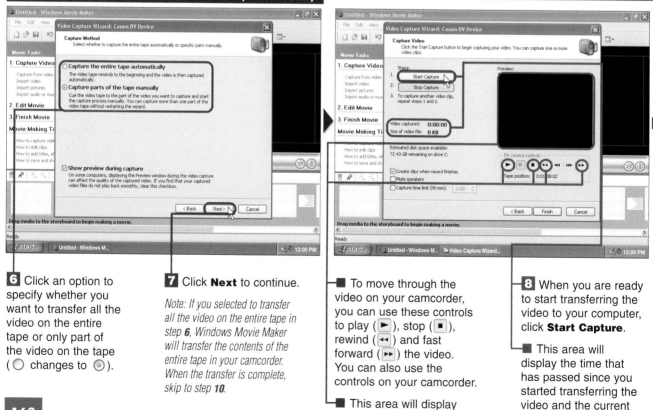

6 Click an option to specify whether you want to transfer all the video on the entire tape or only part of the video on the tape (○ changes to ◉).

7 Click **Next** to continue.

*Note: If you selected to transfer all the video on the entire tape in step **6**, Windows Movie Maker will transfer the contents of the entire tape in your camcorder. When the transfer is complete, skip to step **10**.*

■ To move through the video on your camcorder, you can use these controls to play (►), stop (■), rewind (◄◄) and fast forward (►►) the video. You can also use the controls on your camcorder.

■ This area will display the video.

8 When you are ready to start transferring the video to your computer, click **Start Capture**.

■ This area will display the time that has passed since you started transferring the video and the current size of the video file.

When transferring video to my computer, can I perform other tasks on my computer?

Transferring video from a camcorder to a computer requires a lot of computer processing power. To ensure the best quality of the transferred video, you should avoid performing any tasks on your computer, such as browsing the Web or editing a document, while the video transfers.

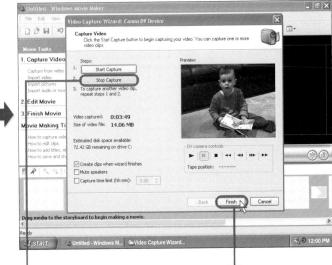

9 When you want to stop transferring the video, click **Stop Capture**.

■ If you want to transfer another part of the video on your camcorder, use the controls in the wizard or the controls on your camcorder to move to the point in the video where you want to start the next transfer. Then repeat steps **8** and **9**.

10 Click **Finish** to close the Video Capture Wizard.

■ When Windows Movie Maker has finished creating the clips for your video, this area displays the name of the collection that stores the video clips. The name of the collection is the name you specified in step **2** on page 167.

■ This area displays the video clips within the collection. To help you identify the video clips, Windows Movie Maker displays the first frame of each clip.

ADD A VIDEO CLIP TO YOUR PROJECT

You must add each video clip that you want to include in your movie to the storyboard.

The storyboard displays the order in which video clips will play in your movie.

You can play a video clip before adding it to your movie to determine if you want to include the video clip in your movie.

ADD A VIDEO CLIP TO YOUR PROJECT

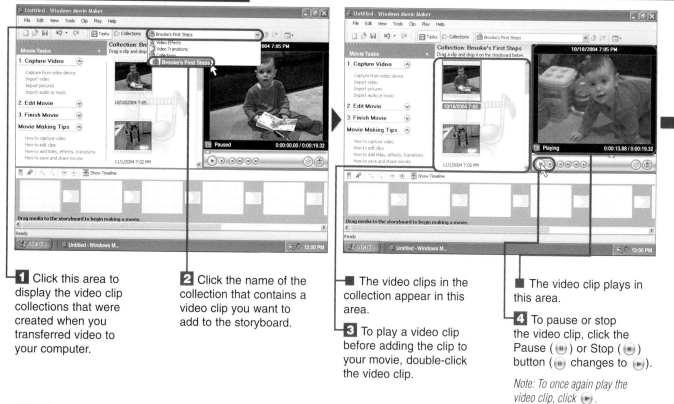

1 Click this area to display the video clip collections that were created when you transferred video to your computer.

2 Click the name of the collection that contains a video clip you want to add to the storyboard.

■ The video clips in the collection appear in this area.

3 To play a video clip before adding the clip to your movie, double-click the video clip.

■ The video clip plays in this area.

4 To pause or stop the video clip, click the Pause (⏸) or Stop (⏹) button (⏸ changes to ▶).

Note: To once again play the video clip, click ▶.

Tip

Can I change the order of the video clips on the storyboard?

Yes. Changing the order of the video clips on the storyboard allows you to change the order in which the clips will play in your movie. To change the location of a video clip in your movie, position the mouse ⥮ over the video clip on the storyboard and then drag the video clip to a new location on the storyboard. A vertical bar will indicate where the video clip will appear. When you move a video clip, the surrounding video clips will move to make room for the video clip.

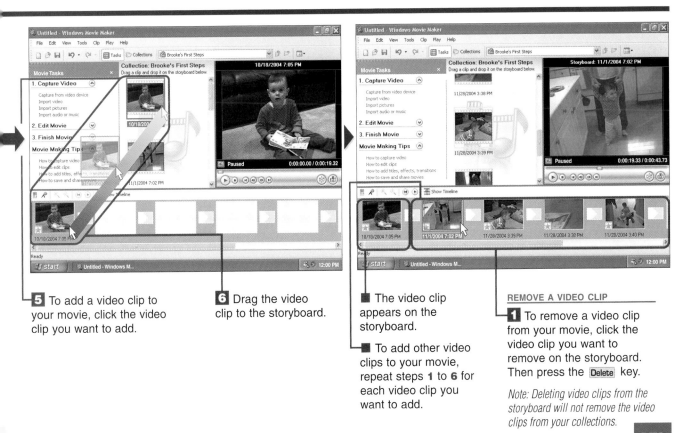

5 To add a video clip to your movie, click the video clip you want to add.

6 Drag the video clip to the storyboard.

■ The video clip appears on the storyboard.

■ To add other video clips to your movie, repeat steps **1** to **6** for each video clip you want to add.

REMOVE A VIDEO CLIP

1 To remove a video clip from your movie, click the video clip you want to remove on the storyboard. Then press the Delete key.

Note: Deleting video clips from the storyboard will not remove the video clips from your collections.

SAVE A PROJECT

You can save a project so you can later review and make changes to the project.

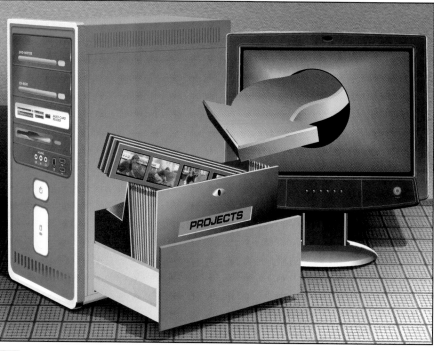

A project is a rough draft of your movie that contains all the video clips you added to the storyboard. You should regularly save changes you make to a project to avoid losing your work.

SAVE A PROJECT

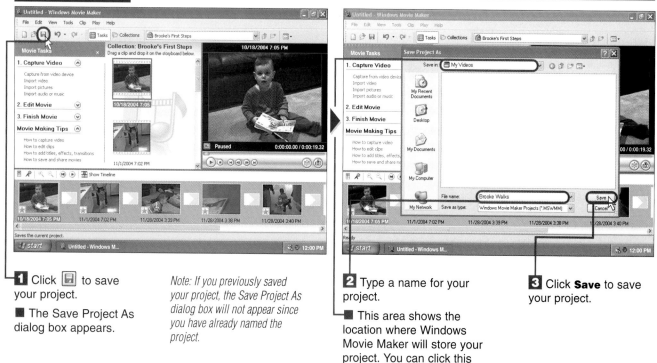

1 Click 🖫 to save your project.

■ The Save Project As dialog box appears.

Note: If you previously saved your project, the Save Project As dialog box will not appear since you have already named the project.

2 Type a name for your project.

■ This area shows the location where Windows Movie Maker will store your project. You can click this area to change the location.

3 Click **Save** to save your project.

OPEN A PROJECT

You can open a saved project to display the video clips in the project. Opening a project allows you to review and make changes to the project.

A project is a rough draft of your movie that contains all the video clips you added to the storyboard.

You can work with only one project at a time. If you are currently working with a project, make sure you save the project before opening another project. To save a project, see page 172.

OPEN A PROJECT

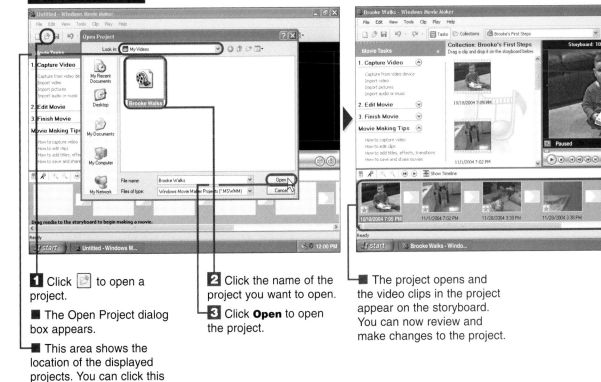

1 Click 📂 to open a project.

■ The Open Project dialog box appears.

■ This area shows the location of the displayed projects. You can click this area to change the location.

2 Click the name of the project you want to open.

3 Click **Open** to open the project.

■ The project opens and the video clips in the project appear on the storyboard. You can now review and make changes to the project.

TRIM A VIDEO CLIP

You can trim a video clip to remove parts of the clip you do not want to play in your movie.

You can trim the beginning of a video clip, the end of a video clip, or both. Trimming a video clip in your movie will not affect the original video clip stored in Windows Movie Maker.

TRIM A VIDEO CLIP

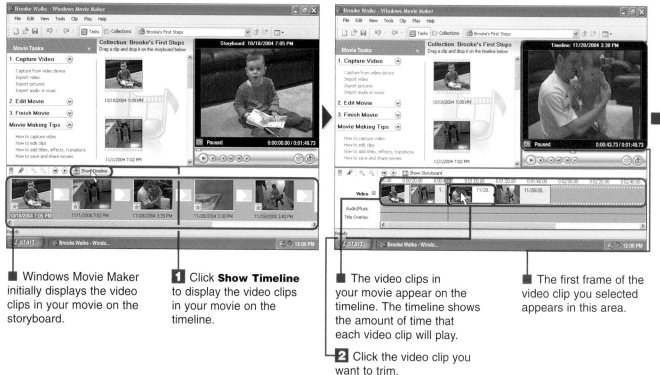

■ Windows Movie Maker initially displays the video clips in your movie on the storyboard.

1 Click **Show Timeline** to display the video clips in your movie on the timeline.

■ The video clips in your movie appear on the timeline. The timeline shows the amount of time that each video clip will play.

2 Click the video clip you want to trim.

■ The first frame of the video clip you selected appears in this area.

Tip

Will trimming a video clip reduce the file size of my movie?

Yes. Trimming video clips will reduce the file size and length of a movie. A movie with a smaller file size will take up less storage space on your computer and transfer more quickly over the Internet. Creating movies with smaller file sizes is especially useful if you plan to send your movies in e-mail messages. Most companies that provide e-mail accounts usually limit the size of the files that you can send in e-mail messages.

Tip

After I trim a video clip, can I undo the change I made?

Yes. If you trimmed too much or too little of a video clip or decide that you no longer want to trim a video clip in your movie, you can undo the change you made. To return a video clip to its original length, click the video clip on the timeline and then perform steps **5** and **6** below, selecting **Clear Trim Points** in step **6**.

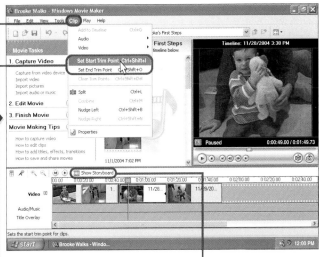

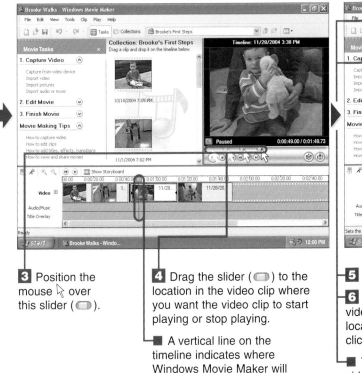

3 Position the mouse ⟍ over this slider (⬭).

4 Drag the slider (⬭) to the location in the video clip where you want the video clip to start playing or stop playing.

■ A vertical line on the timeline indicates where Windows Movie Maker will trim the video clip.

5 Click **Clip**.

6 To remove the part of the video clip before the current location of the slider (⬭), click **Set Start Trim Point**.

■ To remove the part of the video clip after the current location of the slider (⬭), click **Set End Trim Point**.

7 To once again display the video clips on the storyboard, click **Show Storyboard**.

Note: To preview how the trimmed video clip will appear in your movie, see page 178 to preview a movie.

ADD A VIDEO TRANSITION

You can create a smooth video transition from one video clip to another in your movie. The first video clip will fade out as the following video clip fades in.

ADD A VIDEO TRANSITION

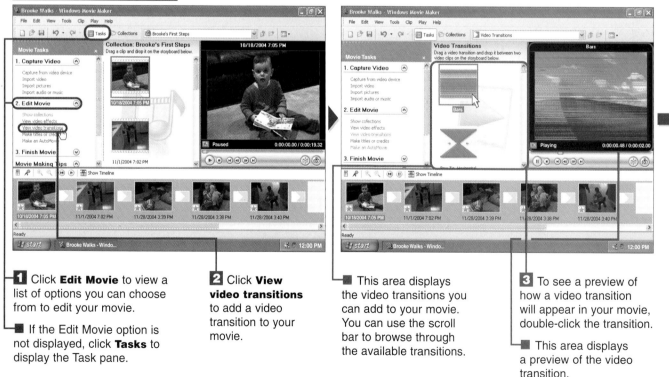

1 Click **Edit Movie** to view a list of options you can choose from to edit your movie.

■ If the Edit Movie option is not displayed, click **Tasks** to display the Task pane.

2 Click **View video transitions** to add a video transition to your movie.

■ This area displays the video transitions you can add to your movie. You can use the scroll bar to browse through the available transitions.

3 To see a preview of how a video transition will appear in your movie, double-click the transition.

■ This area displays a preview of the video transition.

Tip

How do I remove a video transition from my movie?

To remove a video transition, click the picture representing the transition between the video clips on the storyboard. Then press the `Delete` key.

Tip

What should I consider when adding video transitions to a movie?

Although Windows Movie Maker offers many different types of video transitions, using too many different transitions in a movie can distract the audience from your movie. If you are trying to create a professional-looking movie, use similar video transitions throughout your movie and add video transitions sparingly.

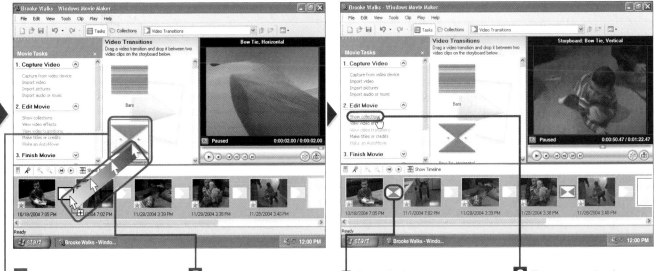

4 To add a video transition to your movie, position the mouse ⌖ over the transition you want to add.

5 Drag the video transition between the video clips on the storyboard where you want to add the transition.

■ A small picture representing the video transition appears between the video clips.

■ To add additional video transitions to your movie, repeat steps **3** to **5** for each transition you want to add.

6 To once again view your video clips instead of the list of available video transitions, click **Show collections**.

Note: To see how your movie plays with the video transitions you have added, see page 178.

PREVIEW AND SAVE A MOVIE

You can preview and save your movie.

Preview a Movie

You can preview a movie by playing all the video clips you have added to the storyboard. Before you save a completed movie, you should preview the movie to make sure you are happy with the movie. You can also preview a movie at any time while you create a movie.

Save a Movie

When your movie is complete, you can save the movie on your computer. Saving a movie allows you to share the movie with family and friends.

PREVIEW A MOVIE

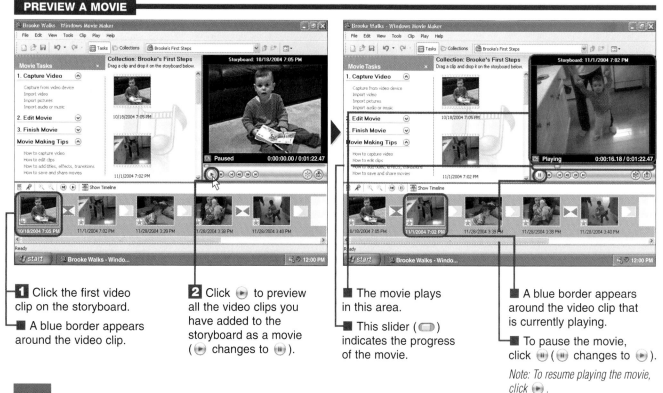

1 Click the first video clip on the storyboard.

■ A blue border appears around the video clip.

2 Click ▶ to preview all the video clips you have added to the storyboard as a movie (▶ changes to ⏸).

■ The movie plays in this area.

■ This slider (▭) indicates the progress of the movie.

■ A blue border appears around the video clip that is currently playing.

■ To pause the movie, click ⏸ (⏸ changes to ▶).

Note: To resume playing the movie, click ▶.

Tip

After I save a movie, how can I share the movie with other people?

Send a Movie in an E-mail Message

You can send a movie in an e-mail message. You should try to keep your movies under 10 megabytes (MB), since most companies that provide e-mail accounts limit the size of the files that you can send and receive over the Internet. To send a movie in an e-mail message, see page 278.

Copy a Movie to a CD

If you have a recordable CD drive, you can copy a movie from your computer to a CD. You can then share the CD with other people. To copy a movie to a CD, see page 92.

SAVE A MOVIE

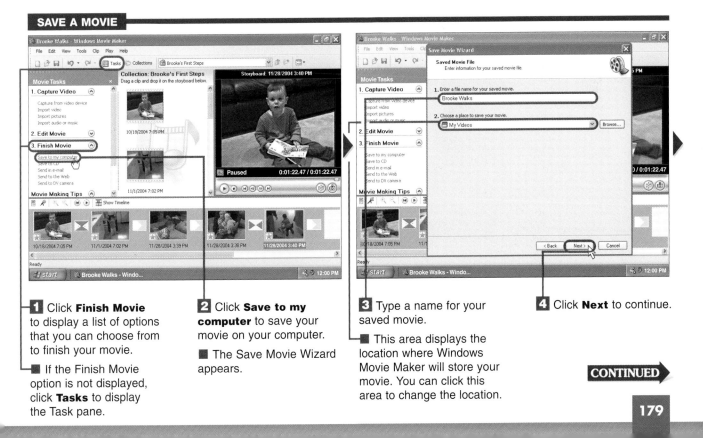

1 Click **Finish Movie** to display a list of options that you can choose from to finish your movie.

■ If the Finish Movie option is not displayed, click **Tasks** to display the Task pane.

2 Click **Save to my computer** to save your movie on your computer.

■ The Save Movie Wizard appears.

3 Type a name for your saved movie.

■ This area displays the location where Windows Movie Maker will store your movie. You can click this area to change the location.

4 Click **Next** to continue.

CONTINUED

PREVIEW AND SAVE A MOVIE

After you save a movie on your computer, the wizard will automatically play the movie in Windows Media Player.

SAVE A MOVIE (CONTINUED)

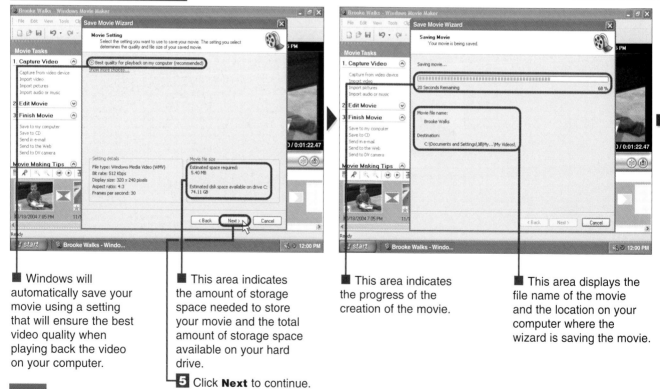

■ Windows will automatically save your movie using a setting that will ensure the best video quality when playing back the video on your computer.

■ This area indicates the amount of storage space needed to store your movie and the total amount of storage space available on your hard drive.

5 Click **Next** to continue.

■ This area indicates the progress of the creation of the movie.

■ This area displays the file name of the movie and the location on your computer where the wizard is saving the movie.

Tip

How can I later play a movie I have saved?

Windows Movie Maker automatically stores your movies in the My Videos folder, which is located within the My Documents folder. You can double-click a movie in the My Videos folder to play the movie. To view the contents of the My Documents folder, see page 44.

Tip

Can I make changes to a movie I have saved?

No. You cannot make changes to a movie you have saved. Windows Movie Maker only allows you to make changes to a project, which is a rough draft of a movie. To open a project so you can make changes to the project, see page 173.

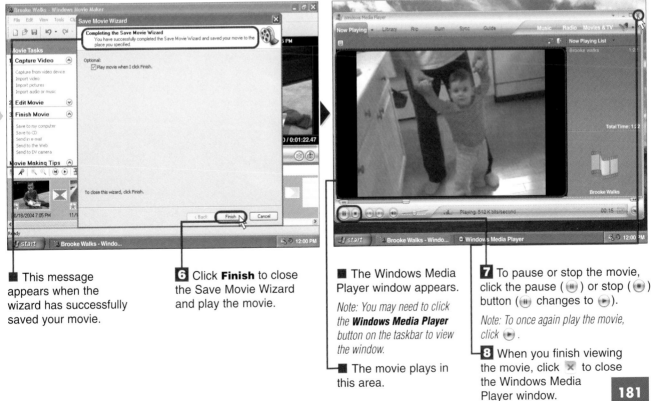

■ This message appears when the wizard has successfully saved your movie.

6 Click **Finish** to close the Save Movie Wizard and play the movie.

■ The Windows Media Player window appears.

*Note: You may need to click the **Windows Media Player** button on the taskbar to view the window.*

■ The movie plays in this area.

7 To pause or stop the movie, click the pause (ⅱ) or stop (▪) button (ⅱ changes to ▶).

Note: To once again play the movie, click ▶ .

8 When you finish viewing the movie, click ✕ to close the Windows Media Player window.

CHAPTER 8

Share Your Computer

If you share your computer with other family members or colleagues, you can create user accounts so each person can use their own personalized files and settings. Read this chapter to learn how to create and work with user accounts on your computer.

CREATE A USER ACCOUNT

If you share your computer with other people, you can create a personalized user account for each person.

You must have a computer administrator account to create a user account. For information on the types of accounts, see page 186.

CREATE A USER ACCOUNT

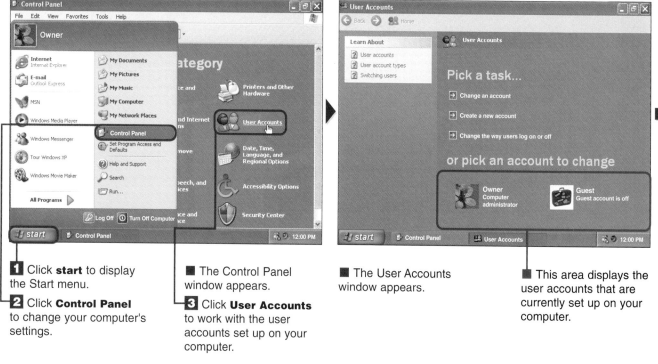

1 Click **start** to display the Start menu.

2 Click **Control Panel** to change your computer's settings.

■ The Control Panel window appears.

3 Click **User Accounts** to work with the user accounts set up on your computer.

■ The User Accounts window appears.

■ This area displays the user accounts that are currently set up on your computer.

Tip
Will Windows keep my personal files separate from the files of other users?

Yes. Windows will keep your personal files separate from the personal files created by other users. For example, your My Documents folder displays only the files you have created. Internet Explorer also keeps your lists of recently visited Web pages and favorite Web pages separate from the lists of other users.

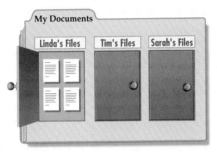

Tip
How can I personalize Windows for my user account?

You can personalize the appearance of Windows for your user account by changing the screen saver, desktop background and many other computer settings.

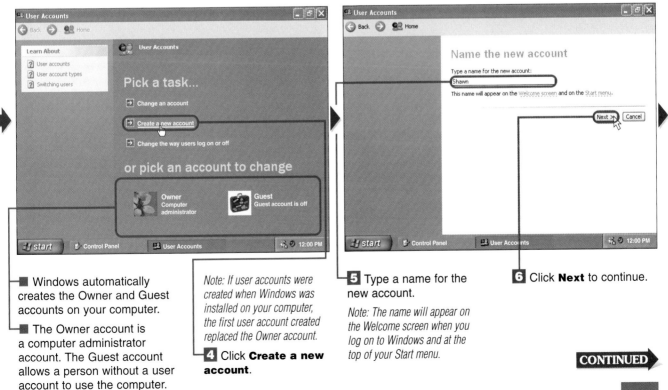

■ Windows automatically creates the Owner and Guest accounts on your computer.

■ The Owner account is a computer administrator account. The Guest account allows a person without a user account to use the computer.

Note: If user accounts were created when Windows was installed on your computer, the first user account created replaced the Owner account.

4 Click **Create a new account**.

5 Type a name for the new account.

Note: The name will appear on the Welcome screen when you log on to Windows and at the top of your Start menu.

6 Click **Next** to continue.

CONTINUED

CREATE A USER ACCOUNT

When you create a user account, you must select the type of account you want to create.

Computer Administrator
The user can perform any task on the computer. For example, the user can create and change all user accounts as well as install programs and hardware.

Limited
The user can perform only certain tasks on the computer. For example, the user can create and change their own password and change some computer settings but cannot delete important files.

CREATE A USER ACCOUNT (CONTINUED)

7 Click the type of account you want to create (◯ changes to ◉).

■ This area displays a description of the account type you selected.

8 Click **Create Account**.

■ This area displays the account you created.

9 Click ☒ to close the User Accounts window.

186

DELETE A USER ACCOUNT

If a person no longer uses your computer, you can delete the person's user account from your computer.

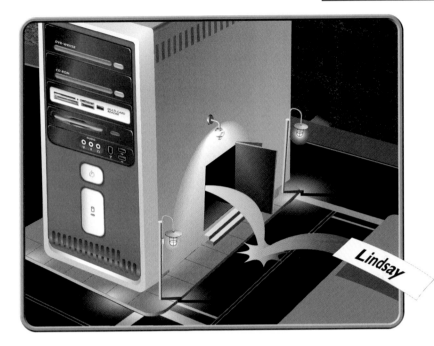

You must have a computer administrator account to delete a user account. For information on the types of accounts, see page 186.

DELETE A USER ACCOUNT

1 Click **start** to display the Start menu.

2 Click **Control Panel** to change your computer's settings.

■ The Control Panel window appears.

3 Click **User Accounts** to work with the user accounts set up on your computer.

CONTINUED

DELETE A USER ACCOUNT

When you delete a user account, you can choose to keep or delete the user's personal files.

If you choose to delete a user's personal files, Windows will permanently delete the files from your computer.

DELETE A USER ACCOUNT (CONTINUED)

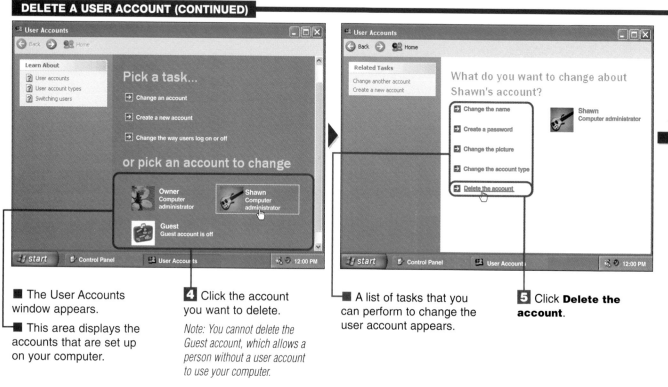

■ The User Accounts window appears.

■ This area displays the accounts that are set up on your computer.

4 Click the account you want to delete.

Note: You cannot delete the Guest account, which allows a person without a user account to use your computer.

■ A list of tasks that you can perform to change the user account appears.

5 Click **Delete the account**.

Tip

If I choose to keep the personal files for a deleted user account, which files will Windows save?

Windows will save the user's personal files that are displayed on the desktop and stored in the My Documents folder. The files will be saved on your desktop in a new folder that has the same name as the deleted account. Windows will not save the user's e-mail messages, list of favorite Web pages and other computer settings.

Tip

Can I delete a computer administrator account?

Yes. If you have a computer administrator account, you can delete other computer administrator accounts. Windows will not allow you to delete the last computer administrator account on your computer. This ensures that one computer administrator account always exists on the computer.

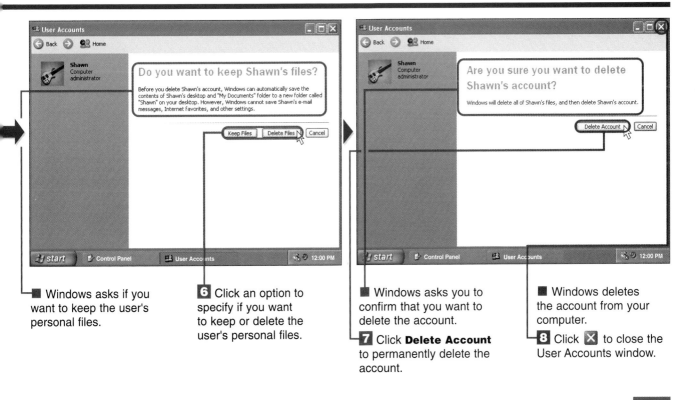

■ Windows asks if you want to keep the user's personal files.

6 Click an option to specify if you want to keep or delete the user's personal files.

■ Windows asks you to confirm that you want to delete the account.

7 Click **Delete Account** to permanently delete the account.

■ Windows deletes the account from your computer.

8 Click **X** to close the User Accounts window.

You can assign a password to your user account to prevent other people from accessing the account. You will need to enter the password each time you want to use Windows.

You should choose a password that is at least eight characters long and contains a random combination of letters, numbers and symbols. Do not use words that people can easily associate with you, such as your name.

If you have a computer administrator account, you can assign passwords to all accounts. If you have a limited account, you can assign a password only to your own account. For information on the types of accounts, see page 186.

ASSIGN A PASSWORD TO A USER ACCOUNT

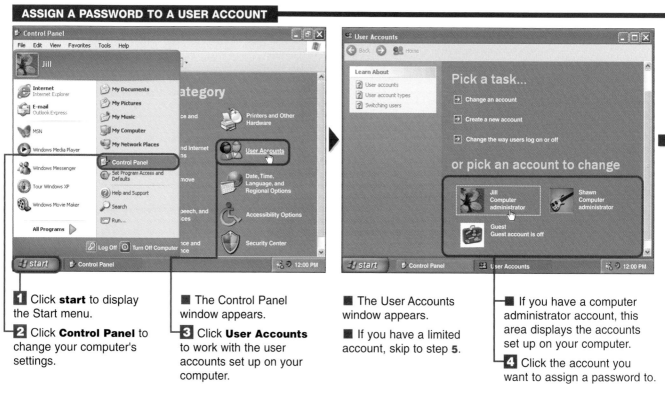

1 Click **start** to display the Start menu.

2 Click **Control Panel** to change your computer's settings.

■ The Control Panel window appears.

3 Click **User Accounts** to work with the user accounts set up on your computer.

■ The User Accounts window appears.

■ If you have a limited account, skip to step **5**.

■ If you have a computer administrator account, this area displays the accounts set up on your computer.

4 Click the account you want to assign a password to.

Tip

When assigning a password to my user account, why does Windows ask if I want to make my files and folders private?

When you assign a password to your user account, other users can still access your files and folders. If you do not want other people to have access to your files and folders, you can make your files and folders private. Click **Yes, Make Private** or **No** to specify if you want to make your files and folders private. For more information on making your files and folders private, see page 196.

Tip

How can I change the password I assigned to my user account?

To change your password, perform steps **1** to **5** below, except click **Change my password** in step **5**. Then type your current password and perform steps **6** to **9** below, except click **Change Password** in step **9**.

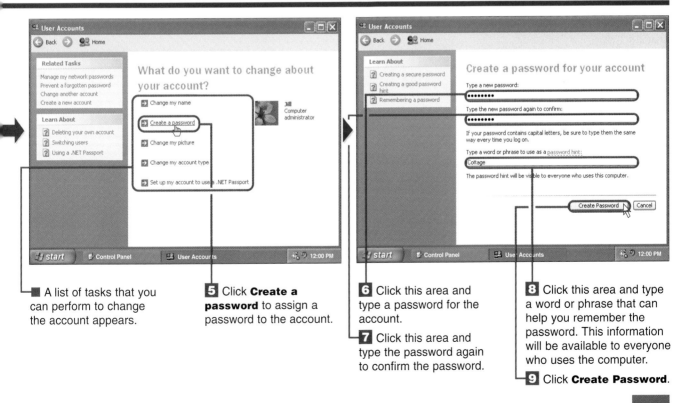

■ A list of tasks that you can perform to change the account appears.

5 Click **Create a password** to assign a password to the account.

6 Click this area and type a password for the account.

7 Click this area and type the password again to confirm the password.

8 Click this area and type a word or phrase that can help you remember the password. This information will be available to everyone who uses the computer.

9 Click **Create Password**.

LOG OFF WINDOWS

You can log off Windows so another person can log on to Windows to use the computer.

When you log off Windows, you can choose to keep your programs and files open while another person uses the computer. This allows you to quickly return to your programs and files after the other person finishes using the computer.

LOG OFF WINDOWS

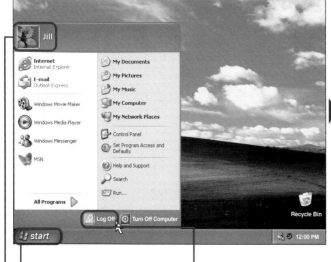

1 Click **start** to display the Start menu.

■ This area displays the name of the current user account.

2 Click **Log Off** to log off Windows.

■ The Log Off Windows dialog box appears.

3 Click one of the following options.

Switch User
Log off Windows, keeping your programs and files open.

Log Off
Log off Windows, closing your open programs and files.

■ The Welcome screen appears, allowing another person to log on to Windows to use the computer. To log on to Windows, see page 193.

If you have set up user accounts on your computer, you will need to log on to Windows to use the computer.

You must log on to Windows each time you turn on your computer or log off Windows to switch between user accounts. For information on logging off Windows, see page 192.

LOG ON TO WINDOWS

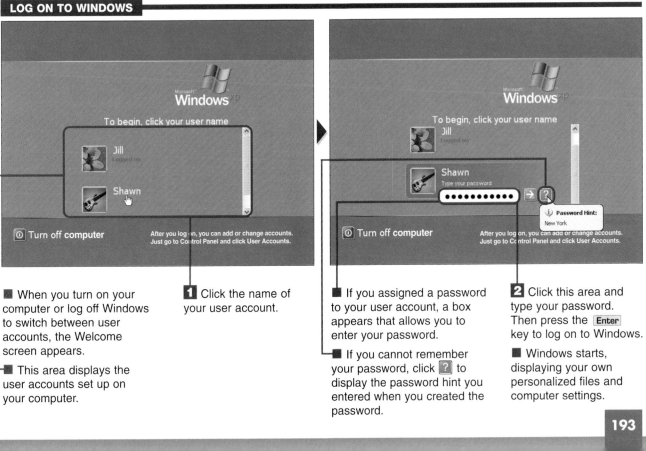

■ When you turn on your computer or log off Windows to switch between user accounts, the Welcome screen appears.

■ This area displays the user accounts set up on your computer.

1 Click the name of your user account.

■ If you assigned a password to your user account, a box appears that allows you to enter your password.

■ If you cannot remember your password, click ? to display the password hint you entered when you created the password.

2 Click this area and type your password. Then press the Enter key to log on to Windows.

■ Windows starts, displaying your own personalized files and computer settings.

VIEW SHARED FILES

You can view the personal files of every user set up on your computer.

In most cases, the contents of every user's My Documents folder and its subfolders are available to every user set up on your computer.

If your computer uses the NTFS file system, you cannot view the personal files of other users if you have a limited user account or a user has made their personal folders private. For information on making personal folders private, see page 196.

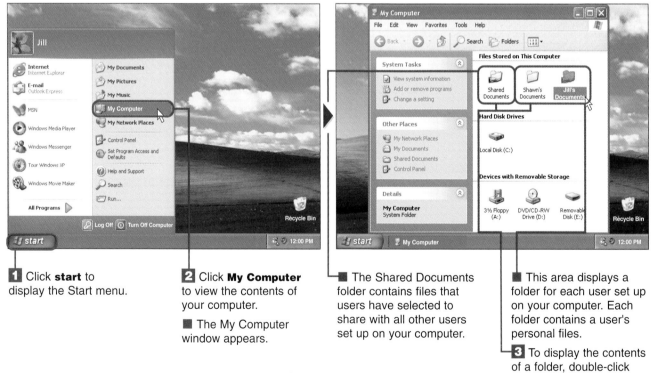

1 Click **start** to display the Start menu.

2 Click **My Computer** to view the contents of your computer.

■ The My Computer window appears.

■ The Shared Documents folder contains files that users have selected to share with all other users set up on your computer.

■ This area displays a folder for each user set up on your computer. Each folder contains a user's personal files.

3 To display the contents of a folder, double-click the folder.

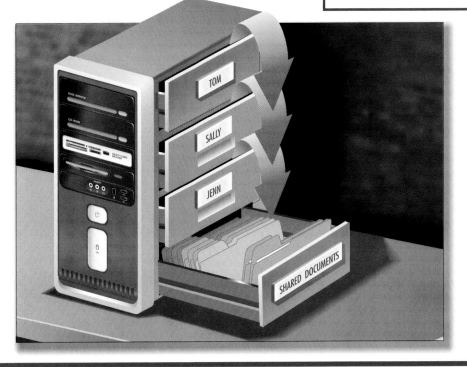

If you want to share files with every user set up on your computer, you can copy the files to the Shared Documents folder.

Copying files to the Shared Documents folder is useful when you want to share files that are not stored in the My Documents folder or if your computer uses the NTFS file system and other users are restricted from viewing the contents of your My Documents folder.

SHARE FILES

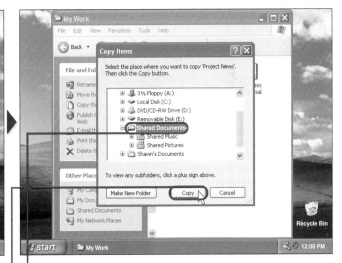

1 Click the file you want to share with every user set up on your computer.

■ To share more than one file, select all the files you want to share. To select multiple files, see page 56.

2 Click **Copy this file**.

*Note: If you selected multiple files, click **Copy the selected items** in step 2.*

■ The Copy Items dialog box appears.

3 Click **Shared Documents**.

4 Click **Copy** to copy the file.

■ Windows places a copy of the file in the Shared Documents folder. The file is now available to every user set up on your computer.

Note: If you no longer want to share a file, delete the file from the Shared Documents folder. To view the contents of the Shared Documents folder, see page 194. To delete a file, see page 62.

MAKE YOUR PERSONAL FOLDERS PRIVATE

You can make the contents of your personal folders private so that only you can access the files within the folders. Your personal folders include the My Documents folder and its subfolders.

You can make your personal folders private only if your computer uses the NTFS file system. The file system is typically determined when you install Windows.

If your computer uses the NTFS file system, the contents of your personal folders are available to every user with an administrator account set up on your computer.

MAKE YOUR PERSONAL FOLDERS PRIVATE

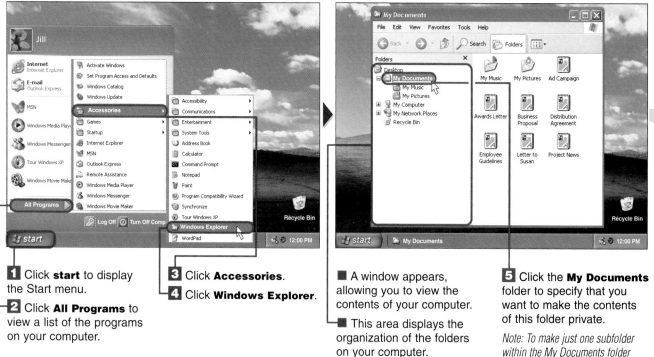

1 Click **start** to display the Start menu.

2 Click **All Programs** to view a list of the programs on your computer.

3 Click **Accessories**.

4 Click **Windows Explorer**.

■ A window appears, allowing you to view the contents of your computer.

■ This area displays the organization of the folders on your computer.

5 Click the **My Documents** folder to specify that you want to make the contents of this folder private.

Note: To make just one subfolder within the My Documents folder private, click the subfolder you want to make private.

Tip

What do I need to consider before making my personal folders private?

Before making your personal folders private, you should assign a password to your user account. If you do not assign a password to your user account, anyone will be able to log on to your account and view the contents of your personal folders even if you make the folders private. To assign a password to your user account, see page 190.

Tip

After making my personal folders private, can I share just one file in the folders?

Yes. To share a specific file with every user set up on your computer, you need to place a copy of the file in the Shared Documents folder. The Shared Documents folder contains files that every user set up on your computer can access. For information on the Shared Documents folder, see page 195.

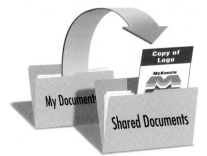

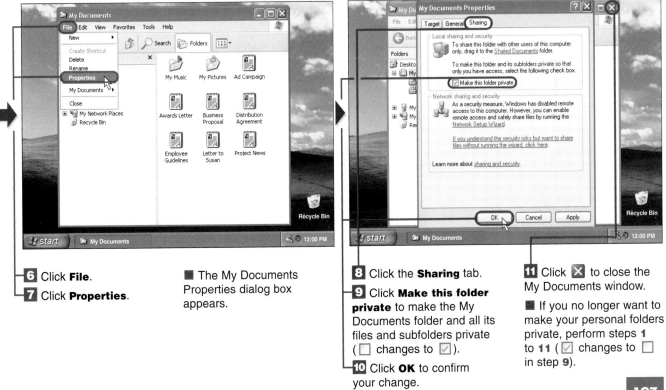

-6 Click **File**.

-7 Click **Properties**.

■ The My Documents Properties dialog box appears.

8 Click the **Sharing** tab.

9 Click **Make this folder private** to make the My Documents folder and all its files and subfolders private (☐ changes to ☑).

10 Click **OK** to confirm your change.

11 Click ☒ to close the My Documents window.

■ If you no longer want to make your personal folders private, perform steps **1** to **11** (☑ changes to ☐ in step **9**).

CHAPTER 9

Optimize Computer Performance

In this chapter, you will discover ways to enhance the performance of your computer. You will learn how to check your computer's security settings, remove unnecessary programs and files to save space on your computer and restore your computer to an earlier time before you encountered any problems.

VIEW AMOUNT OF DISK SPACE

You can view the amount of used and free space on a disk.

You should check the amount of free space on your computer's hard disk (C:) at least once a month. Your computer will operate most effectively when at least 20% of your total hard disk space is free.

You may also want to check the amount of free space on your computer's hard disk before installing a program that requires a lot of disk space.

VIEW AMOUNT OF DISK SPACE

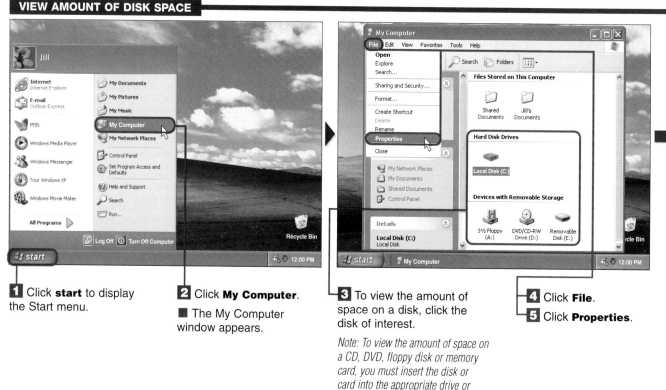

1 Click **start** to display the Start menu.

2 Click **My Computer**.

■ The My Computer window appears.

3 To view the amount of space on a disk, click the disk of interest.

Note: To view the amount of space on a CD, DVD, floppy disk or memory card, you must insert the disk or card into the appropriate drive or slot before performing step 3.

4 Click **File**.

5 Click **Properties**.

Tip

How can I increase the amount of free space on my hard disk?

Delete Files

Delete files you no longer need from your computer. To delete files, see page 62.

Use Disk Cleanup

Use Disk Cleanup to remove unnecessary files from your computer. To use Disk Cleanup, see page 204.

Remove Programs

Remove programs you no longer use from your computer. To remove programs, see page 202.

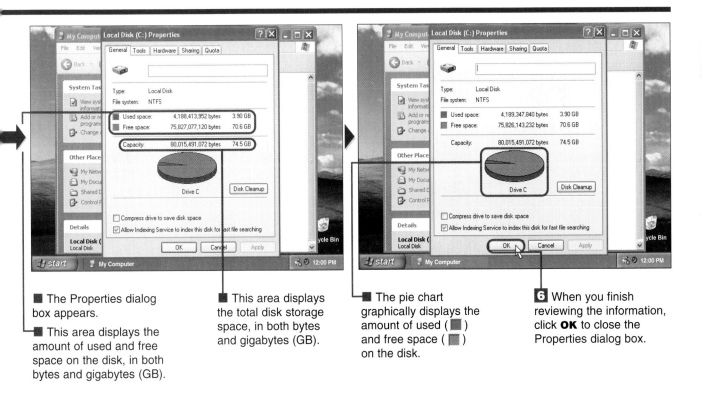

■ The Properties dialog box appears.

■ This area displays the amount of used and free space on the disk, in both bytes and gigabytes (GB).

■ This area displays the total disk storage space, in both bytes and gigabytes (GB).

■ The pie chart graphically displays the amount of used (■) and free space (■) on the disk.

6 When you finish reviewing the information, click **OK** to close the Properties dialog box.

REMOVE A PROGRAM

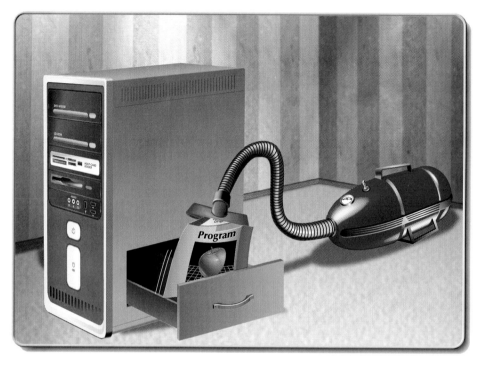

You can remove a program you no longer use from your computer. Removing a program will free up space on your computer.

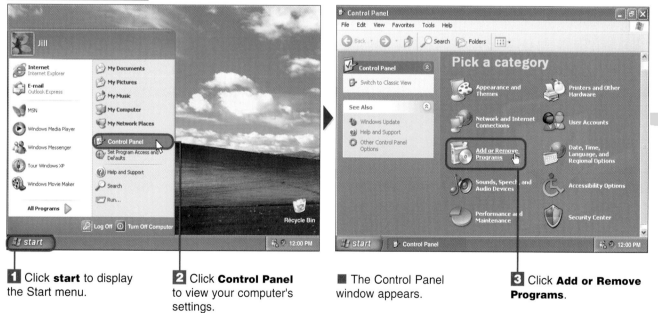

1 Click **start** to display the Start menu.

2 Click **Control Panel** to view your computer's settings.

■ The Control Panel window appears.

3 Click **Add or Remove Programs**.

Tip

Why doesn't the program I want to remove appear in the Add or Remove Programs window?

You can only use the Add or Remove Programs window to remove programs designed for Windows. For all other programs, you can check the documentation supplied with the program to determine how to remove the program from your computer.

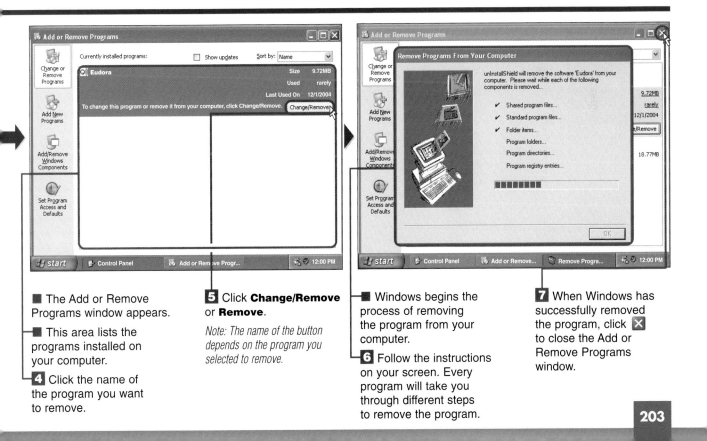

■ The Add or Remove Programs window appears.

■ This area lists the programs installed on your computer.

4 Click the name of the program you want to remove.

5 Click **Change/Remove** or **Remove**.

Note: The name of the button depends on the program you selected to remove.

■ Windows begins the process of removing the program from your computer.

6 Follow the instructions on your screen. Every program will take you through different steps to remove the program.

7 When Windows has successfully removed the program, click ⊠ to close the Add or Remove Programs window.

203

USING DISK CLEANUP

You can use Disk Cleanup to remove unnecessary files from your computer to free up disk space.

USING DISK CLEANUP

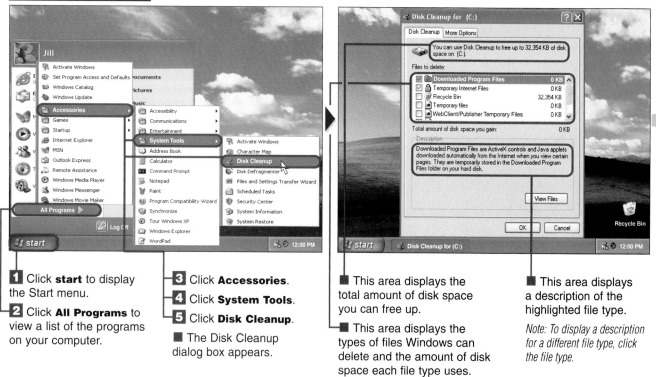

1 Click **start** to display the Start menu.

2 Click **All Programs** to view a list of the programs on your computer.

3 Click **Accessories**.

4 Click **System Tools**.

5 Click **Disk Cleanup**.

■ The Disk Cleanup dialog box appears.

■ This area displays the total amount of disk space you can free up.

■ This area displays the types of files Windows can delete and the amount of disk space each file type uses.

■ This area displays a description of the highlighted file type.

Note: To display a description for a different file type, click the file type.

Tip

What are some types of files that Disk Cleanup can remove?

	File Type	Description
	Downloaded Program Files	Program files transferred automatically from the Internet and stored on your computer when you view certain Web pages.
	Temporary Internet Files	Web pages stored on your computer for quick viewing.
	Recycle Bin	Stores files you have deleted from your computer.
	Temporary files	Files created by programs to store temporary information.
	WebClient/Publisher Temporary Files	Copies of files you have accessed on your computer.
	Compress old files	Compresses, or squeezes, files you have not opened in a while.
	Catalog files for the Content Indexer	Files previously used to speed up and improve file searches.

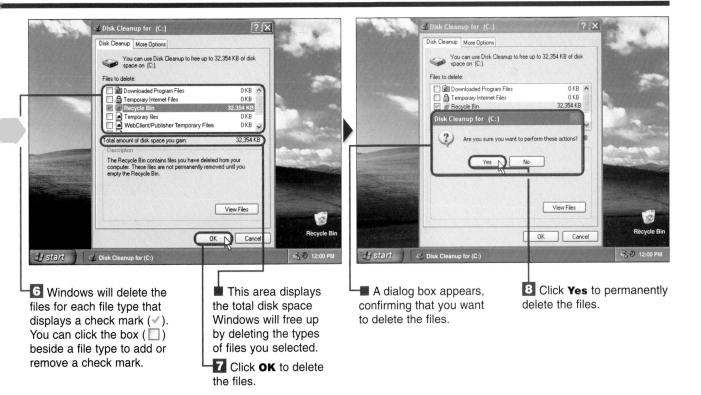

6 Windows will delete the files for each file type that displays a check mark (✔). You can click the box (☐) beside a file type to add or remove a check mark.

■ This area displays the total disk space Windows will free up by deleting the types of files you selected.

7 Click **OK** to delete the files.

■ A dialog box appears, confirming that you want to delete the files.

8 Click **Yes** to permanently delete the files.

INSTALL A PRINTER

Before you can use a printer that attaches directly to your computer, you need to install the printer on your computer. You need to install a printer only once.

Windows provides a wizard that guides you step by step through the process of installing a printer.

Before installing a printer, make sure you connect the printer to your computer and turn on the printer.

INSTALL A PRINTER

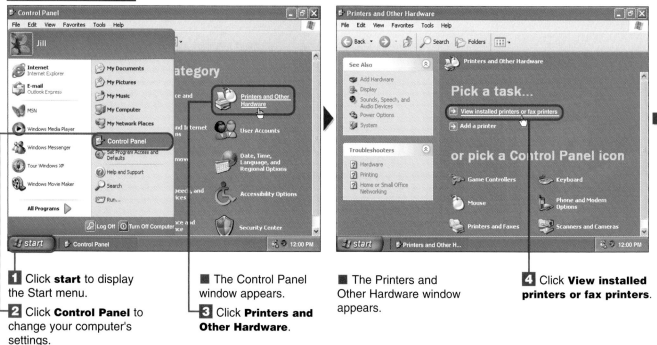

1 Click **start** to display the Start menu.

2 Click **Control Panel** to change your computer's settings.

■ The Control Panel window appears.

3 Click **Printers and Other Hardware**.

■ The Printers and Other Hardware window appears.

4 Click **View installed printers or fax printers**.

Tip

Why do I need to install a printer?

Installing a printer allows you to install the printer driver that Windows needs to work with the printer. A printer driver is special software that enables Windows to communicate with a printer.

Tip

How do I install a Plug and Play printer?

A Plug and Play printer is a printer that Windows can automatically detect and install. Most new printers are Plug and Play. The first time you connect a Plug and Play printer to your computer and turn on the printer, Windows will usually install the printer without requiring you to make any selections. In some cases, the Found New Hardware Wizard appears, displaying instructions you can follow to install the printer.

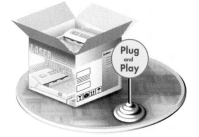

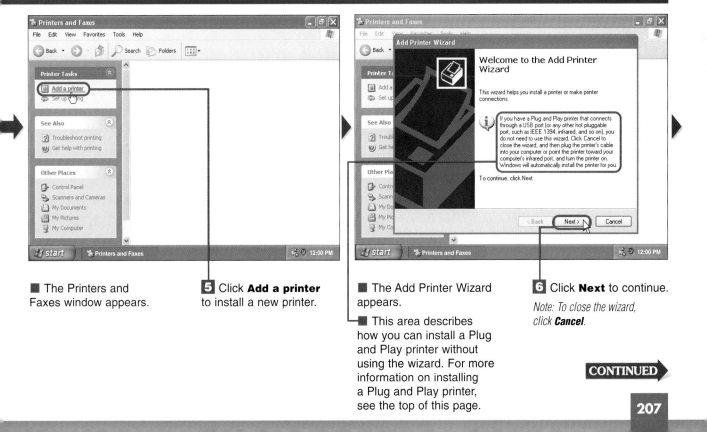

■ The Printers and Faxes window appears.

5 Click **Add a printer** to install a new printer.

■ The Add Printer Wizard appears.

■ This area describes how you can install a Plug and Play printer without using the wizard. For more information on installing a Plug and Play printer, see the top of this page.

6 Click **Next** to continue.

*Note: To close the wizard, click **Cancel**.*

CONTINUED

INSTALL A PRINTER

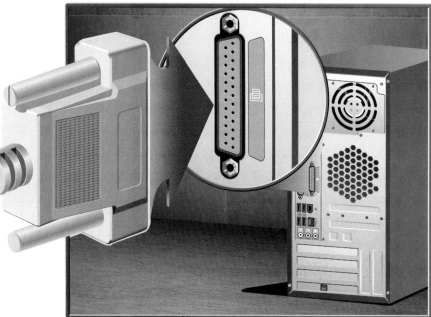

When installing a printer, you need to specify which port the printer uses. A port is a socket where you plug a device into a computer.

A printer port is usually located at the back of a computer and allows a computer to communicate with a printer.

INSTALL A PRINTER (CONTINUED)

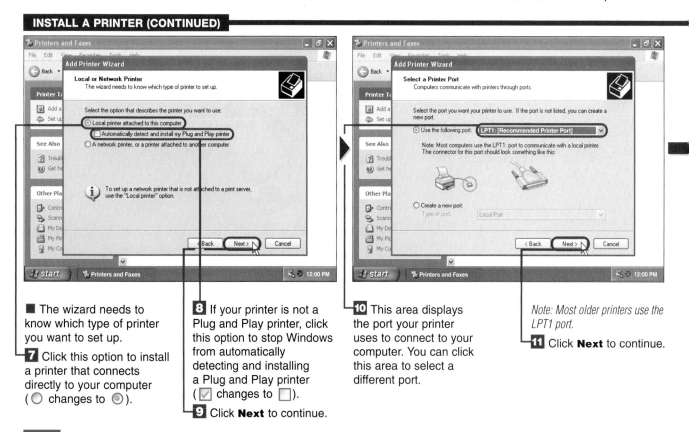

■ The wizard needs to know which type of printer you want to set up.

7 Click this option to install a printer that connects directly to your computer (○ changes to ◉).

8 If your printer is not a Plug and Play printer, click this option to stop Windows from automatically detecting and installing a Plug and Play printer (☑ changes to ☐).

9 Click **Next** to continue.

10 This area displays the port your printer uses to connect to your computer. You can click this area to select a different port.

Note: Most older printers use the LPT1 port.

11 Click **Next** to continue.

Tip

What should I do if the printer I want to install does not appear in the list?

If the printer you want to install does not appear in the list of printers, you can use the installation disk that came with your printer. An installation disk is usually a CD that comes with a printer and contains the installation files for the printer.

1 Insert the installation disk into the appropriate drive on your computer.

2 Click **Have Disk** to use the installation disk to install the printer.

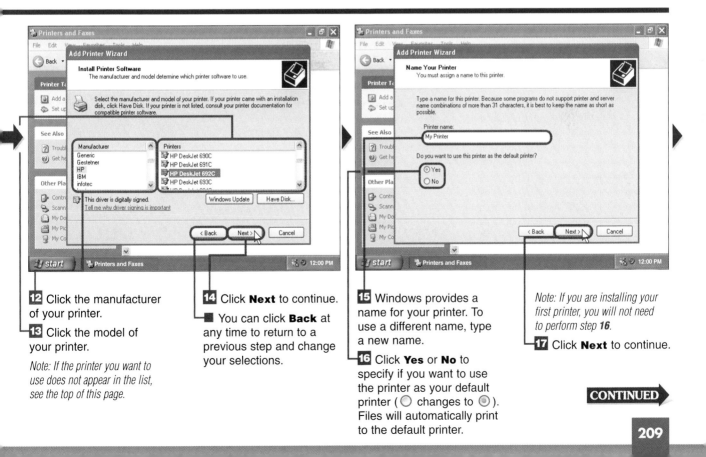

12 Click the manufacturer of your printer.

13 Click the model of your printer.

Note: If the printer you want to use does not appear in the list, see the top of this page.

14 Click **Next** to continue.

■ You can click **Back** at any time to return to a previous step and change your selections.

15 Windows provides a name for your printer. To use a different name, type a new name.

16 Click **Yes** or **No** to specify if you want to use the printer as your default printer (○ changes to ●). Files will automatically print to the default printer.

Note: If you are installing your first printer, you will not need to perform step 16.

17 Click **Next** to continue.

CONTINUED

If your computer is set up on a network, you can share your printer with other people on the network. Sharing a printer allows other people to use your printer to print documents.

Sharing a printer allows individuals and companies to save money since several people on a network can use the same printer.

INSTALL A PRINTER (CONTINUED)

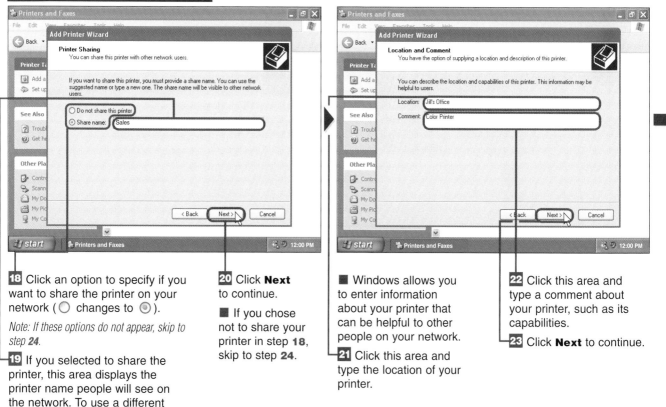

18 Click an option to specify if you want to share the printer on your network (○ changes to ⊙).

Note: If these options do not appear, skip to step 24.

19 If you selected to share the printer, this area displays the printer name people will see on the network. To use a different printer name, type a new name.

20 Click **Next** to continue.

■ If you chose not to share your printer in step **18**, skip to step **24**.

21 Click this area and type the location of your printer.

■ Windows allows you to enter information about your printer that can be helpful to other people on your network.

22 Click this area and type a comment about your printer, such as its capabilities.

23 Click **Next** to continue.

Tip

How can I view the printer I installed on my computer?

The Printers and Faxes window displays an icon for the printer you installed on your computer. If you chose to share your printer with other people on your network, a hand (🖐) appears under the icon for the shared printer. The Printers and Faxes window may also display an icon for each printer on your network that is available for you to use. A check mark (✅) indicates which printer will automatically print your files, known as the default printer. To view the Printers and Faxes window, perform steps **1** to **4** on page 206.

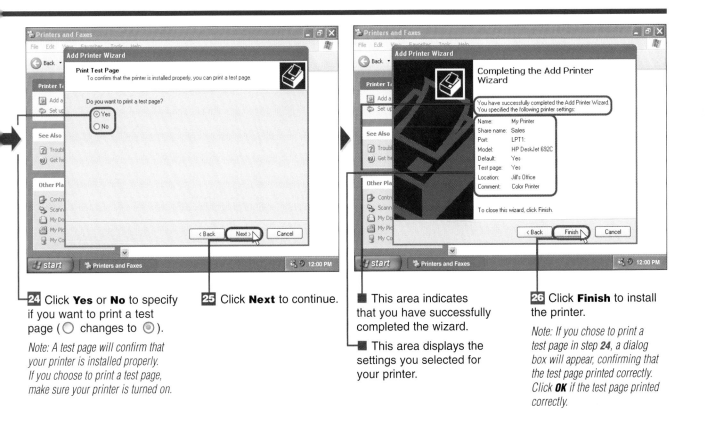

24 Click **Yes** or **No** to specify if you want to print a test page (◯ changes to ◉).

Note: A test page will confirm that your printer is installed properly. If you choose to print a test page, make sure your printer is turned on.

25 Click **Next** to continue.

■ This area indicates that you have successfully completed the wizard.

■ This area displays the settings you selected for your printer.

26 Click **Finish** to install the printer.

*Note: If you chose to print a test page in step **24**, a dialog box will appear, confirming that the test page printed correctly. Click **OK** if the test page printed correctly.*

ADD A BLUETOOTH DEVICE

What is Bluetooth?

Bluetooth wireless technology allows computers and devices to communicate without cables. Bluetooth devices use radio signals to transmit information and operate over a distance of up to 30 feet. Bluetooth was named after a tenth-century Danish king named Harald Bluetooth.

Can my computer use Bluetooth devices?

Computers do not usually come with the capability to use Bluetooth devices. To add Bluetooth capability to a computer, you can plug in an external Bluetooth adapter, or transceiver, to a computer. Once you add Bluetooth capability to a computer, any Bluetooth device can communicate with the computer.

How can I use Bluetooth technology?

✓ Use a Bluetooth wireless mouse or keyboard to prevent clutter on your desk.

✓ Print to a Bluetooth wireless printer.

✓ Transfer information between a computer and a Personal Digital Assistant (PDA), such as a Pocket PC or Palm handheld device.

✓ Connect wirelessly to the Internet using a Bluetooth cell phone when traveling with a notebook computer.

What must I do before adding a Bluetooth device to my computer?

✓ Attach a Bluetooth adapter, or transceiver, to your computer.

✓ Insert batteries into the Bluetooth device.

✓ Turn the Bluetooth device on.

✓ Make sure the Bluetooth device is "discoverable," which means that your computer can see the device. If you are adding a Bluetooth mouse or keyboard, the device may have a button that you can press to make the device discoverable. To determine how to make your Bluetooth device discoverable, refer to the documentation that came with your device.

✓ If you are adding a Bluetooth mouse or keyboard, you must have a mouse or keyboard with a cable connected to your computer.

Before you can use a Bluetooth device, you need to add the device to your computer.

You can obtain many types of Bluetooth devices, including a mouse, keyboard, cell phone, printer and Personal Digital Assistant (PDA) such as a Pocket PC or Palm handheld device.

ADD A BLUETOOTH DEVICE

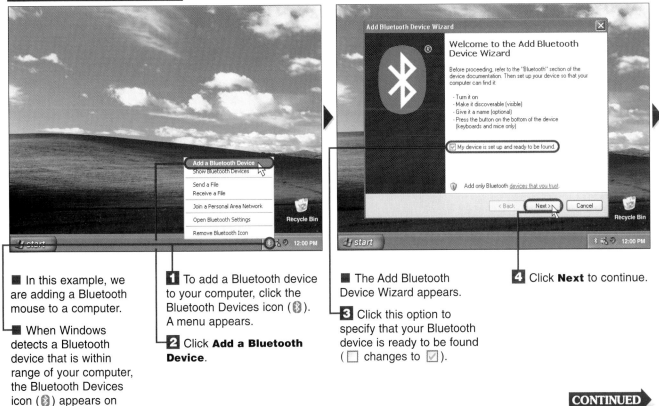

■ In this example, we are adding a Bluetooth mouse to a computer.

■ When Windows detects a Bluetooth device that is within range of your computer, the Bluetooth Devices icon (⬧) appears on the taskbar.

1 To add a Bluetooth device to your computer, click the Bluetooth Devices icon (⬧). A menu appears.

2 Click **Add a Bluetooth Device**.

■ The Add Bluetooth Device Wizard appears.

3 Click this option to specify that your Bluetooth device is ready to be found (☐ changes to ☑).

4 Click **Next** to continue.

CONTINUED ▶

ADD A BLUETOOTH DEVICE

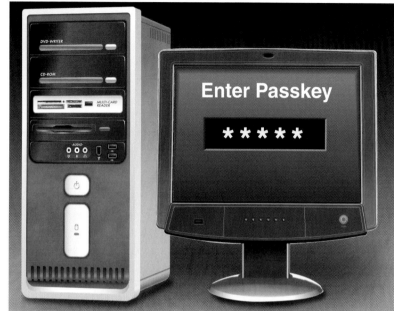

When adding a Bluetooth device to your computer, you may need to enter a passkey for the device.

A passkey enables Windows to identify your Bluetooth device and helps to secure the data passing between your computer and the device. Some Bluetooth devices do not use a passkey.

You should refer to the documentation that came with your Bluetooth device to determine if your device requires a specific passkey.

ADD A BLUETOOTH DEVICE (CONTINUED)

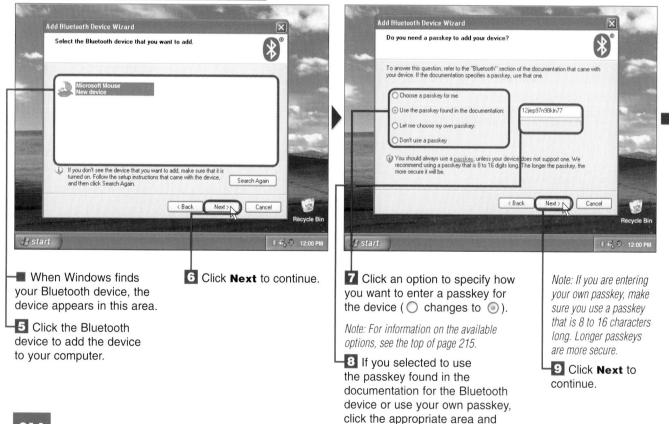

■ When Windows finds your Bluetooth device, the device appears in this area.

5 Click the Bluetooth device to add the device to your computer.

6 Click **Next** to continue.

7 Click an option to specify how you want to enter a passkey for the device (○ changes to ⊙).

Note: For information on the available options, see the top of page 215.

8 If you selected to use the passkey found in the documentation for the Bluetooth device or use your own passkey, click the appropriate area and type the passkey.

Note: If you are entering your own passkey, make sure you use a passkey that is 8 to 16 characters long. Longer passkeys are more secure.

9 Click **Next** to continue.

Tip

When adding a Bluetooth device, how can I enter a passkey for the device?

Choose a passkey for me

Select this option if the documentation for the Bluetooth device does not specify a passkey, but the device can accept a passkey. Typically, Bluetooth devices such as keyboards, cell phones and Personal Digital Assistants (PDAs) can accept a passkey.

Let me choose my own passkey

Select this option if you want to create your own passkey.

Use the passkey found in the documentation

Select this option if the documentation for the Bluetooth device specifies a passkey. Typically, devices such as Bluetooth headsets and mice specify a passkey in the documentation.

Don't use a passkey

Select this option if the documentation for the Bluetooth device does not specify a passkey and the device cannot accept a passkey.

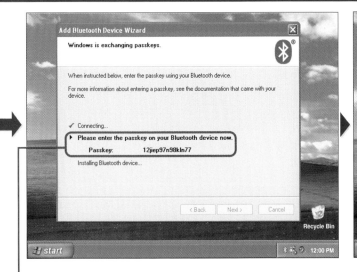

■ Windows starts adding the Bluetooth device to your computer.

■ If your Bluetooth device requires a passkey, the wizard indicates when you must enter the passkey on your device and displays the passkey you need to enter.

Note: You can refer to the documentation that came with your Bluetooth device to determine how to enter a passkey on the device.

■ This message appears when you have successfully added the Bluetooth device to your computer. Your computer and the device can now communicate whenever the device is within range of your computer.

10 Click **Finish** to close the wizard.

Note: Depending on the Bluetooth device you added, you may need to perform other steps to allow the device to communicate with your computer. You can refer to the documentation that came with your device to determine what steps, if any, you need to perform.

CHECK YOUR COMPUTER'S SECURITY SETTINGS

You can view and manage the security settings that help protect your computer.

CHECK YOUR COMPUTER'S SECURITY SETTINGS

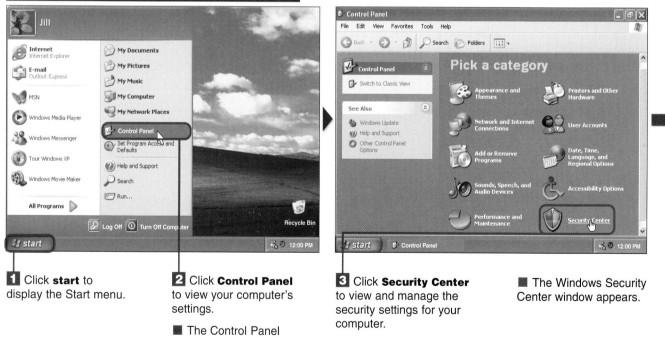

1 Click **start** to display the Start menu.

2 Click **Control Panel** to view your computer's settings.

■ The Control Panel window appears.

3 Click **Security Center** to view and manage the security settings for your computer.

■ The Windows Security Center window appears.

Tip

Will Windows alert me if there is a problem with my computer's security settings?

Yes. If Windows detects a problem with any of the three main security settings, including Firewall, Automatic Updates or Virus Protection, Windows displays an icon (🛡) in the taskbar and displays a message. For example, if you do not have an antivirus program installed on your computer, the icon and a message will appear. You can click the icon to instantly display the Windows Security Center window to find information on how to fix the problem.

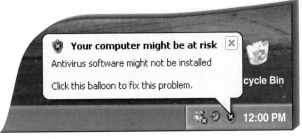

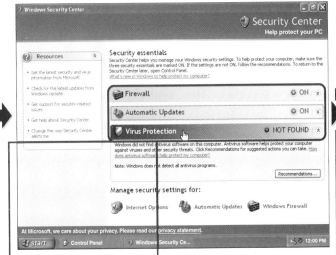

■ This area displays the status of the three most important security settings. To best protect your computer, each setting should be marked "ON."

■ Windows uses different colors to indicate the status of each security setting—blue for a more secure status, yellow for a warning status and red for an alert status.

4 To display or hide information for a security setting, click the heading bar for the security setting.

FIREWALL

■ Windows comes with firewall software that helps protect your computer by preventing unauthorized people or unwanted programs, such as viruses, from accessing your computer from the Internet or a network.

■ The firewall software included with Windows is turned on automatically. To keep your computer more secure, you should leave the Firewall setting turned on.

CONTINUED

CHECK YOUR COMPUTER'S SECURITY SETTINGS

Windows helps keep your computer safe by automatically installing the latest Windows updates from the Internet free of charge.

Windows regularly checks Microsoft's Web site for the latest important updates for your computer. Important updates help protect your computer against viruses and other security threats.

You need an Internet connection for Windows to be able to update your computer automatically.

CHECK YOUR COMPUTER'S SECURITY SETTINGS (CONTINUED)

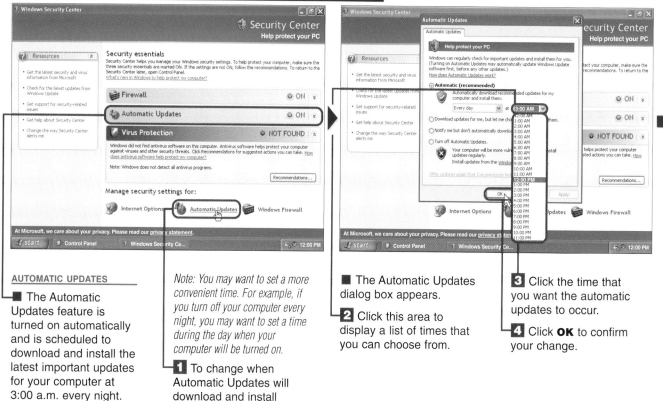

AUTOMATIC UPDATES

■ The Automatic Updates feature is turned on automatically and is scheduled to download and install the latest important updates for your computer at 3:00 a.m. every night.

Note: You may want to set a more convenient time. For example, if you turn off your computer every night, you may want to set a time during the day when your computer will be turned on.

1 To change when Automatic Updates will download and install updates, click **Automatic Updates**.

■ The Automatic Updates dialog box appears.

2 Click this area to display a list of times that you can choose from.

3 Click the time that you want the automatic updates to occur.

4 Click **OK** to confirm your change.

Tip

What is a virus?

A virus is a program that disrupts the normal operation of a computer. A virus can cause a variety of problems, such as the appearance of annoying messages on a screen, the destruction of information or the slowing down of a computer. Files you receive on removable storage media, such as a CD, memory card or floppy disk, can contain viruses. Files you obtain on the Internet and files sent as attachments in e-mail messages can also contain viruses.

Tip

How can I keep my antivirus software up to date?

Keeping your antivirus software up to date is important since new viruses are discovered every day. Many antivirus programs can update automatically when you are connected to the Internet. If your antivirus program cannot update automatically, you can check for updates at the company's Web site on a regular basis.

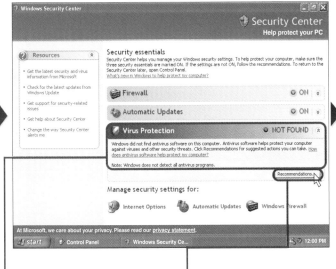

VIRUS PROTECTION

■ Windows checks to see if your computer is using an antivirus program and whether the program is up to date. An antivirus program helps protect your computer against viruses and other security threats.

Note: Windows does not come with an antivirus program and cannot detect some antivirus programs.

1 To obtain an antivirus program, click **Recommendations**.

■ The Recommendation dialog box appears.

2 Click **How?** to get an antivirus program for your computer.

■ A Microsoft Web page will appear, displaying companies that offer antivirus programs. You can select the company that provides the antivirus program you want to use and follow the instructions on your screen to install the program on your computer.

3 When you finish installing an antivirus program on your computer, click **OK** to close the dialog box.

DEFRAGMENT YOUR HARD DISK

You can improve the performance of your computer by defragmenting your hard disk. Defragmenting your hard disk will make your programs run faster and your files open more quickly.

Before defragmenting your hard disk, Windows can analyze the disk to determine if you need to defragment the disk. You should have Windows analyze your hard disk at least once a week.

DEFRAGMENT YOUR HARD DISK

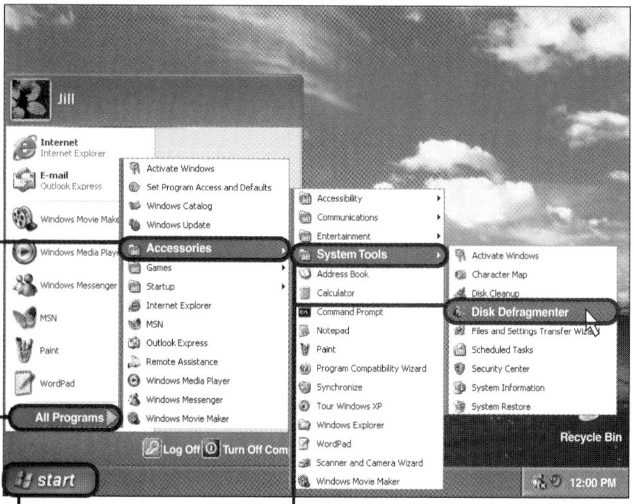

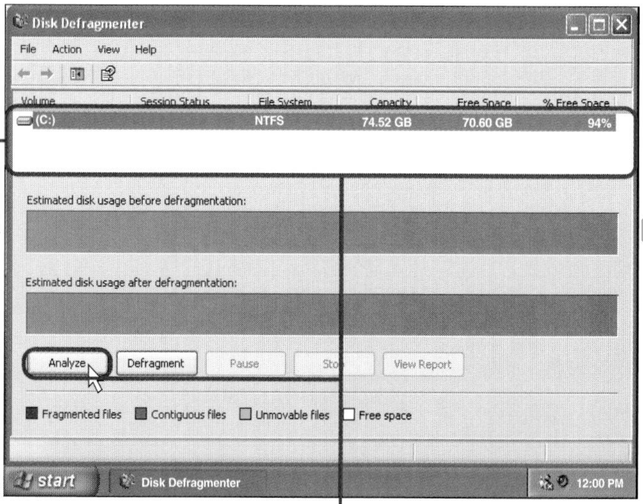

1 Click **start** to display the Start menu.

2 Click **All Programs** to view a list of the programs on your computer.

3 Click **Accessories**.

4 Click **System Tools**.

5 Click **Disk Defragmenter**.

■ The Disk Defragmenter window appears.

■ This area lists the hard disks on your computer as well as the storage capacity and the amount of free space on each disk.

Note: A hard disk must have at least 15% of free space for Windows to properly defragment the disk.

6 Click the hard disk you want to defragment.

7 Click **Analyze** to determine if you need to defragment the hard disk.

Why would I need to defragment my hard disk?

A fragmented hard disk stores parts of each file in many different locations on the disk. Your computer must search many areas on the disk to retrieve a file. You can use Disk Defragmenter to place all the parts of each file in one location, which reduces the time your computer will spend locating files.

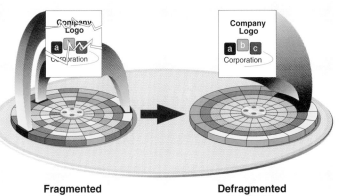

Fragmented Hard Disk

Defragmented Hard Disk

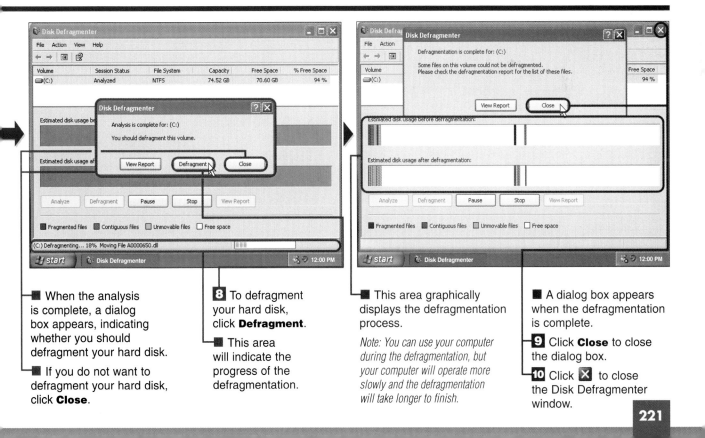

■ When the analysis is complete, a dialog box appears, indicating whether you should defragment your hard disk.

■ If you do not want to defragment your hard disk, click **Close**.

8 To defragment your hard disk, click **Defragment**.

■ This area will indicate the progress of the defragmentation.

■ This area graphically displays the defragmentation process.

Note: You can use your computer during the defragmentation, but your computer will operate more slowly and the defragmentation will take longer to finish.

■ A dialog box appears when the defragmentation is complete.

9 Click **Close** to close the dialog box.

10 Click ✕ to close the Disk Defragmenter window.

RESTORE YOUR COMPUTER

If you are experiencing problems with your computer, you can use the System Restore feature to return your computer to a time before the problems occurred.

For example, if your computer does not work properly after you install a program, you can restore your computer to a time before you installed the program.

RESTORE YOUR COMPUTER

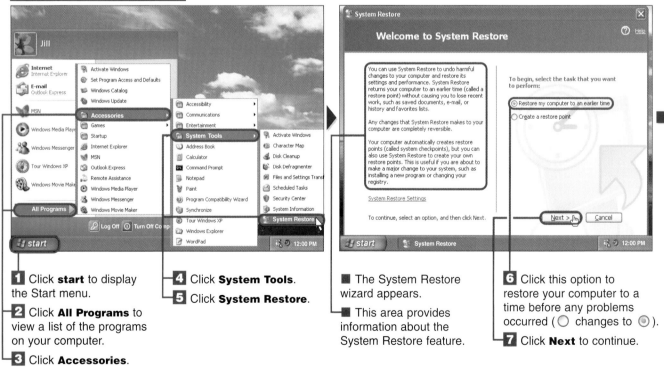

1 Click **start** to display the Start menu.

2 Click **All Programs** to view a list of the programs on your computer.

3 Click **Accessories**.

4 Click **System Tools**.

5 Click **System Restore**.

■ The System Restore wizard appears.

■ This area provides information about the System Restore feature.

6 Click this option to restore your computer to a time before any problems occurred (○ changes to ◉).

7 Click **Next** to continue.

Tip

What types of restore points are available?

When restoring your computer, you can select from several types of restore points. A restore point is an earlier, more stable time that you can return your computer to.

Windows can store between one to three weeks of restore points. Here are two common types of restore points.

System Checkpoint

Restore points created automatically by Windows on a regular basis.

Installed (*Program*)

Restore points created automatically when you install certain programs. The name of the program appears beside the word "Installed."

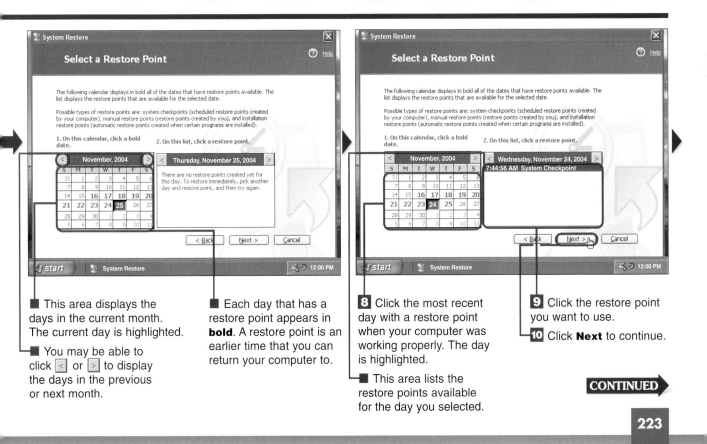

■ This area displays the days in the current month. The current day is highlighted.

■ You may be able to click < or > to display the days in the previous or next month.

■ Each day that has a restore point appears in **bold**. A restore point is an earlier time that you can return your computer to.

8 Click the most recent day with a restore point when your computer was working properly. The day is highlighted.

■ This area lists the restore points available for the day you selected.

9 Click the restore point you want to use.

10 Click **Next** to continue.

CONTINUED

RESTORE YOUR COMPUTER

When you restore your computer to an earlier time, you will not lose any of your recent work, such as your documents or e-mail messages.

Before restoring your computer to an earlier time, you should close all open files and programs.

RESTORE YOUR COMPUTER (CONTINUED)

■ This area displays information about the restore point you selected.

■ You can click **Back** to return to the previous screen and change the restore point you selected.

■ This area displays information about the System Restore feature.

11 Click **Next** to restore your computer.

Tip

Will I need to re-install any programs after restoring my computer?

When you restore your computer to an earlier time, any programs you installed after that date may be uninstalled. Files you created using the program will not be deleted, but you may need to re-install the program to work with the files again.

Tip

Can I reverse the changes made when I restored my computer to an earlier time?

Yes. Any changes that the System Restore feature makes to your computer are completely reversible. To undo your last restoration, perform steps **1** to **7** on page 222, except select **Undo my last restoration** in step **6**. Then perform steps **11** and **12** below.

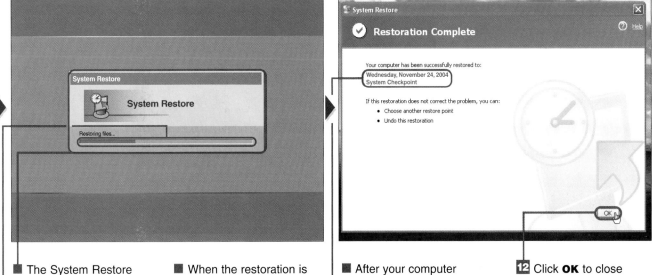

■ The System Restore dialog box appears.

■ This area shows the progress of the restoration.

■ When the restoration is complete, your computer will automatically restart.

■ After your computer restarts, a dialog box appears, indicating that your computer has been successfully restored.

■ This area displays the date to which your computer was restored.

12 Click **OK** to close the dialog box.

CHAPTER 10

Work on a Network

This chapter teaches you how to share information and equipment, such as a printer, on a network. You will learn how to set up a wired network as well as a wireless network, which does not use any cables to exchange information.

SET UP A NETWORK

If you have more than one computer at home or at a small office, you can set up a network so the computers can exchange information as well as share equipment and an Internet connection.

Computers

You will need two or more computers to set up a network. One computer on your network must use Windows XP. All the other computers on your network must use Windows XP, Windows Me or Windows 98.

Ethernet Network Card

Each computer requires an Ethernet network card or connection. An Ethernet network card or connection attaches each computer to a network and allows the computers on a network to communicate.

Hub or Switch

A network may require a hub or switch, which is a device that provides a central location where all the cables on the network meet.

Cables

Cables physically connect each computer to the network.

Set Up a Network with Only Two Computers

If you want to connect only two computers that are located close together on a network, you can use a special type of cable, known as crossover cable, to connect the computers. This eliminates the need for a hub or switch.

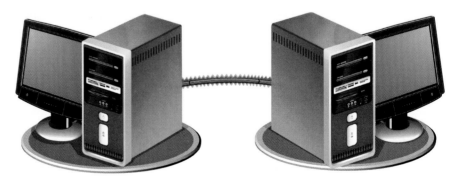

SHARE AN INTERNET CONNECTION ON A NETWORK

Share One Computer's Internet Connection

Computer

You can share one computer's Internet connection with all the other computers on a network. The computer sharing its Internet connection should be using Windows XP. When other computers on the network want to access the Internet, the computer sharing its Internet connection must be turned on.

Internet Connection Device

You will need a device that allows you to connect to the Internet, such as a cable modem or Digital Subscriber Line (DSL).

Use a Router to Share an Internet Connection

Router

A router is a device that you can use to share one Internet connection with all the computers on a network. Using a router to connect to the Internet offers more security and better performance than when one computer on a network shares its Internet connection. Most routers include a built-in hub or switch. A router is also known as a residential gateway.

Internet Connection Device

You will need a device that allows you to connect to the Internet, such as a cable modem or Digital Subscriber Line (DSL).

SET UP A NETWORK

Windows provides the Network Setup Wizard that will take you step by step through the process of setting up a computer on your network.

You must run the Network Setup Wizard on each computer you want to set up on your network. If the computers on your network will share an Internet connection, you should run the wizard on the computer that has the Internet connection first.

SET UP A NETWORK

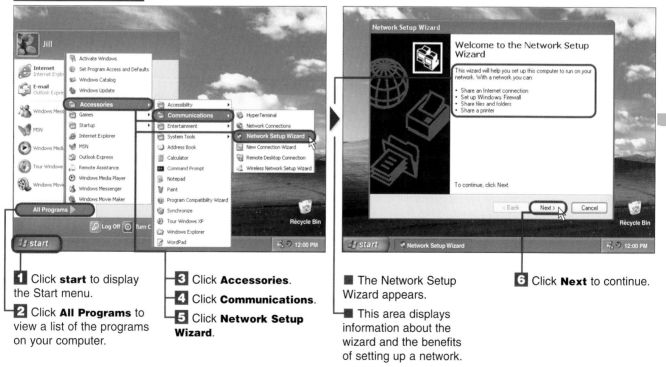

1 Click **start** to display the Start menu.

2 Click **All Programs** to view a list of the programs on your computer.

3 Click **Accessories**.

4 Click **Communications**.

5 Click **Network Setup Wizard**.

■ The Network Setup Wizard appears.

■ This area displays information about the wizard and the benefits of setting up a network.

6 Click **Next** to continue.

Tip

What are the advantages of setting up a network?

✓ Share information.

✓ Share equipment, such as a printer.

✓ Share one Internet connection.

✓ Play multiplayer games with each player using a different computer.

Tip

Can Windows help protect my network?

Yes. Windows comes with firewall software that helps protect computers on a network. Firewall software prevents unauthorized people or unwanted programs, such as viruses, from accessing computers on a network through the Internet or through other computers on the network.

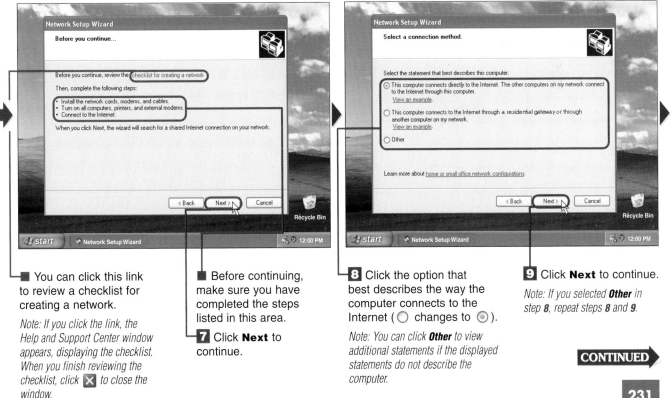

■ You can click this link to review a checklist for creating a network.

Note: If you click the link, the Help and Support Center window appears, displaying the checklist. When you finish reviewing the checklist, click ☒ to close the window.

■ Before continuing, make sure you have completed the steps listed in this area.

7 Click **Next** to continue.

8 Click the option that best describes the way the computer connects to the Internet (○ changes to ⊙).

*Note: You can click **Other** to view additional statements if the displayed statements do not describe the computer.*

9 Click **Next** to continue.

*Note: If you selected **Other** in step **8**, repeat steps **8** and **9**.*

CONTINUED ▶

SET UP A NETWORK

When setting up a
computer on your
network, you need to
provide a description,
computer name and
workgroup name for
the computer.

A computer name
identifies the computer
on your network.
A workgroup name
identifies the group
of computers on
your network that the
computer belongs to.

SET UP A NETWORK (CONTINUED)

■ This area lists the
possible connections
the computer can use to
connect to the Internet.
The wizard automatically
selects the connection that
the computer most likely
uses.

10 To select a different
connection to the Internet,
click the connection the
computer uses.

*Note: This screen may not appear,
depending on the statement you
selected in step 8. If the screen
does not appear, skip to step 12.*

11 Click **Next** to continue.

12 Type a brief description
for the computer.

13 Double-click this area
and type a name that will
identify the computer on
the network.

*Note: For information on choosing
a computer name, see the top of
page 233.*

14 Click **Next** to continue.

Tip

What should I consider when choosing a computer name?

✓ Each computer on your network must have a different name.

✓ A computer name can contain up to 15 characters.

✓ A computer name cannot contain spaces or the following special characters: ; : , " < > * + = \ | or ?

✓ Your Internet Service Provider (ISP), which is the company that gives you access to the Internet, may require you to use a specific name for the computer that shares its Internet connection. If this is true for your ISP, make sure you use the name your ISP specifies.

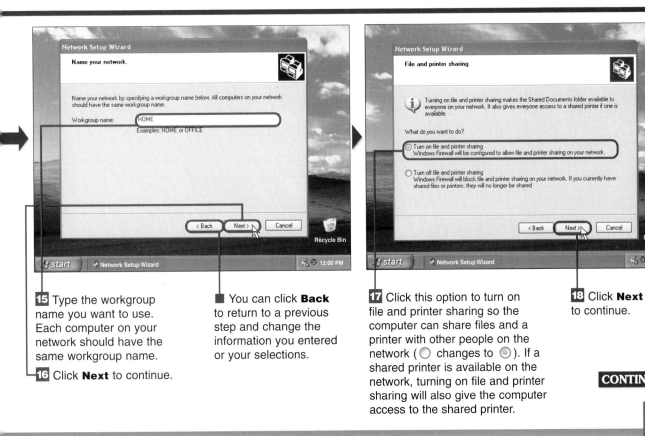

15 Type the workgroup name you want to use. Each computer on your network should have the same workgroup name.

16 Click **Next** to continue.

■ You can click **Back** to return to a previous step and change the information you entered or your selections.

17 Click this option to turn on file and printer sharing so the computer can share files and a printer with other people on the network (○ changes to ◉). If a shared printer is available on the network, turning on file and printer sharing will also give the computer access to the shared printer.

18 Click **Next** to continue.

CONTINUED

You need to specify how you want to set up other computers that are not running Windows XP on your network.

To set up other computers that use Windows 98 or Windows Me, you can create a Network Setup disk or use the CD used to install Windows XP.

To set up other computers that use Windows XP, perform the steps for the Network Setup Wizard starting on page 230 on each computer.

SET UP A NETWORK (CONTINUED)

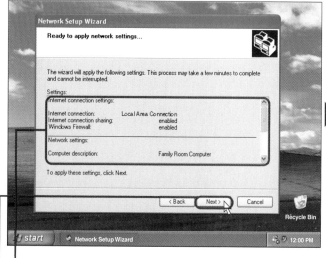

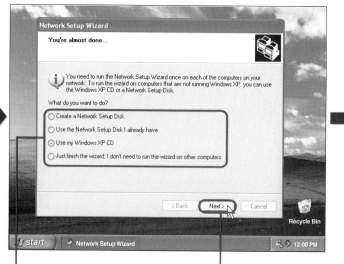

■ This area displays the network settings that the wizard will apply to the computer.

19 Click **Next** to apply the network settings.

■ The wizard may take a few minutes to apply the network settings. This process cannot be interrupted.

20 Click an option to specify the task you want to perform to set up other computers on your network (○ changes to ◉).

Note: If all the computers on your network are running Windows XP, select Just finish the wizard. If one or more computers are not running Windows XP, select Create a Network Setup Disk or Use my Windows XP CD.

21 Click **Next** to continue.

Note: If you chose to create a network setup disk, follow the instructions on your screen to create the disk and then skip to step 22. If you chose to just finish the wizard, skip to step 23.

Tip **How do I share resources on my network?**

The Network Setup Wizard automatically shares your printer and your Shared Documents folder with other people on the network. After setting up your network, you can specify other folders that you want to share. For information on the Shared Documents folder, see page 195. To share a specific folder, see page 238.

Tip **How can I view all the folders that are shared on my network?**

You can use **My Network Places** to view all the folders that are shared by your computer and other computers on your network. To use My Network Places, see page 236.

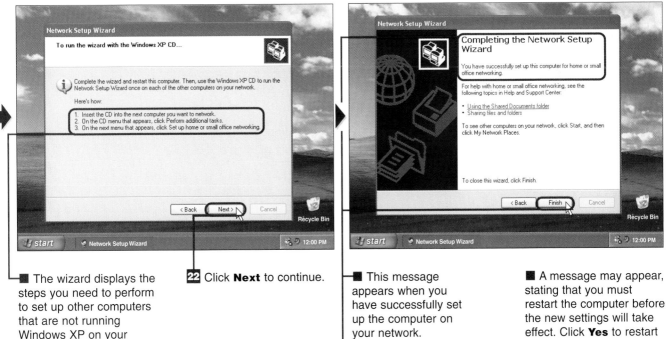

■ The wizard displays the steps you need to perform to set up other computers that are not running Windows XP on your network. The displayed steps depend on the option you selected in step **20**.

22 Click **Next** to continue.

■ This message appears when you have successfully set up the computer on your network.

23 Click **Finish** to close the wizard.

■ A message may appear, stating that you must restart the computer before the new settings will take effect. Click **Yes** to restart the computer.

BROWSE THROUGH A NETWORK

You can use My Network Places to browse through the information available on your network.

You can work with the files available on your network as you would work with files stored on your own computer.

BROWSE THROUGH A NETWORK

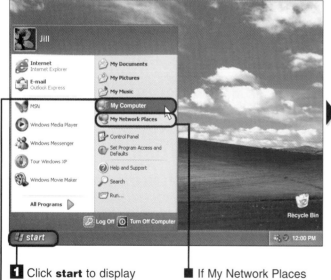

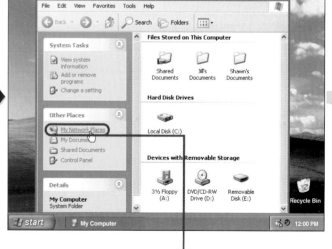

1 Click **start** to display the Start menu.

2 Click **My Computer** to view the contents of your computer.

■ If My Network Places appears on the Start menu, click **My Network Places** and then skip to step **4**.

■ The My Computer window appears.

3 Click **My Network Places** to browse through the information available on your network.

236

Tip

Why can I no longer access a folder on my network?

You will not be able to access a folder on your network if the computer that stores the folder is turned off or if the owner of the computer stops sharing the folder.

Tip

How can I view the shared folders on only one computer on my network?

In the My Network Places window, click **View workgroup computers**. An icon ( ) will appear for each computer on your network that belongs to the same workgroup. To view the shared folders and other shared resources on a computer, double-click the computer.

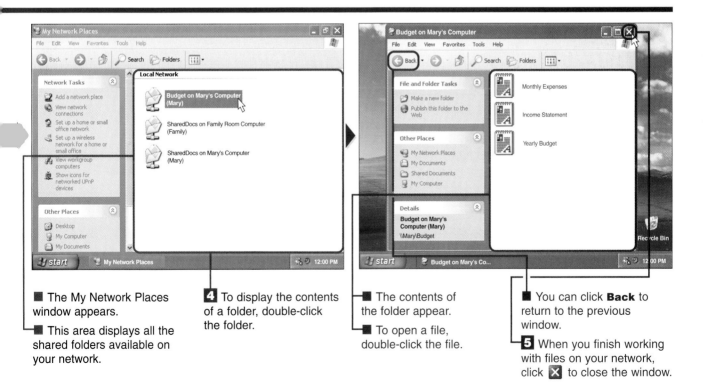

■ The My Network Places window appears.

■ This area displays all the shared folders available on your network.

4 To display the contents of a folder, double-click the folder.

■ The contents of the folder appear.

■ To open a file, double-click the file.

■ You can click **Back** to return to the previous window.

5 When you finish working with files on your network, click **X** to close the window.

SHARE INFORMATION

You can specify the information on your computer that you want to share with other people on your network.

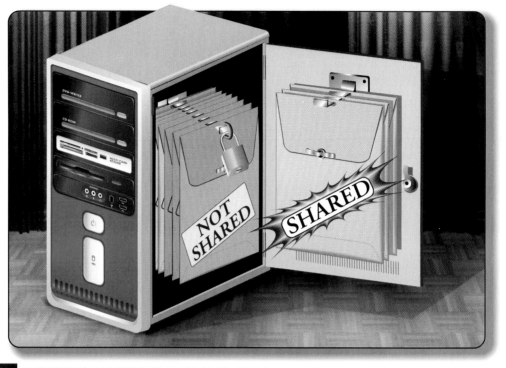

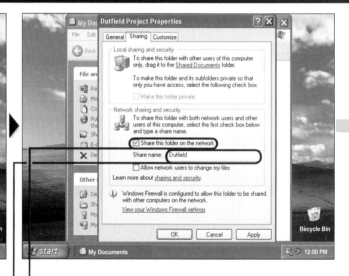

1 Click the folder you want to share with other people on your network.

2 Click **Share this folder**.

■ A Properties dialog box appears.

3 Click this option to share the folder with other people on your network (☐ changes to ☑).

4 This area displays the name of the folder people will see on your network. To change the folder name, drag the mouse I over the current name and then type a new name.

Note: If the name of the folder is longer than 12 characters, other computers that are not running Windows XP on the network may not be able to access the folder. Changing the name of the folder will not change the name of the folder on your computer.

Tip

What must I do before I can share information on my computer?

Before you can share information on your computer with other people on your network, your computer must be set up on the network. To set up your computer on a network, see page 228.

When you set up your computer on a network, Windows automatically shares your Shared Documents folder. For information on the Shared Documents folder, see page 195.

Tip

How can I share a folder located on my desktop?

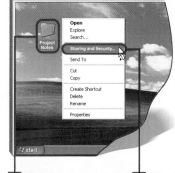

1 To share a folder located on your desktop, right-click the folder. A menu appears.

2 Click **Sharing and Security**. Then perform steps **3** to **6** below to share the folder.

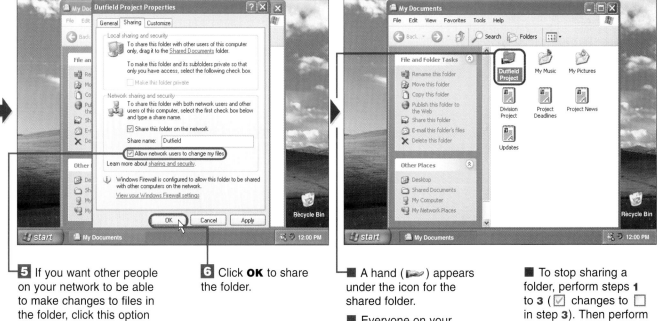

5 If you want other people on your network to be able to make changes to files in the folder, click this option (☐ changes to ☑).

6 Click **OK** to share the folder.

■ A hand (👉) appears under the icon for the shared folder.

■ Everyone on your network will be able to access all the files within the shared folder.

■ To stop sharing a folder, perform steps **1** to **3** (☑ changes to ☐ in step **3**). Then perform step **6**.

239

SHARE A PRINTER

You can share your printer with other people on a network. Sharing a printer allows other people to use your printer to print documents.

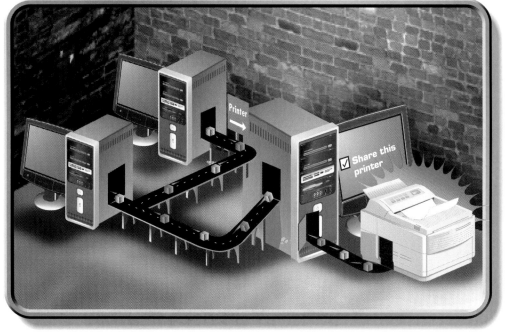

Sharing a printer allows individuals and companies to save money since several people on a network can use the same printer.

To share a printer on a network, your computer must be set up on a network. To set up a computer on a network, see page 228.

SHARE A PRINTER

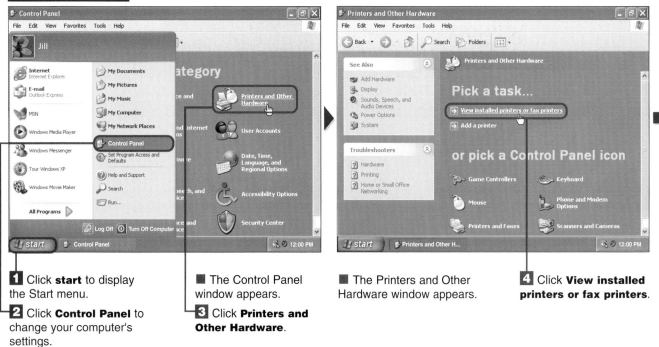

1 Click **start** to display the Start menu.

2 Click **Control Panel** to change your computer's settings.

■ The Control Panel window appears.

3 Click **Printers and Other Hardware**.

■ The Printers and Other Hardware window appears.

4 Click **View installed printers or fax printers**.

Tip

How can I tell if my printer is shared?

In the Printers and Faxes window, a hand ( ) appears under the icon for your shared printer. Windows may have already shared your printer when you set up your computer on the network or installed the printer. You should make sure both your computer and the shared printer are turned on and are accessible when other people want to use the printer.

Tip

How do I stop sharing a printer?

When you no longer want people on the network to use your printer, you can stop sharing your printer. To stop sharing a printer, perform steps **1** to **10** below, except select **Do not share this printer** in step **7**.

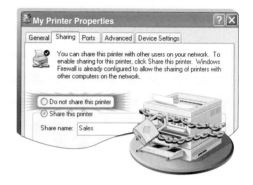

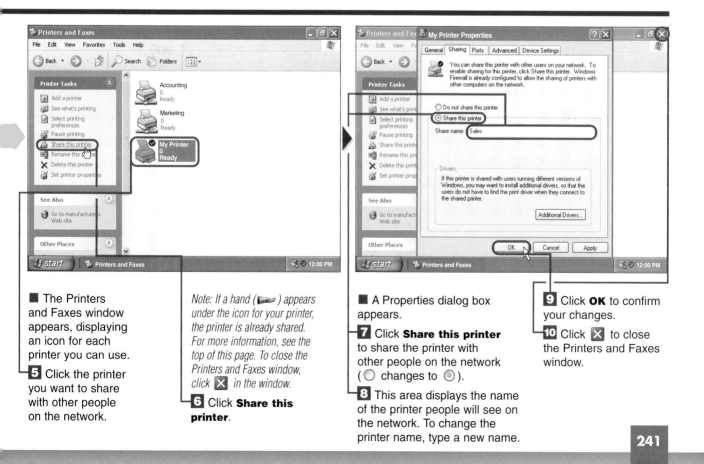

■ The Printers and Faxes window appears, displaying an icon for each printer you can use.

5 Click the printer you want to share with other people on the network.

Note: If a hand ( ) appears under the icon for your printer, the printer is already shared. For more information, see the top of this page. To close the Printers and Faxes window, click ✕ in the window.

6 Click **Share this printer**.

■ A Properties dialog box appears.

7 Click **Share this printer** to share the printer with other people on the network (○ changes to ⊙).

8 This area displays the name of the printer people will see on the network. To change the printer name, type a new name.

9 Click **OK** to confirm your changes.

10 Click ✕ to close the Printers and Faxes window.

SET UP A WIRELESS NETWORK

Windows provides the Wireless Network Setup Wizard that will take you step by step through the process of setting up a wireless network.

A wireless network allows computers to share information on a network without using any cables.

Wireless networks are useful when computers are located where cables are not practical or economical. Wireless networks also allow notebook computers to access a network from many locations in a home or office.

SET UP A WIRELESS NETWORK

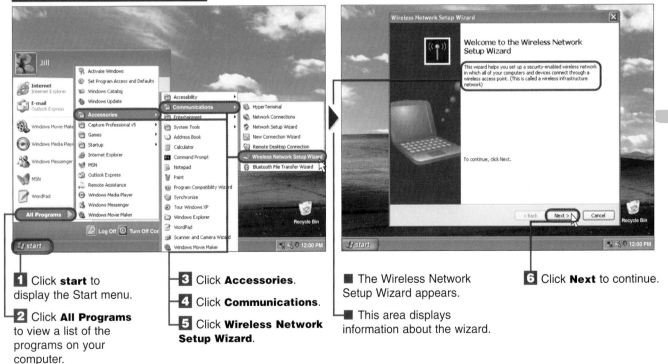

1 Click **start** to display the Start menu.

2 Click **All Programs** to view a list of the programs on your computer.

3 Click **Accessories**.

4 Click **Communications**.

5 Click **Wireless Network Setup Wizard**.

■ The Wireless Network Setup Wizard appears.

■ This area displays information about the wizard.

6 Click **Next** to continue.

Tip

What equipment do I need to set up a wireless network?

Wireless Network Card
Each computer requires an internal wireless network card or an external wireless network adapter. A wireless network card or adapter allows computers on a wireless network to communicate using radio signals.

Wireless Router or Wireless Access Point
A wireless router or wireless access point is a device that uses radio signals to transmit and receive data between computers on a network. To set up a wireless network using the steps below, you need a wireless router or wireless access point that supports the Windows Connect Now feature.

Flash Drive
A flash drive is a small, portable, lightweight storage device that plugs into a Universal Serial Bus (USB) port on a computer. A flash drive is also known as a USB key.

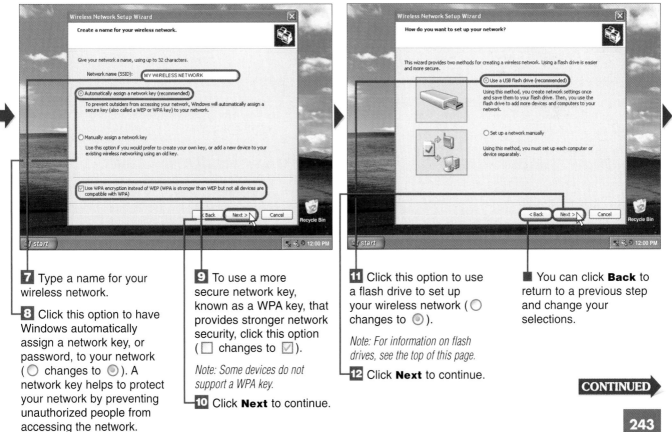

7 Type a name for your wireless network.

8 Click this option to have Windows automatically assign a network key, or password, to your network (○ changes to ◉). A network key helps to protect your network by preventing unauthorized people from accessing the network.

9 To use a more secure network key, known as a WPA key, that provides stronger network security, click this option (☐ changes to ☑).

Note: Some devices do not support a WPA key.

10 Click **Next** to continue.

11 Click this option to use a flash drive to set up your wireless network (○ changes to ◉).

Note: For information on flash drives, see the top of this page.

12 Click **Next** to continue.

■ You can click **Back** to return to a previous step and change your selections.

CONTINUED

When setting up a wireless network, you can use a flash drive to easily transfer your network settings to all the other computers on your network.

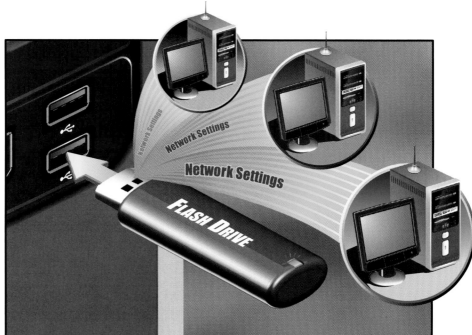

SET UP A WIRELESS NETWORK (CONTINUED)

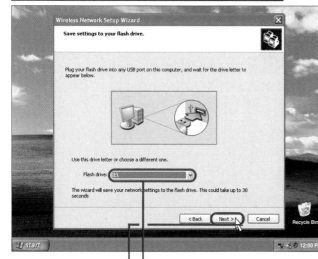

13 Plug your flash drive into a USB port on your computer.

■ This area displays the drive letter for the flash drive. If the wizard does not show the correct drive letter, you can click this area to select a different drive letter.

14 Click **Next** to save the network settings to the flash drive.

■ This area displays the steps you need to perform to transfer the network settings to your other computers and devices on the network.

15 Unplug the flash drive from your computer.

16 Plug the flash drive into your wireless router or wireless access point. Wait about 30 seconds or until the device blinks its lights three times to indicate the data transfer is complete.

Tip

Can I share an Internet connection on a wireless network?

Yes. If you have a wireless router on your network, you can connect an Internet connection device, such as a cable modem or Digital Subscriber Line (DSL), directly to the router. Once connected, all the computers on the network will be able to use the device to connect to the Internet. If you have a wireless access point that does not have router capabilities on your network, you can connect an Internet connection device directly to one computer on your network to share its Internet connection.

Tip

Is there anything I need to do after setting up a wireless network?

Yes. After you set up a wireless network, you should run the Network Setup Wizard on each computer on your network. The Network Setup Wizard allows you to turn on file and printer sharing for each computer on the network to enable the computers to share files and printers.

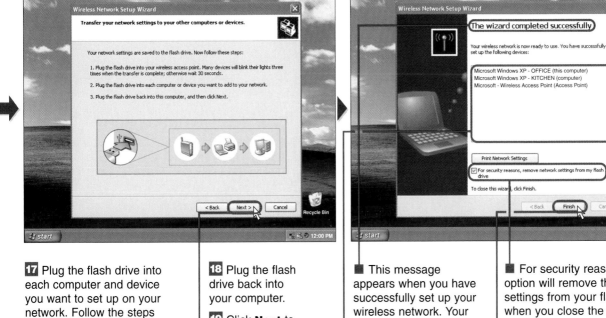

17 Plug the flash drive into each computer and device you want to set up on your network. Follow the steps that appear on each screen to set up each computer on the network.

18 Plug the flash drive back into your computer.

19 Click **Next** to continue.

■ This message appears when you have successfully set up your wireless network. Your wireless network is now ready to use.

■ This area lists the computers and devices that you have set up on your wireless network.

■ For security reasons, this option will remove the network settings from your flash drive when you close the wizard. If you want to use the flash drive to set up other computers at a later time, click this option to turn the option off (☑ changes to ☐).

20 Click **Finish** to close the wizard.

CONNECT TO A WIRELESS NETWORK

You can easily connect to a wireless network at home or at the office to access the information and equipment available on the network.

If a wireless network is connected to the Internet, connecting to the network will also allow you to access the Internet.

CONNECT TO A WIRELESS NETWORK

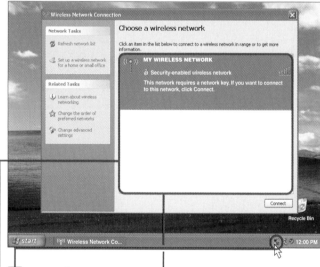

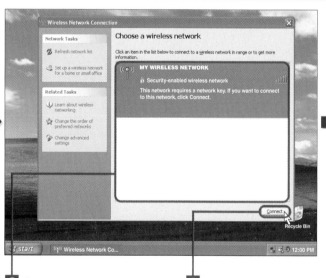

1 Click 📶 to connect to a wireless network.

■ The Wireless Network Connection dialog box appears.

■ This area lists all the wireless networks that are available to you.

■ Windows provides information about each wireless network. For example, a lock symbol (🔒) indicates a network that is secure. A series of bars indicates the signal strength of a network.

Note: You can position the mouse over the series of bars to display a brief description of the signal strength.

2 Click the wireless network you want to connect to.

3 Click **Connect** to connect to the wireless network.

Tip

Can I connect to a wireless network when I am away from home or the office?

Increasing numbers of public places, such as coffee shops, hotels and airports, are allowing people to connect to the Internet through wireless networks set up on their premises. These locations are called wi-fi hotspots, or wireless hotspots, and provide a convenient way of accessing the Internet while you are away from home or the office.

Tip

How can I ensure a good connection to a wireless network?

When connecting to a wireless network, the strength of the radio signal used to connect to the network is very important. For the best signal, try to avoid obstacles between your computer and the wireless router or wireless access point. Also try to avoid using devices that use the same frequency as your wireless network, such as a cordless phone, near the network.

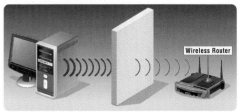

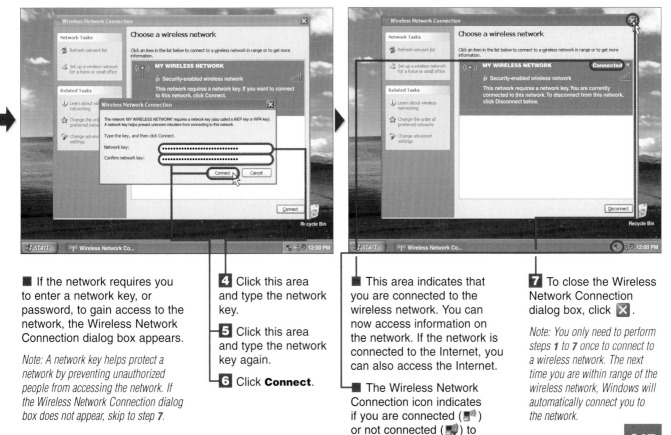

■ If the network requires you to enter a network key, or password, to gain access to the network, the Wireless Network Connection dialog box appears.

Note: A network key helps protect a network by preventing unauthorized people from accessing the network. If the Wireless Network Connection dialog box does not appear, skip to step 7.

4 Click this area and type the network key.

5 Click this area and type the network key again.

6 Click **Connect**.

■ This area indicates that you are connected to the wireless network. You can now access information on the network. If the network is connected to the Internet, you can also access the Internet.

■ The Wireless Network Connection icon indicates if you are connected (📶) or not connected (📵) to a wireless network.

7 To close the Wireless Network Connection dialog box, click ❌.

Note: You only need to perform steps 1 to 7 once to connect to a wireless network. The next time you are within range of the wireless network, Windows will automatically connect you to the network.

CHAPTER 11

Browse the Web

In this chapter, you will learn how to browse through information on the Web, search for specific information on the Web, keep a list of your favorite Web pages, and much more.

INTRODUCTION TO THE WEB

The Web consists of a huge collection of electronic documents stored on computers around the world. The Web is also known as the World Wide Web.

Web Page

A Web page is a document on the Web. Web pages can include text, pictures, sounds and videos. You can find Web pages on every subject imaginable. Web pages can offer information such as newspaper and magazine articles, movie clips, recipes, job listings, travel guides, airline schedules and more.

Web Server

A Web server is a computer that stores Web pages and makes the pages available on the Web for other people to view.

URL

Each Web page has a unique address, called a Uniform Resource Locator (URL). You can display any Web page if you know its URL.

The three letters at the end of a Web page address can help identify the type of organization or the country that offers a Web page. Here are some common endings.

.com (commercial)
.edu (educational)
.gov (government)
.org (organization)
.au (Australia)
.uk (United Kingdom)

Web Site

A Web site is a collection of Web pages maintained by a company, school, government agency, non-profit organization or individual.

Web Browser

A Web browser is a program that allows you to view and explore information on the Web. Windows XP comes with the Microsoft Internet Explorer Web browser, which is currently the most popular Web browser.

Links

Web pages contain highlighted text or images, called links or hyperlinks, that connect to other pages on the Web. You can select a link to display a Web page located on the same computer or on a computer across the city, country or world.

Links allow you to easily navigate through a vast amount of information by jumping from one Web page to another, which is known as "browsing the Web."

Connecting to the Internet

You use a company called an Internet Service Provider (ISP) to connect to the Internet. Once you pay an ISP to connect to the Internet, you can view and exchange information on the Internet free of charge.

Most people connect to the Internet by using a cable modem, a Digital Subscriber Line (DSL) or a modem. A cable modem connects to the Internet using the same type of cable that attaches to a television set, while a digital subscriber line uses a high-speed digital telephone line. A modem offers the slowest type of connection and transmits information over telephone lines.

You can start
Internet Explorer
to browse
through the
information
on the Web.

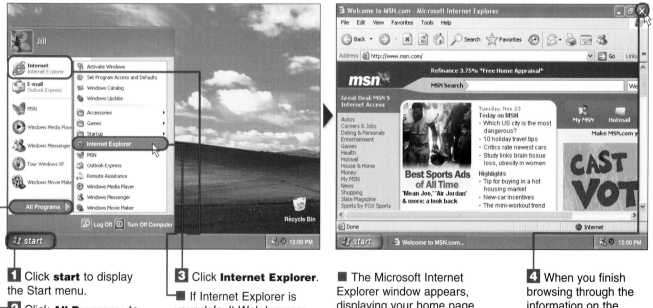

1 Click **start** to display
the Start menu.

2 Click **All Programs** to
view a list of the programs
on your computer.

3 Click **Internet Explorer**.

■ If Internet Explorer is
your default Web browser,
you can click **Internet**
instead of performing
steps **2** and **3**.

■ The Microsoft Internet
Explorer window appears,
displaying your home page.

*Note: Your home page is the Web
page that appears each time you
start Internet Explorer. To change
your home page, see page 258.*

4 When you finish
browsing through the
information on the
Web, click ☒ to close
the Microsoft Internet
Explorer window.

SELECT A LINK

A link connects text or an image on one Web page to another Web page. When you select the text or image, the linked Web page appears.

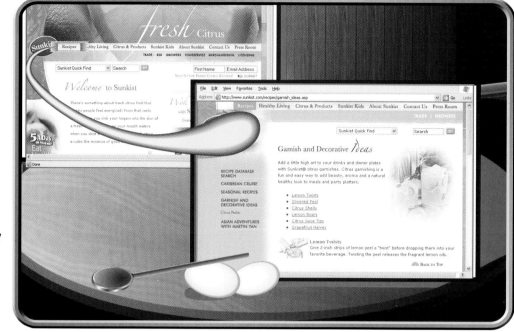

Links allow you to easily navigate through a vast amount of information by jumping from one Web page to another. Links are also known as hyperlinks.

SELECT A LINK

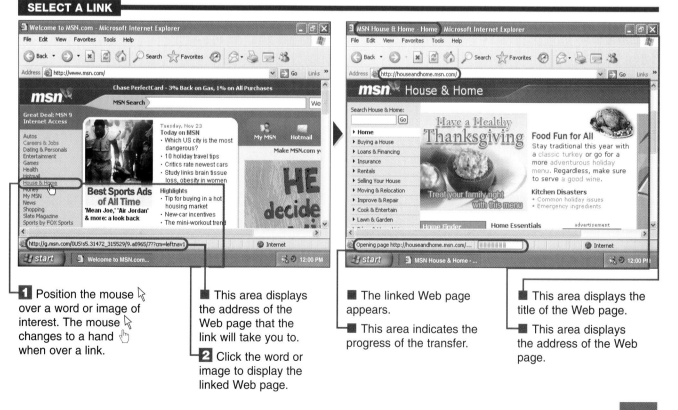

1 Position the mouse over a word or image of interest. The mouse changes to a hand when over a link.

■ This area displays the address of the Web page that the link will take you to.

2 Click the word or image to display the linked Web page.

■ The linked Web page appears.

■ This area indicates the progress of the transfer.

■ This area displays the title of the Web page.

■ This area displays the address of the Web page.

DISPLAY A SPECIFIC WEB PAGE

You can display any Web page on the Web that you have heard or read about.

You need to know the address of the Web page that you want to view. Each page on the Web has a unique address.

DISPLAY A SPECIFIC WEB PAGE

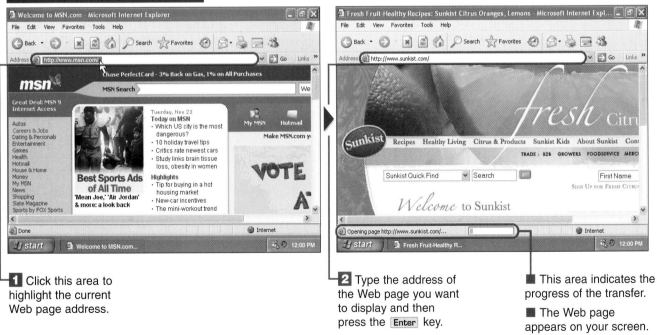

1 Click this area to highlight the current Web page address.

2 Type the address of the Web page you want to display and then press the Enter key.

■ This area indicates the progress of the transfer.

■ The Web page appears on your screen.

Tip

When displaying Web pages, what type of content does Internet Explorer block?

Internet Explorer blocks most pop-up windows from appearing. Pop-up windows are small windows that are often used to display advertisements and usually appear as soon as you visit a Web site. When blocking pop-up windows, Internet Explorer may block some useful pop-up windows. For example, if you click an image to see a larger version of the image, Internet Explorer may block the pop-up window that displays the larger image.

Internet Explorer also prevents Web sites from downloading potentially harmful files and running software on your computer without your knowledge. When blocking some content, Internet Explorer may prevent some Web pages from displaying properly.

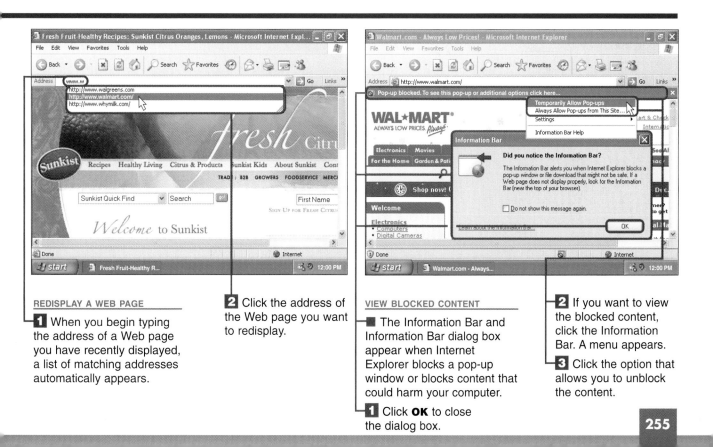

REDISPLAY A WEB PAGE

1 When you begin typing the address of a Web page you have recently displayed, a list of matching addresses automatically appears.

2 Click the address of the Web page you want to redisplay.

VIEW BLOCKED CONTENT

■ The Information Bar and Information Bar dialog box appear when Internet Explorer blocks a pop-up window or blocks content that could harm your computer.

1 Click **OK** to close the dialog box.

2 If you want to view the blocked content, click the Information Bar. A menu appears.

3 Click the option that allows you to unblock the content.

STOP TRANSFER OF A WEB PAGE

If a Web page is taking a long time to appear on your screen, you can stop the transfer of the Web page.

You may also want to stop the transfer of a Web page if you realize a page contains information that does not interest you.

STOP TRANSFER OF A WEB PAGE

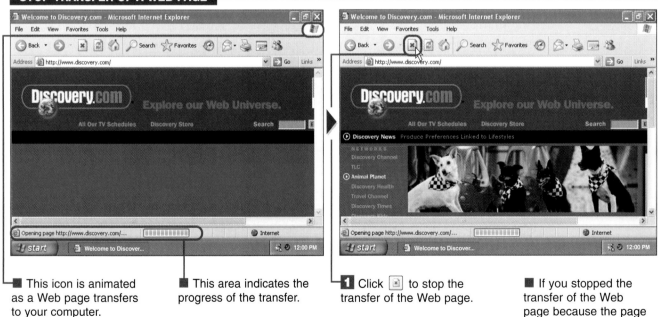

■ This icon is animated as a Web page transfers to your computer.

■ This area indicates the progress of the transfer.

1 Click 🗷 to stop the transfer of the Web page.

■ If you stopped the transfer of the Web page because the page was taking too long to appear, you may want to try displaying the page at a later time.

You can easily move back and forth through the Web pages you have viewed since you last started Internet Explorer.

MOVE THROUGH WEB PAGES

MOVE BACK

1 Click **Back** to return to the last Web page you viewed.

Note: The Back button is only available if you have viewed more than one Web page since you last started Internet Explorer.

MOVE FORWARD

1 Click ⊙ to move forward through the Web pages you have viewed.

Note: The ⊙ button is only available after you use the Back button to return to a Web page.

DISPLAY AND CHANGE YOUR HOME PAGE

You can display and change the Web page that appears each time you start Internet Explorer. This page is called your home page.

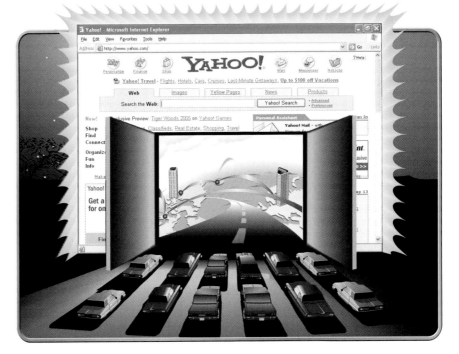

DISPLAY AND CHANGE YOUR HOME PAGE

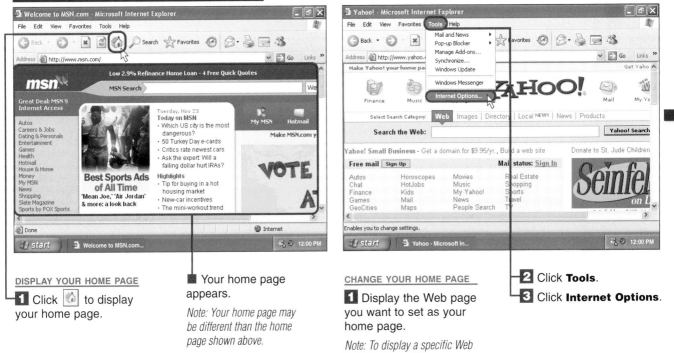

DISPLAY YOUR HOME PAGE

1 Click 🏠 to display your home page.

■ Your home page appears.

Note: Your home page may be different than the home page shown above.

CHANGE YOUR HOME PAGE

1 Display the Web page you want to set as your home page.

Note: To display a specific Web page, see page 254.

2 Click **Tools**.

3 Click **Internet Options**.

Tip

Which Web page should I set as my home page?

You can set any page on the Web as your home page. The Web page you choose should be a page you want to frequently visit. You may want to choose a Web page that provides a good starting point for exploring the Web, such as www.yahoo.com, or a page that provides information relevant to your personal interests or work.

Tip

How can I once again use my original home page?

To once again use your original home page, perform steps **2** to **5** starting on page 258, except select **Use Default** in step **4**. In most cases, the www.msn.com Web page is the original home page.

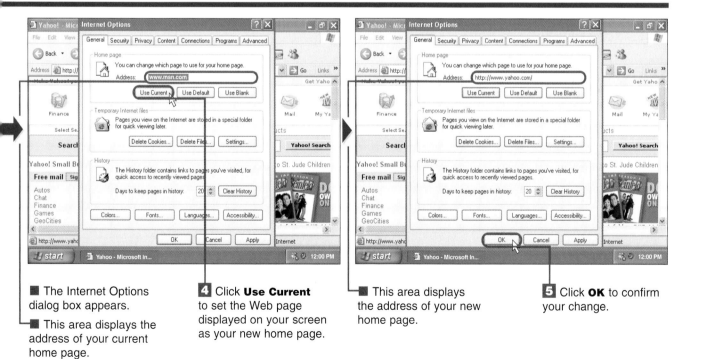

■ The Internet Options dialog box appears.

■ This area displays the address of your current home page.

4 Click **Use Current** to set the Web page displayed on your screen as your new home page.

■ This area displays the address of your new home page.

5 Click **OK** to confirm your change.

SEARCH THE WEB

You can search for Web pages that discuss topics of interest to you.

Web sites that allow you to search for information on the Web are known as search engines. Google is the most popular search engine on the Web. Other popular search engines include:

Yahoo! (www.yahoo.com)

MSN (www.msn.com)

SEARCH THE WEB

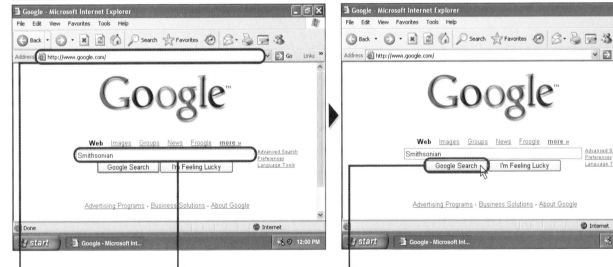

1 To visit the Google Web site, click this area and type **www.google.com**. Then press the Enter key.

■ The Google Web page appears.

2 Click this area and type the words that best describe the information you want to find. Google will find Web pages that contain all the words you type.

*Note: To find words that appear side by side on a Web page, surround the words with quotation marks (").
For example, type "Star Wars."*

3 Click **Google Search** or press the Enter key to start the search.

*Note: You can click **I'm Feeling Lucky** if you want to bypass the list of matching Web pages and display the first matching Web page that Google finds.*

Tip

Can I use Google to search for images and other types of information on the Web?

Yes. Google allows you to search for various types of information on the Web. Before performing a search, you can click the type of information you want to search for.

Web
Search for Web pages. Google is automatically set up to search for Web pages.

Images
Search for images, such as photographs and drawings.

Groups
Search for discussion groups that allow you to communicate with people who share similar interests.

News
Search for news of interest and display the top news headlines.

Froogle
Search for products you can purchase.

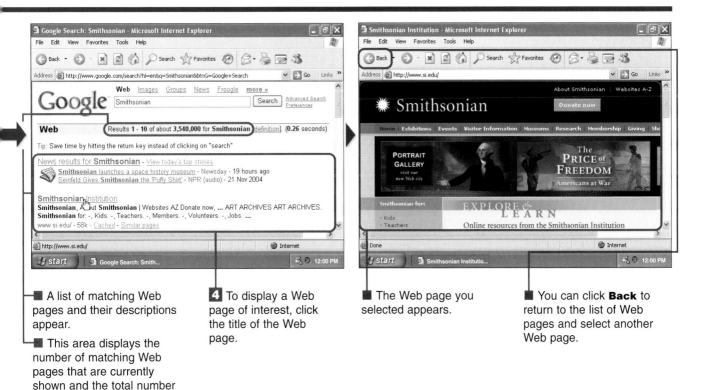

■ A list of matching Web pages and their descriptions appear.

■ This area displays the number of matching Web pages that are currently shown and the total number of matching Web pages.

4 To display a Web page of interest, click the title of the Web page.

■ The Web page you selected appears.

■ You can click **Back** to return to the list of Web pages and select another Web page.

DISPLAY HISTORY OF VIEWED WEB PAGES

Internet Explorer uses the History list to keep track of the Web pages you have recently viewed. You can display the History list at any time to redisplay a Web page.

DISPLAY HISTORY OF VIEWED WEB PAGES

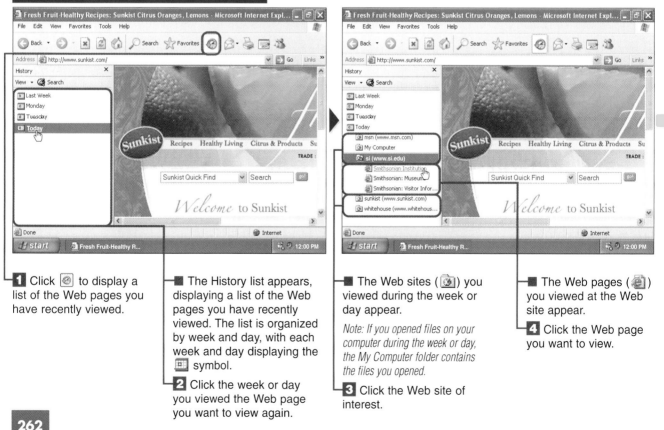

1 Click to display a list of the Web pages you have recently viewed.

■ The History list appears, displaying a list of the Web pages you have recently viewed. The list is organized by week and day, with each week and day displaying the 📅 symbol.

2 Click the week or day you viewed the Web page you want to view again.

■ The Web sites (📑) you viewed during the week or day appear.

Note: If you opened files on your computer during the week or day, the My Computer folder contains the files you opened.

3 Click the Web site of interest.

■ The Web pages (📄) you viewed at the Web site appear.

4 Click the Web page you want to view.

Tip

How long does the History list keep track of the Web pages I have viewed?

By default, the History list keeps track of the Web pages you have viewed over the last 20 days.

1 To change the number of days the History list keeps track of the Web pages you have viewed, perform steps **1** and **2** on page 263 to display the Internet Options dialog box.

2 Double-click this area and type a new number of days.

3 Click **OK** to confirm your change.

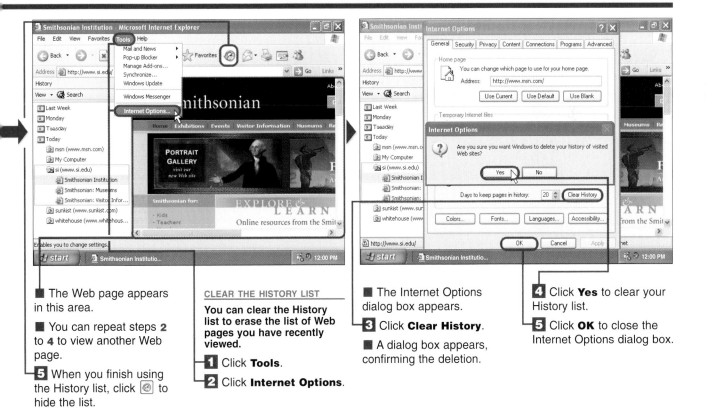

■ The Web page appears in this area.

■ You can repeat steps **2** to **4** to view another Web page.

5 When you finish using the History list, click 📷 to hide the list.

CLEAR THE HISTORY LIST

You can clear the History list to erase the list of Web pages you have recently viewed.

1 Click **Tools**.

2 Click **Internet Options**.

■ The Internet Options dialog box appears.

3 Click **Clear History**.

■ A dialog box appears, confirming the deletion.

4 Click **Yes** to clear your History list.

5 Click **OK** to close the Internet Options dialog box.

ADD A WEB PAGE TO FAVORITES

You can use the Favorites feature to create a list of Web pages that you frequently visit. The Favorites feature allows you to quickly display a favorite Web page at any time.

Selecting Web pages from your list of favorites saves you from having to remember and constantly retype the same Web page addresses over and over again.

ADD A WEB PAGE TO FAVORITES

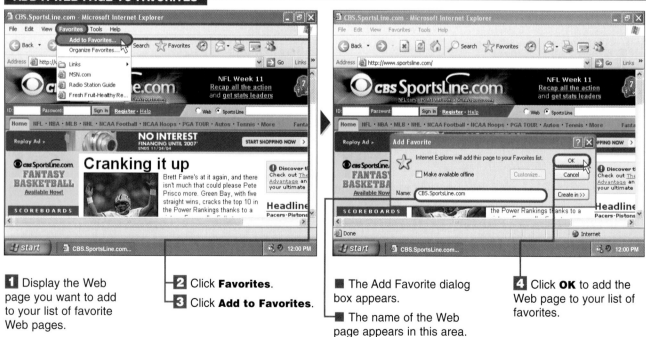

1 Display the Web page you want to add to your list of favorite Web pages.

Note: To display a specific Web page, see page 254.

2 Click **Favorites**.

3 Click **Add to Favorites**.

■ The Add Favorite dialog box appears.

■ The name of the Web page appears in this area.

4 Click **OK** to add the Web page to your list of favorites.

Tip

Does Internet Explorer automatically add Web pages to my list of favorites?

Yes. Internet Explorer automatically adds the Links folder and two Web pages to your list of favorites.

Links folder

Contains several useful Web pages, such as the Free Hotmail page, which allows you to set up and use a free e-mail account.

MSN.com

A Web site provided by Microsoft that offers a great starting point for exploring the Web.

Radio Station Guide

Allows you to listen to radio stations from around the world that broadcast on the Internet.

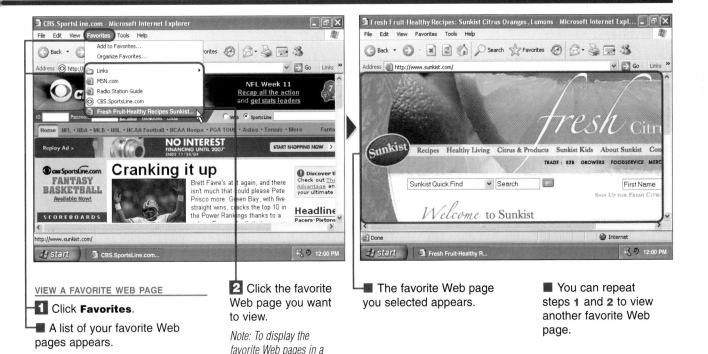

VIEW A FAVORITE WEB PAGE

1 Click **Favorites**.

■ A list of your favorite Web pages appears.

Note: If you have a long list of favorite Web pages, you can position the mouse over the bottom of the menu to view any hidden Web pages in the list.

2 Click the favorite Web page you want to view.

Note: To display the favorite Web pages in a folder, click the folder (📁) before performing step 2.

■ The favorite Web page you selected appears.

■ You can repeat steps **1** and **2** to view another favorite Web page.

CHAPTER 12

Exchange E-Mail

You can exchange e-mail messages with friends, family members and colleagues from around the world. In this chapter, you will learn how to read and send messages, use the address book and more.

You can start
Outlook Express to
open and read the
contents of your
e-mail messages.

The first time you start
Outlook Express, a
wizard will appear if you
have not yet set up your
e-mail account. Follow
the instructions in the
wizard to set up your
e-mail account.

READ MESSAGES

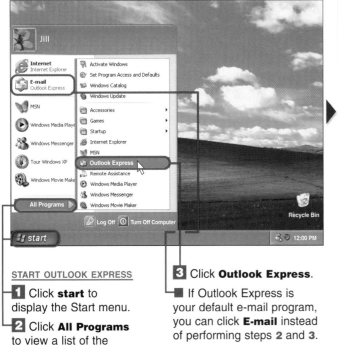

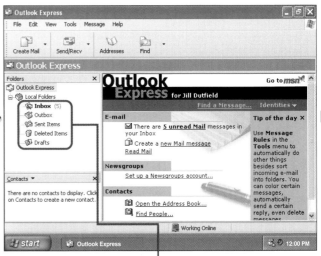

START OUTLOOK EXPRESS

1 Click **start** to
display the Start menu.

2 Click **All Programs**
to view a list of the
programs on your
computer.

3 Click **Outlook Express**.

■ If Outlook Express is
your default e-mail program,
you can click **E-mail** instead
of performing steps **2** and **3**.

■ The Outlook Express
window appears.

READ MESSAGES

■ This area displays the
folders that contain your
messages.

*Note: A number in brackets beside
a folder indicates how many unread
messages the folder contains. The
number disappears when you have
read all the messages in the folder.*

Tip

What folders does Outlook Express use to store my messages?

Inbox
Stores messages sent to you.

Outbox
Temporarily stores messages that have not yet been sent.

Sent Items
Stores copies of messages you have sent.

Deleted Items
Stores messages you have deleted.

Drafts
Stores messages you have not yet completed.

Tip

Why does Outlook Express block pictures and other content in my e-mail messages?

Outlook Express blocks pictures and other content from displaying in your messages to help you avoid viewing potentially offensive material. Blocking content also helps reduce the amount of junk mail you receive. If pictures are displayed in junk mail, a message is sent back to the sender, notifying the sender that your e-mail address works, which often results in you receiving more junk mail.

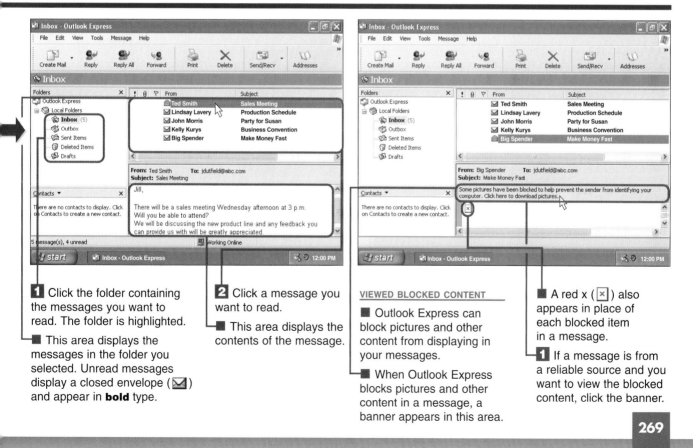

1 Click the folder containing the messages you want to read. The folder is highlighted.

■ This area displays the messages in the folder you selected. Unread messages display a closed envelope ( ) and appear in **bold** type.

2 Click a message you want to read.

■ This area displays the contents of the message.

VIEWED BLOCKED CONTENT

■ Outlook Express can block pictures and other content from displaying in your messages.

■ When Outlook Express blocks pictures and other content in a message, a banner appears in this area.

■ A red x (☒) also appears in place of each blocked item in a message.

1 If a message is from a reliable source and you want to view the blocked content, click the banner.

SEND A MESSAGE

You can send a message to express an idea or request information.

To practice sending a message, you can send a message to yourself.

SEND A MESSAGE

1 Click **Create Mail** to send a new message.

■ The New Message window appears.

2 Type the e-mail address of the person you want to receive the message.

3 To send a copy of the message to a person who is not directly involved but would be interested in the message, click this area and then type the person's e-mail address.

Note: To send the message to more than one person, separate each e-mail address with a semicolon (;).

Tip

How can I express emotions in my e-mail messages?

You can use special combinations of characters, called smileys, to express emotions in e-mail messages. These characters resemble human faces if you turn them sideways.

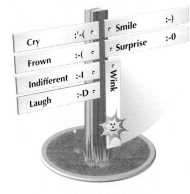

Emotion	Smiley
Cry	:'-(
Frown	:-(
Indifferent	:-I
Laugh	:-D
Smile	:-)
Surprise	:-0
Wink	;-)

Tip

What should I consider when sending a message?

A MESSAGE WRITTEN IN CAPITAL LETTERS IS ANNOYING AND DIFFICULT TO READ. THIS IS CALLED SHOUTING. Always use upper and lower case letters when typing e-mail messages.

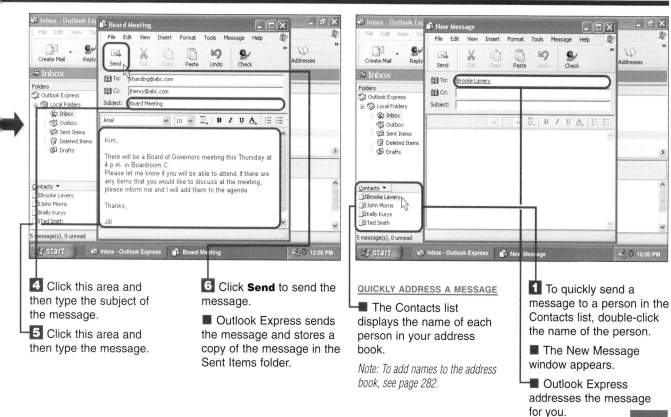

4 Click this area and then type the subject of the message.

5 Click this area and then type the message.

6 Click **Send** to send the message.

■ Outlook Express sends the message and stores a copy of the message in the Sent Items folder.

QUICKLY ADDRESS A MESSAGE

■ The Contacts list displays the name of each person in your address book.

Note: To add names to the address book, see page 282.

1 To quickly send a message to a person in the Contacts list, double-click the name of the person.

■ The New Message window appears.

■ Outlook Express addresses the message for you.

SAVE A DRAFT OF A MESSAGE

You can save a draft of a message so you can send the message at a later time.

Saving a draft of a message allows you to later review and make changes to a message.

SAVE A DRAFT OF A MESSAGE

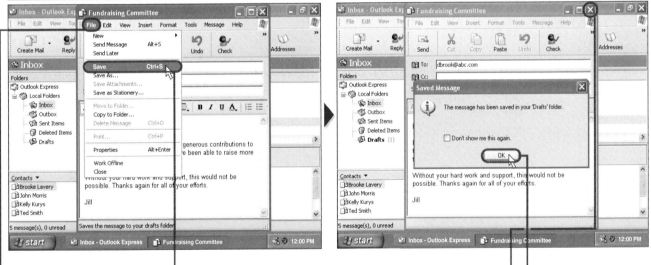

1 To create a message, perform steps **1** to **5** starting on page 270.

2 Click **File**.

3 Click **Save** to save the message as a draft so you can send the message at a later time.

■ The Saved Message dialog box appears, stating that your message was saved in your Drafts folder.

4 Click **OK** to close the dialog box.

5 Click **X** to close the window that displays the message.

Tip

I am still not ready to send a draft message. What should I do?

While reviewing a message you have saved as a draft, you can once again save the message so you can send the message at a later time. You can review a draft message as many times as you need until you are happy with the contents of the message. To save changes you have made to a draft message and close the message window, repeat steps **2** to **5** on page 272.

Tip

I no longer want to send a message I saved as a draft. How can I delete the message?

If you no longer want to send a message you saved as a draft, you can delete the message from the Drafts folder as you would delete any message. To delete a message, see page 281.

SEND A DRAFT MESSAGE

■ When you save a draft of a message, Outlook Express stores the message in the Drafts folder until you are ready to send the message.

1 Click the **Drafts** folder to display the messages in the folder.

■ This area lists the messages you have saved as drafts.

2 Double-click the message you want to send.

■ A window appears, displaying the contents of the message. You can review and make changes to the message.

3 To send the message, click **Send**.

■ Outlook Express removes the message from the Drafts folder and places a copy of the message in the Sent Items folder.

REPLY TO A MESSAGE

You can reply to a message to answer a question, express an opinion or supply additional information.

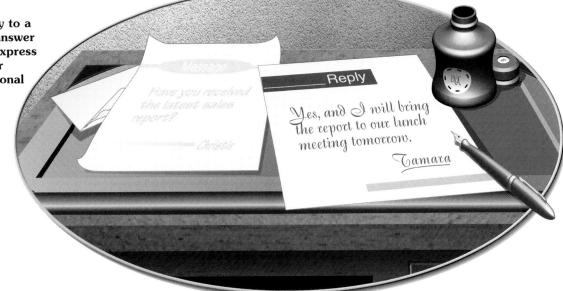

REPLY TO A MESSAGE

1 Click the message you want to reply to.

2 Click the reply option you want to use.

Reply
Sends a reply to only the author.

Reply All
Sends a reply to the author and everyone who received the original message.

■ A window appears for you to compose your reply.

■ Outlook Express fills in the e-mail address(es) for you.

■ Outlook Express also fills in the subject, starting the subject with **Re:**.

Tip

How can I save time when typing a message?

You can use abbreviations for words and phrases to save time when typing messages. Here are some commonly used abbreviations.

Abbreviation	Meaning	Abbreviation	Meaning
BTW	by the way	LOL	laughing out loud
FAQ	frequently asked questions	MOTAS	member of the appropriate sex
FOAF	friend of a friend	MOTOS	member of the opposite sex
FWIW	for what it's worth		
FYI	for your information	MOTSS	member of the same sex
IMHO	in my humble opinion	ROTFL	rolling on the floor laughing
IMO	in my opinion		
IOW	in other words	SO	significant other
L8R	later	WRT	with respect to

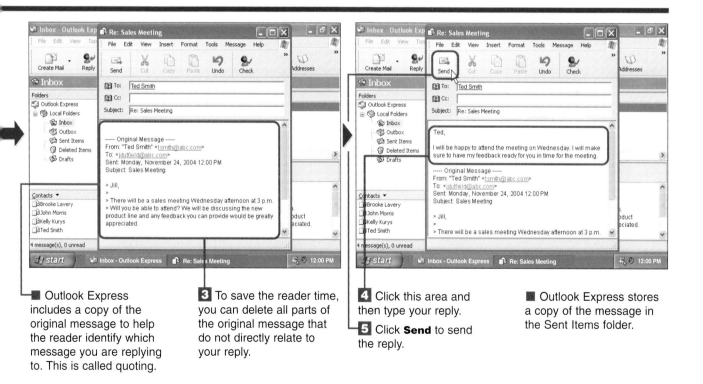

■ Outlook Express includes a copy of the original message to help the reader identify which message you are replying to. This is called quoting.

3 To save the reader time, you can delete all parts of the original message that do not directly relate to your reply.

4 Click this area and then type your reply.

5 Click **Send** to send the reply.

■ Outlook Express stores a copy of the message in the Sent Items folder.

FORWARD A MESSAGE

After reading a message, you can add comments and then forward the message to a friend, family member or colleague.

Forwarding a message is useful when you know another person would be interested in a message.

FORWARD A MESSAGE

1 Click the message you want to forward.

2 Click **Forward**.

■ A window appears, displaying the contents of the message you are forwarding.

3 Type the e-mail address of the person you want to receive the message.

■ Outlook Express fills in the subject for you, starting the subject with **Fw:**.

4 Click this area and then type any comments about the message you are forwarding.

5 Click **Send** to forward the message.

CHECK FOR NEW MESSAGES

If you are waiting for an important message, you can have Outlook Express immediately check for new messages.

You can also change how often Outlook Express checks for new messages. Outlook Express initially checks for new messages every 30 minutes when you are connected to the Internet.

CHECK FOR NEW MESSAGES

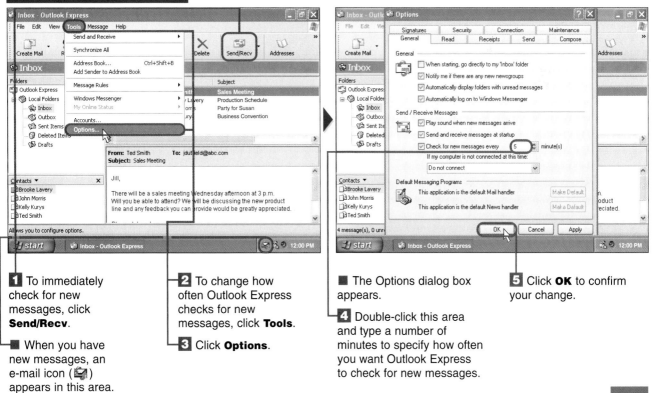

1 To immediately check for new messages, click **Send/Recv**.

■ When you have new messages, an e-mail icon (📧) appears in this area.

2 To change how often Outlook Express checks for new messages, click **Tools**.

3 Click **Options**.

■ The Options dialog box appears.

4 Double-click this area and type a number of minutes to specify how often you want Outlook Express to check for new messages.

5 Click **OK** to confirm your change.

ATTACH A FILE TO A MESSAGE

You can attach a file to a message you are sending. Attaching a file to a message is useful when you want to include additional information with a message.

From:
To:
Subject:
Cc:

This year's charity golf
was a huge success! I would like to
thank all the volunteers for organizing
a fantastic event. This year's winner was
Mike Taylor. I have attached a photo of
one of his winning drives!

ATTACH A FILE TO A MESSAGE

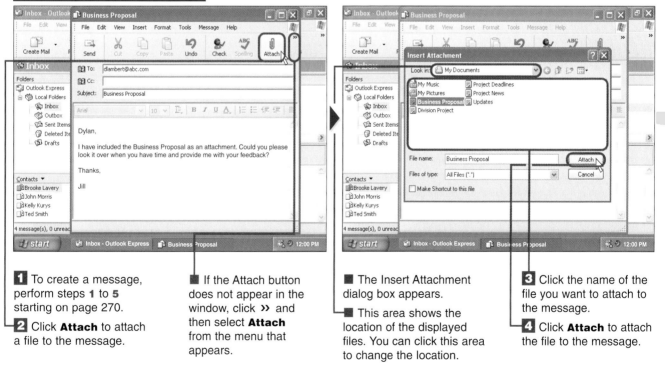

1 To create a message, perform steps **1** to **5** starting on page 270.

2 Click **Attach** to attach a file to the message.

■ If the Attach button does not appear in the window, click **»** and then select **Attach** from the menu that appears.

■ The Insert Attachment dialog box appears.

■ This area shows the location of the displayed files. You can click this area to change the location.

3 Click the name of the file you want to attach to the message.

4 Click **Attach** to attach the file to the message.

Tip

What types of files can I attach to a message?

You can attach many types of files to a message, including documents, photos, videos, sounds and programs. The computer receiving the message must have the necessary hardware and software installed to display or play the file you attach.

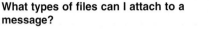

Tip

Can I attach a large file to a message?

The company that provides your e-mail account will usually limit the size of the messages that you can send and receive over the Internet. Most companies do not allow you to send or receive messages larger than 10 MB, which includes all attached files.

LIMIT
10 MB

■ This area displays the name and size of the file you selected.

■ To attach additional files to the message, perform steps **2** to **4** for each file you want to attach.

5 Click **Send** to send the message.

■ Outlook Express will send the message and the attached file(s) to the e-mail address(es) you specified.

OPEN AN ATTACHED FILE

You can easily open a file attached to a message you receive.

Before opening an attached file, make sure the file is from a reliable source. Some files can contain viruses, which can damage the information on your computer. You can use an antivirus program to check files for viruses. To obtain an antivirus program, see page 219.

OPEN AN ATTACHED FILE

1 Click a message with an attached file. A message with an attached file displays a paper clip icon (📎).

2 Click the paper clip icon (📎) in this area to display a list of the files attached to the message.

3 Click the name of the file you want to open.

■ A dialog box may appear, asking if you want to open the file.

4 Click **Open** to open the file.

*Note: If you no longer want to open the file, click **Cancel**.*

You can delete a
message you no
longer need. Deleting
messages prevents
your folders from
becoming cluttered
with messages.

DELETE A MESSAGE

1 Click the message
you want to delete.

2 Click **Delete** to delete
the message.

■ Outlook Express removes
the message from the current
folder and places the message
in the Deleted Items folder.

*Note: Deleting a message from the
Deleted Items folder will permanently
remove the message from your
computer.*

■ When you delete
a message from the
Deleted Items folder,
a dialog box will
appear, confirming the
deletion. Click **Yes** to
delete the message.

ADD A NAME TO THE ADDRESS BOOK

You can use the address book to store the e-mail addresses of people you frequently send messages to.

Selecting a name from the address book helps you avoid typing mistakes when entering an e-mail address. Typing mistakes can result in a message being delivered to the wrong person or being returned to you.

1 Click **Addresses** to display the address book.

■ The Address Book window appears.

■ This area displays the name and e-mail address of each person in your address book.

2 Click **New** to add a name to the address book.

3 Click **New Contact**.

■ The Properties dialog box appears.

Can Outlook Express automatically add names to my address book?

Yes. Each time you reply to a message, the name and e-mail address of the person who sent the message is automatically added to your address book.

How do I delete a name from the address book?

To delete a person's name from the address book, click their name in the Address Book window and then press the `Delete` key. When a confirmation dialog box appears, click **Yes** to confirm the deletion. Outlook Express permanently removes the person's name from your address book.

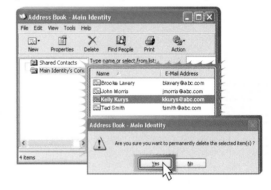

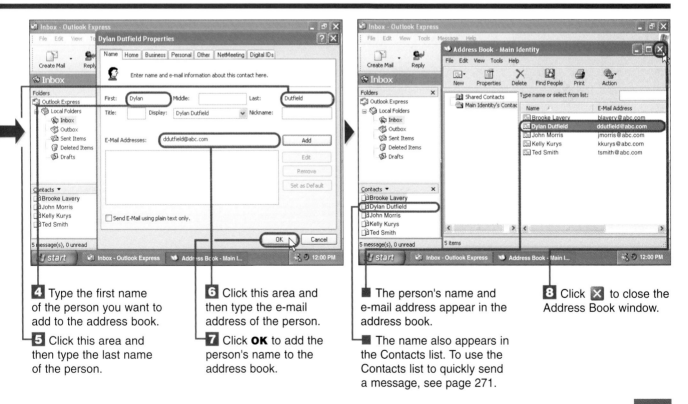

4 Type the first name of the person you want to add to the address book.

5 Click this area and then type the last name of the person.

6 Click this area and then type the e-mail address of the person.

7 Click **OK** to add the person's name to the address book.

■ The person's name and e-mail address appear in the address book.

■ The name also appears in the Contacts list. To use the Contacts list to quickly send a message, see page 271.

8 Click ✕ to close the Address Book window.

ADD A GROUP TO THE ADDRESS BOOK

You can add a group to your address book so you can quickly send the same messages to every person in the group.

You can create as many groups as you need. A person can belong to more than one group.

ADD A GROUP TO THE ADDRESS BOOK

1 Click **Addresses** to display the address book.

■ The Address Book window appears.

2 Click **New** to add a group to the address book.

3 Click **New Group**.

■ The Properties dialog box appears.

4 Type a name for your group.

5 Click **Select Members** to select the people from your address book that you want to include in the group.

Note: To add names to the address book, see page 282.

Tip **How do I send a message to a group?**

When composing a message, you can type the name of the group to send the message to every person in the group. To compose and send a message, see page 270.

Tip **How do I delete a group from the address book?**

To delete a group from the address book, click the plus sign (⊞) beside the Main Identity's Contacts folder in the Address Book window to view a list of the groups you have created. Then click the name of the group you want to delete and press the Delete key. In the confirmation dialog box that appears, click **Yes** to confirm the deletion. Outlook Express will not remove the people within the group from your address book.

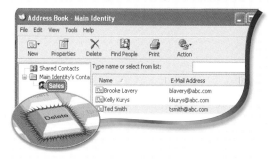

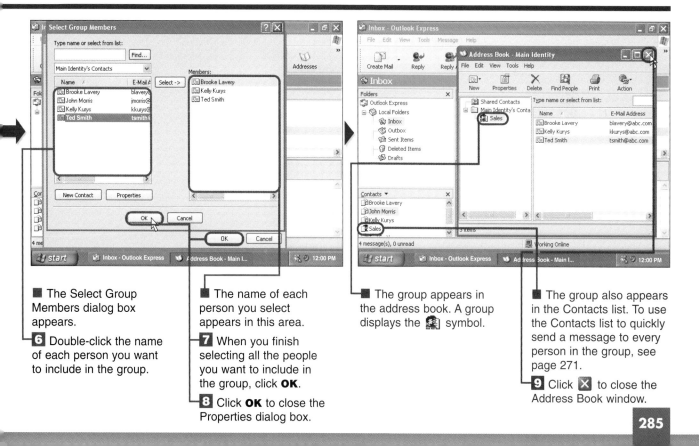

■ The Select Group Members dialog box appears.

6 Double-click the name of each person you want to include in the group.

■ The name of each person you select appears in this area.

7 When you finish selecting all the people you want to include in the group, click **OK**.

8 Click **OK** to close the Properties dialog box.

■ The group appears in the address book. A group displays the 🔁 symbol.

■ The group also appears in the Contacts list. To use the Contacts list to quickly send a message to every person in the group, see page 271.

9 Click ✕ to close the Address Book window.

SELECT A NAME FROM THE ADDRESS BOOK

When sending a message, you can select the name of the person you want to receive the message from the address book.

jthomas@abc.com

E-MAIL AD...

Name	Address
Jack Thomas	jthomas@abc.com
Sue Jones	sjones@abc.com
Bill Carey	bcarey@abc.com
Henry Kim	hkim@abc.com

Name	Address
Silvia Parker	sparker@abc.com
Joy Smart	jsmart@abc.com

Selecting names from the address book saves you from having to remember the e-mail addresses of people you often send messages to.

SELECT A NAME FROM THE ADDRESS BOOK

1 Click **Create Mail** to create a new message.

■ The New Message window appears.

2 To select a name from the address book, click **To:**.

■ The Select Recipients dialog box appears.

3 Click the name of the person you want to receive the message.

4 Click **To:**.

■ This area displays the name of the person you selected.

■ You can repeat steps **3** and **4** for each person you want to receive the message.

Tip

How can I address a message I want to send?

To

Sends the message to the person you specify.

Carbon Copy (Cc)

Sends an exact copy of the message to a person who is not directly involved, but would be interested in the message.

Blind Carbon Copy (Bcc)

Sends an exact copy of the message to a person without anyone else knowing that the person received the message.

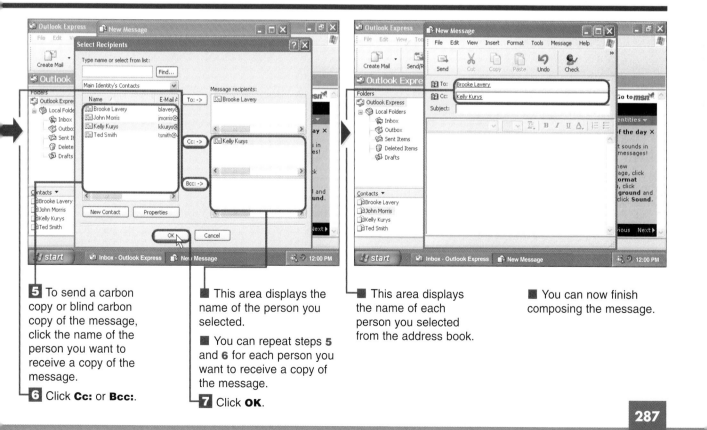

■ **5** To send a carbon copy or blind carbon copy of the message, click the name of the person you want to receive a copy of the message.

■ **6** Click **Cc:** or **Bcc:**.

■ This area displays the name of the person you selected.

■ You can repeat steps **5** and **6** for each person you want to receive a copy of the message.

■ **7** Click **OK**.

■ This area displays the name of each person you selected from the address book.

■ You can now finish composing the message.

ADD A SIGNATURE TO MESSAGES

You can have Outlook Express add personal information to the end of every message you send. This information is called a signature.

A signature saves you from having to type the same information every time you send a message.

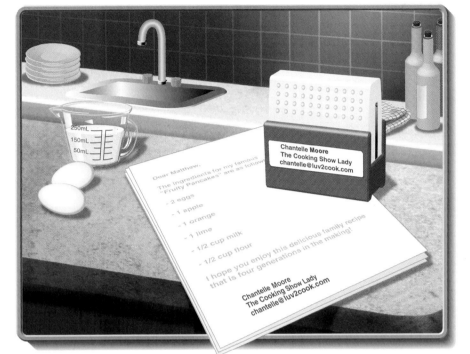

ADD A SIGNATURE TO MESSAGES

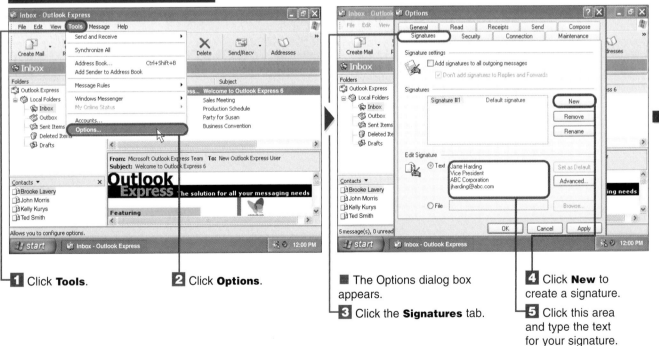

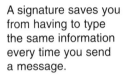

1 Click **Tools**.

2 Click **Options**.

■ The Options dialog box appears.

3 Click the **Signatures** tab.

4 Click **New** to create a signature.

5 Click this area and type the text for your signature.

> **Tip**
>
> **What can I include in a signature?**
>
> A signature can include information such as your name, e-mail address, mailing address, phone number, occupation, favorite quotation and Web page address. As a courtesy to people who will receive your messages, you should limit your signature to four or five lines.

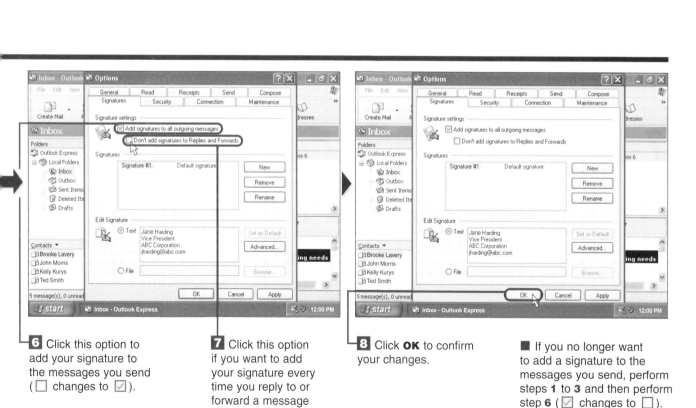

6 Click this option to add your signature to the messages you send (☐ changes to ☑).

7 Click this option if you want to add your signature every time you reply to or forward a message (☑ changes to ☐).

8 Click **OK** to confirm your changes.

■ If you no longer want to add a signature to the messages you send, perform steps **1** to **3** and then perform step **6** (☑ changes to ☐). Then press the **Enter** key.

CHAPTER 13

Exchange Instant Messages

Read this chapter to discover how to use Windows Messenger to exchange instant messages and files with other people over the Internet.

Windows Messenger

START WINDOWS MESSENGER

You can use Windows Messenger to see when your friends are online and exchange instant messages with them.

START WINDOWS MESSENGER

1 Click **start** to display the Start menu.

2 Click **All Programs** to view a list of the programs on your computer.

3 Click **Windows Messenger**.

■ You can also start Windows Messenger by double-clicking the Windows Messenger icon (🎮 or 🎮).

Note: If the Windows Messenger icon is hidden, you can click ◀ on the taskbar to display the icon.

■ The Windows Messenger window appears.

4 Click this link to sign in to Windows Messenger.

Note: If the .Net Passport Wizard appears, see the top of page 293 for information on the wizard. If you are already signed in to Windows Messenger, you do not need to perform step 4.

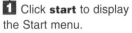

Tip

Why does a wizard appear when I try to sign in to Windows Messenger?

The first time you try to sign in to Windows Messenger, the .Net Passport Wizard appears, helping you add a Passport to your user account. You must add a Passport to your user account to use Windows Messenger. Follow the instructions in the wizard to add a Passport to your user account.

Tip

If I close the Windows Messenger window, can I still receive instant messages?

Yes. If you are signed in to Windows Messenger and you close the Windows Messenger window to free up space on your screen, you will still be able to receive instant messages. To close the Windows Messenger window, click ☒ in the window. To redisplay the Windows Messenger window at any time, double-click its icon (👤 or 👥) in the taskbar.

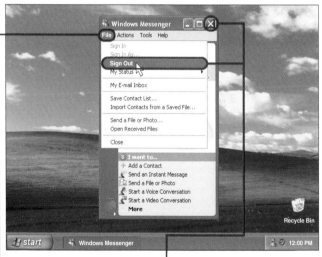

■ If you have added contacts to your contacts list, this area displays the contacts. Windows Messenger indicates if each contact is online (👤) or offline (👤).

Note: To add contacts to your list of contacts, see page 294.

■ After you sign in to Windows Messenger for the first time, Windows Messenger will sign you in automatically each time you start your computer and connect to the Internet. This allows you to start sending instant messages right away.

SIGN OUT OF WINDOWS MESSENGER

■ When you finish using Windows Messenger, you can sign out of the service. Signing out of Windows Messenger prevents other people from sending you instant messages.

1 Click **File**.

2 Click **Sign Out**.

3 Click ☒ to close the Windows Messenger window.

Note: The Windows Messenger icon changes from 👤 to 👥 to indicate that you have signed out.

ADD A CONTACT

You can add people
to your contact list
to see when they are
online and available
to exchange instant
messages.

Each person you want
to add to your contact list
requires a Passport, which
can be obtained when
Windows Messenger is
set up on a computer.

ADD A CONTACT

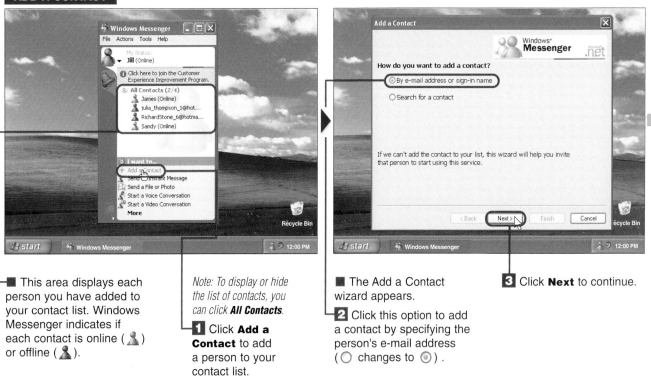

■ This area displays each
person you have added to
your contact list. Windows
Messenger indicates if
each contact is online (🧑)
or offline (🧑).

*Note: To display or hide
the list of contacts, you
can click **All Contacts**.*

1 Click **Add a
Contact** to add
a person to your
contact list.

■ The Add a Contact
wizard appears.

2 Click this option to add
a contact by specifying the
person's e-mail address
(○ changes to ◉).

3 Click **Next** to continue.

Tip

Can other people add me to their own contact lists without my knowledge?

No. When a person adds your name to their contact list, Windows Messenger displays a dialog box on your screen, indicating the name and e-mail address of the person who has added you to their contact list. You can click **Allow** or **Block** to specify whether or not you want the person to be able to add you to their contact list (◯ changes to ◉). Click **OK** to close the dialog box. If you select **Allow**, the person's name is also automatically added to your contact list.

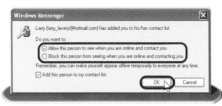

Tip

How do I remove a person from my contact list?

In the Windows Messenger window, click the name of the person you want to remove from your contact list and then press the ⎡Delete⎤ key. In the confirmation dialog box that appears, click **Yes** to remove the person from your contact list. Removing a person from your contact list does not stop the person from being able to send you instant messages.

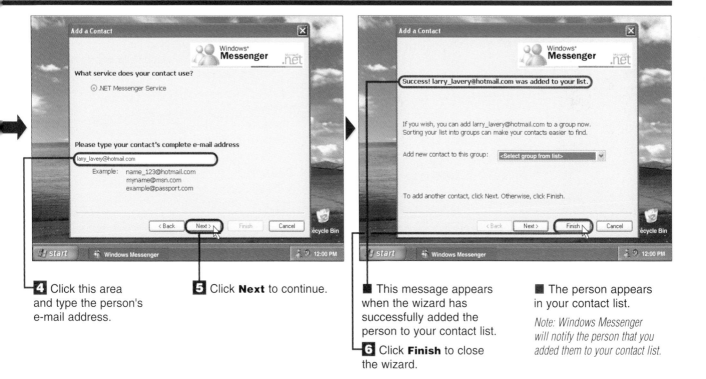

4 Click this area and type the person's e-mail address.

5 Click **Next** to continue.

■ This message appears when the wizard has successfully added the person to your contact list.

6 Click **Finish** to close the wizard.

■ The person appears in your contact list.

Note: Windows Messenger will notify the person that you added them to your contact list.

SEND AN INSTANT MESSAGE

You can send an instant message to a person in your contact list. The person must be currently signed in to Windows Messenger.

For information on adding a person to your contact list, see page 294.

When sending instant messages, never give out your password or credit card information.

SEND AN INSTANT MESSAGE

1 Double-click the name of the person you want to send an instant message to.

Note: The person you want to send an instant message to must currently be online.

■ The Conversation window appears.

2 Click this area and type your message.

Note: A message can be up to 400 characters long.

3 Click **Send** to send the message.

Note: You can also press the `Enter` *key to send the message.*

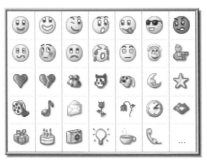

Tip

How can I express emotions in my instant messages?

You can use emoticons in your instant messages to express emotions, such as happiness (😊) or sadness (😞). To add an emoticon to a message you are sending, click 😊▾ in the Conversation window and then click the emoticon you want to add.

Tip

How can I save time when typing instant messages?

To save time when typing instant messages, many people type abbreviations for commonly used words and phrases, such as "cu l8r" for "see you later."

COMMON ABBREVIATIONS

Abbreviation	Meaning	Abbreviation	Meaning
LOL	Laughing Out Loud	GMTA	Great Minds Think Alike
ROTF	Rolling On The Floor (laughing)	F2F	Face-to-Face
BTW	By The Way	TTFN	Ta Ta For Now
RSN	Real Soon Now		
IMHO	In My Humble Opinion	AFK	Away From Keyboard/Keys
CU L8R	See You Later	BRB	Be Right Back

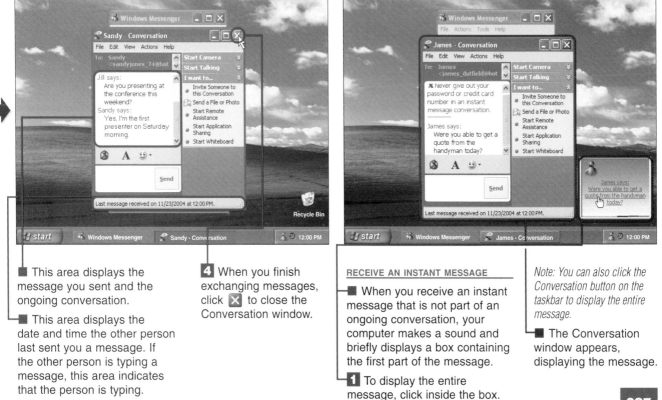

■ This area displays the message you sent and the ongoing conversation.

■ This area displays the date and time the other person last sent you a message. If the other person is typing a message, this area indicates that the person is typing.

4 When you finish exchanging messages, click ☒ to close the Conversation window.

RECEIVE AN INSTANT MESSAGE

■ When you receive an instant message that is not part of an ongoing conversation, your computer makes a sound and briefly displays a box containing the first part of the message.

1 To display the entire message, click inside the box.

Note: You can also click the Conversation button on the taskbar to display the entire message.

■ The Conversation window appears, displaying the message.

SEND A FILE

While exchanging instant messages with another person, you can send the person a file.

If your computer is connected to a corporate network with a firewall or your computer uses virus protection software that includes a firewall, you may not be able to send a file.

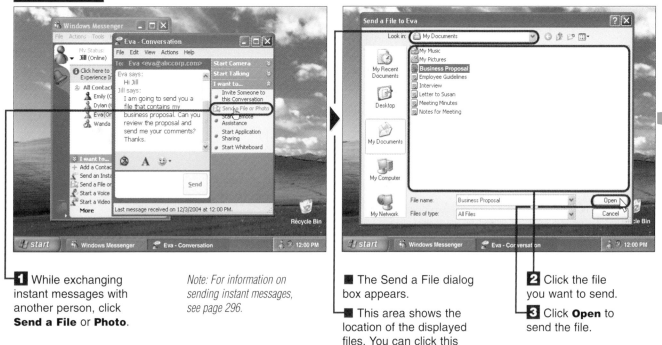

1 While exchanging instant messages with another person, click **Send a File** or **Photo**.

Note: For information on sending instant messages, see page 296.

■ The Send a File dialog box appears.

■ This area shows the location of the displayed files. You can click this area to change the location.

2 Click the file you want to send.

3 Click **Open** to send the file.

Tip

What types of files can I send?

You can send many types of files, including documents, pictures, sounds and videos. The computer receiving the file must have the necessary hardware and software installed to display or play the file.

Tip

Is there another way that I can send a file?

You can also send a file by attaching the file to an e-mail message. This is useful when you want to send a file to a person who is not currently signed in to Windows Messenger. To attach a file to an e-mail message, see page 278.

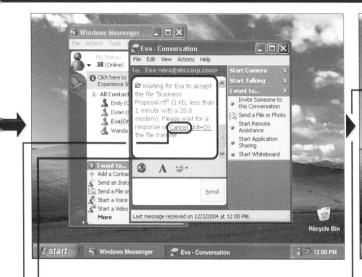

■ This area displays the status of the file transfer. The other person must accept the file before the file will transfer.

■ If you no longer want to send the file, you can click **Cancel** to stop the transfer of the file.

*Note: After the other person accepts the file, the **Cancel** option is no longer available.*

■ This message appears when the other person accepts the file.

■ This message appears when the file transfer is complete.

RECEIVE A FILE

While exchanging instant messages with another person, you can receive a file from the other person.

RECEIVE A FILE

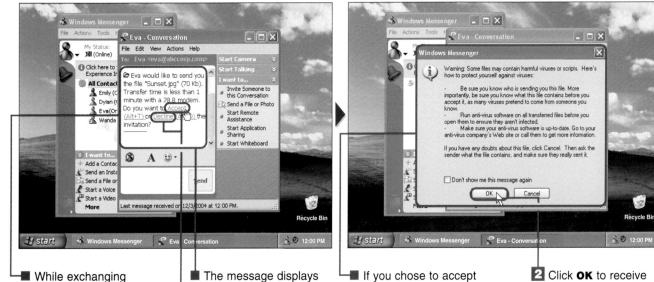

■ While exchanging instant messages with another person, a message appears when the other person sends you a file.

Note: For information on sending instant messages, see page 296.

■ The message displays information about the file, including the file name, file size and transfer time.

1 Click **Accept** or **Decline** to accept or decline the file.

■ If you chose to accept the file, a dialog box appears, warning that some files may contain harmful viruses that can damage the information on your computer.

2 Click **OK** to receive the file.

Tip

What should I consider before opening a file I received?

Before opening a file you received, you should use an antivirus program, such as McAfee VirusScan, to check the file for viruses. Some files may contain viruses, which can damage the information on your computer. You should be very cautious of files you receive from people you do not know.

Tip

How can I later open a file I received?

Windows automatically saves files you received in the My Received Files folder, which is a subfolder within your My Documents folder. You can open the files in this folder at any time. To view the contents of your My Documents folder, see page 44.

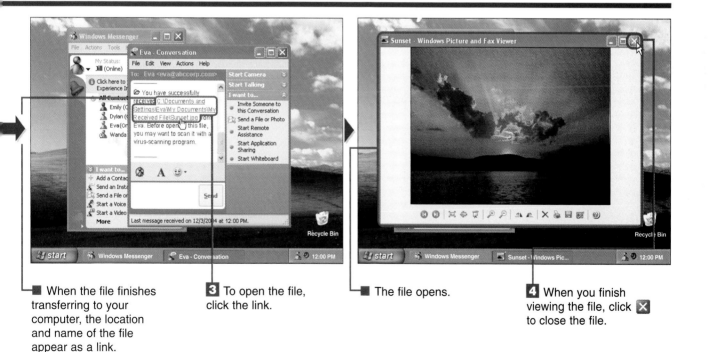

■ When the file finishes transferring to your computer, the location and name of the file appear as a link.

3 To open the file, click the link.

■ The file opens.

4 When you finish viewing the file, click ✕ to close the file.

INDEX

INDEX

INDEX

INDEX

INDEX

Other books by MARAN ILLUSTRATED™...

GUITAR

MARAN ILLUSTRATED™ Guitar is an excellent resource for people who want to learn to play the guitar, as well as for current musicians who want to fine tune their technique. This full-color guide includes over 500 photographs, accompanied by step-by-step instructions that teach you the basics of playing the guitar and reading music, as well as advanced guitar techniques. You will also learn what to look for when purchasing a guitar or accessories, how to maintain and repair your guitar and much more.

Whether you want to learn to strum your favorite tunes or play professionally, MARAN ILLUSTRATED™ Guitar provides all the information you need to become a proficient guitarist.

BOOK BONUS!

Visit **www.maran.com/guitar** to download MP3 files you can listen to and play along with for all the chords, scales, exercises and practice pieces in the book.

ISBN: 1-59200-860-7
Price: $24.99 US; $33.95 CDN
Page count: 320

PIANO

MARAN ILLUSTRATED™ Piano is an information-packed resource for people who want to learn to play the piano, as well as current musicians looking to hone their skills. Combining full-color photographs and easy-to-follow instructions, this guide covers everything from the basics of piano playing to more advanced techniques. Not only does MARAN ILLUSTRATED™ Piano show you how to read music, play scales and chords and improvise while playing with other musicians, it also provides you with helpful information for purchasing and caring for your piano. You will also learn what to look for when you buy a piano or piano accessories, how to find the best location for your piano and how to clean your piano.

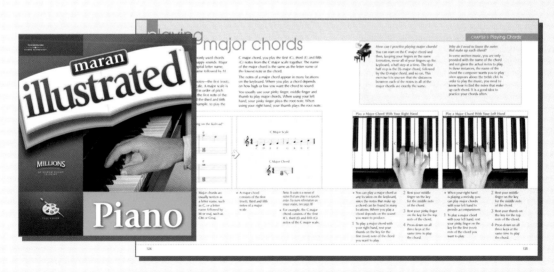

ISBN: 1-59200-864-X
Price: $24.99 US; $33.95 CDN
Page count: 304

Other books by MARAN ILLUSTRATED™...

DOG TRAINING

MARAN ILLUSTRATED™ Dog Training is an excellent guide for both current dog owners and people considering making a dog part of their family. Using clear, step-by-step instructions accompanied by over 400 full-color photographs, MARAN ILLUSTRATED™ Dog Training is perfect for any visual learner who prefers seeing what to do rather than reading lengthy explanations.

Beginning with insights into popular dog breeds and puppy development, this book emphasizes positive training methods to guide you through socializing, housetraining and teaching your dog many commands. You will also learn how to work with problem behaviors, such as destructive chewing, excessive barking and separation anxiety.

ISBN: 1-59200-858-5
Price: $19.99 US; $26.95 CDN
Page count: 256

KNITTING & CROCHETING

MARAN ILLUSTRATED™ Knitting & Crocheting contains a wealth of information about these two increasingly popular crafts. Whether you are just starting out or you are an experienced knitter or crocheter interested in picking up new tips and techniques, this information-packed resource will take you from the basics, such as how to hold the knitting needles or crochet hook and create different types of stitches, to more advanced skills, such as how to add decorative touches to your projects and fix mistakes. The easy-to-follow information is communicated through clear, step-by-step instructions and accompanied by over 600 full-color photographs—perfect for any visual learner.

This book also includes numerous easy-to-follow patterns for all kinds of items, from simple crocheted scarves to cozy knitted baby outfits.

ISBN: 1-59200-862-3
Price: $24.99 US; $33.95 CDN
Page count: 304

WEIGHT TRAINING

MARAN ILLUSTRATED™ Weight Training is an information-packed guide that covers all the basics of weight training, as well as more advanced techniques and exercises.

MARAN ILLUSTRATED™ Weight Training contains more than 500 full-color photographs of exercises for every major muscle group, along with clear, step-by-step instructions for performing the exercises. Useful tips provide additional information and advice to help enhance your weight training experience.

MARAN ILLUSTRATED™ Weight Training provides all the information you need to start weight training or to refresh your technique if you have been weight training for some time.

ISBN: 1-59200-866-6
Price: $24.99 US; $33.95 CDN
Page count: 320

YOGA

MARAN ILLUSTRATED™ **Yoga** provides a wealth of simplified, easy-to-follow information about the increasingly popular practice of Yoga. This easy-to-use guide is a must for visual learners who prefer to see and do without having to read lengthy explanations.

Using clear, step-by-step instructions accompanied by over 500 full-color photographs, this book includes all the information you need to get started with yoga or to enhance your technique if you have already made yoga a part of your life. MARAN ILLUSTRATED™ Yoga shows you how to safely and effectively perform a variety of yoga poses at various skill levels, how to breathe more efficiently, how to customize your yoga practice to meet your needs and much more.

ISBN: 1-59200-868-2
Price: $24.99 US; $33.95 CDN
Page count: 320

Did you like this book? MARAN ILLUSTRATED™ offers books on the most popular computer topics, using the same easy-to-use format of this book. We always say that if you like one of our books, you'll love the rest of our books too!

Here's a list of some of our best-selling computer titles:

Guided Tour Series - 240 pages, Full Color

MARAN ILLUSTRATED's Guided Tour series features a friendly disk character that walks you through each task step by step. The full-color screen shots are larger than in any of our other series and are accompanied by clear, concise instructions.

	ISBN	Price
MARAN ILLUSTRATED™ Computers Guided Tour	1-59200-880-1	$24.99 US/$33.95 CDN
MARAN ILLUSTRATED™ Windows XP Guided Tour	1-59200-886-0	$24.99 US/$33.95 CDN

MARAN ILLUSTRATED™ Series - 320 pages, Full Color

This series covers 30% more content than our Guided Tour series. Learn new software fast using our step-by-step approach and easy-to-understand text. Learning programs has never been this easy!

	ISBN	Price
MARAN ILLUSTRATED™ Windows XP	1-59200-870-4	$24.99 US/$33.95 CDN
MARAN ILLUSTRATED™ Office 2003	1-59200-890-9	$29.99 US/$40.95 CDN
MARAN ILLUSTRATED™ Excel 2003	1-59200-876-3	$24.99 US/$33.95 CDN
MARAN ILLUSTRATED™ Access 2003	1-59200-872-0	$24.99 US/$33.95 CDN

101 Hot Tips Series - 240 pages, Full Color

Progress beyond the basics with MARAN ILLUSTRATED's 101 Hot Tips series. This series features 101 of the coolest shortcuts, tricks and tips that will help you work faster and easier.

	ISBN	Price
MARAN ILLUSTRATED™ Windows XP 101 Hot Tips	1-59200-882-8	$19.99 US/$26.95 CDN